D0214606

SHAPING AMERICAN MILITARY CAPABILITIES AFTER THE COLD WAR

SHAPING AMERICAN MILITARY CAPABILITIES AFTER THE COLD WAR

Richard A. Lacquement Jr.

Westport, Connecticut
London

Library of Congress Cataloging-in-Publication Data

Lacquement, Richard Arlynn, 1962–
   Shaping American military capabilities after the cold war / Richard A.
Lacquement, Jr.
      p. cm.
   Includes bibliographical references and index.
   ISBN 0–275–97764–1 (alk. paper)
   1.   United States—Armed Forces.   2.   United States—Military policy.
   3.   World politics—1989–.   I.   Title.
UA23.L223   2003
355′.033273—dc21   2002072800

British Library Cataloguing in Publication Data is available.

Library of Congress Catalog Card Number: 2002072800
ISBN: 0–275–97764–1

First published in 2003

Praeger Publishers, 88 Post Road West, Westport, CT 06881
An imprint of Greenwood Publishing Group, Inc.
www.praeger.com

Printed in the United States of America

The paper used in this book complies with the
Permanent Paper Standard issued by the National
Information Standards Organization (Z39.48–1984).

10 9 8 7 6 5 4 3 2 1

For her love and untiring support, I dedicate this to Kathleen.

Contents

Illustrations

Preface

The end of the Cold War removed the Soviet threat that had defined U.S. national-security policy and provided the dominant rationale for force structure and doctrine of American armed forces. Over a decade after the collapse of the Soviet Union, however, the force structure and doctrine of the U.S. armed forces have changed very little. It is a smaller but essentially similar force to the one prepared for large-scale conventional war with the U.S.S.R.

This study provides a description and explanation of defense-policy decision making regarding the selection of military capabilities in the post–Cold War era from 1989–2001. This study also evaluates decisions in light of the substantially different military challenges of the post–Cold War era, in particular the challenges of the revolution in military affairs (RMA), frequent peace operations, and new demands of homeland security.

The explanation for lack of military restructuring is relatively simple and somewhat unsurprising: The military leadership of the U.S. armed forces—army, navy, marines, and air force—have been united in their support for incremental reduction of the armed forces while avoiding dramatic changes to doctrine or force structure. The military is a very large, powerful, and popular institution that has defended its preferred position successfully during a series of post–Cold War American defense policy reviews (the 1990 Base Force, 1993 Bottom Up Review, 1995 Commission on Roles and Missions, the 1997 Quadrennial Defense Review, and the 2001 Quadrennial Defense Review). The military leadership's preferences were accepted by civilian leaders in the executive branch and Congress. This inertia was permitted by the general lack of public concern about defense issues since the Cold War.

In September 2001, terrorist attacks on the United States created a fundamentally different context within which issues of national security will be addressed. Increased emphasis on homeland security is the most obvious initial response. Nonetheless, as this study goes to publication, there has been little change to the fundamental force structure and doctrine of the U.S. armed forces.

This study evaluates this inertia as a negative outcome for two main reasons. First, given the technological advancements that represent the RMA, failure to adapt force structure and doctrine means that U.S. armed forces may be largely unprepared for the next major war. Second, such Cold War forces are not well designed for use in the many peace operations that have been common in the post–Cold War era.

This work has taken much time to complete and owes much to the inspiration, encouragement, and support of many others. Any errors, omissions, or lapses are mine, but much of the credit for what is good in this study is a reflection of the guidance, mentorship, support, and friendship I have received from others. The successful completion of this study would not have been possible without the sustaining strength of my academic advisers, professional mentors in the military, and, most importantly, my loving family—especially my wife.

Professionally, I owe a tremendous debt of gratitude to the U.S. Army. The institution and its culture are responsible for providing me the opportunity for academic enrichment that made this study possible. However, the views expressed in this study are entirely my own and do not represent the official views of the U.S. Government, the Department of Defense, or the Department of the Army.

The army's validation and support of academic enrichment began when I was a cadet at West Point. The many professors that I had there nurtured my excitement for learning and encouraged my interest in further study. In particular, I owe the USMA Department of Social Sciences (Sosh) my thanks for supporting and fueling my interest in international relations and security studies. The many superb professors and professional officers I worked with as a cadet gave me the inspiration to excel and gave me truly excellent role models to emulate. After nine years in tactical army units, I was fortunate to be selected by the Sosh Department to go to graduate school at Princeton en route to an assignment back at USMA as a Sosh professor.

As a graduate student, I am greatly indebted to the Woodrow Wilson School that provided such a superlative environment for academic advancement. I was blessed with Woodrow Wilson School and Politics department professors and classmates who contributed in innumerable ways to my education. In particular, I owe thanks to Dave McCormick, Michele Penner, Danielle Rollmann, and Phil Saunders. Discussion partners, willing sounding boards, and friends—they were particularly responsible for making Princeton fun as well as enlightening.

As a faculty member of the Sosh Department, I was also encouraged and supported by the department leadership—in particular Brigadier General (ret) Jim Golden, Brigadier General Dan Kaufman, and Colonel Jay Parker—who provided a stimulating environment and professional support during the time I undertook the majority of the research for this study. In the hallways of Sosh, I fed off the energy and intellect of a fantastic faculty of civilian and military professors. Too numerous to name them all, I must single out a handful of peers and friends who were a constant source of support and feedback throughout the initial stages of drafting this study. Chris Gibson, Lew Irwin, and John Nagl—officers and doctors all—were critical sources of moral and substantive support as I worked on the initial drafts.

I also appreciate the help from Brad Lee and Tom Mahnken at the Naval War College. Their critiques and comments on various parts of the manuscript were very useful as I prepared this for publication.

Academically, I am indebted to the mentorship and friendship of Dick Ullman. A long-time friend of the Sosh department and advisor to many officers who have moved through WWS, Dick is the consummate teacher and academic role model. He is easily accessible, always willing to help, and virtually incapable of saying no to requests for time and attention for his students. His intellectual skills and ability to facilitate learning are second only to his extraordinary, caring support for his students. His optimism and encouragement buoyed me to see past obstacles and discouraging moments. He often raised my spirits and helped renew my enthusiasm to continue with this daunting undertaking.

I am also indebted to the valuable academic leadership of Professor Aaron Friedberg at Princeton and Dr. Don Snider at West Point, who, along with Dick Ullman, were my doctoral dissertation committee for five years. Professor Friedberg many times helped me to better organize the scattered thoughts and ideas that I often had throughout the years. His ability to help me integrate, organize, and focus my thoughts was remarkable. Similarly, Dr. Snider, a retired army colonel with a tremendous record of national service in peace and war, helped me to better understand the defense policy process that is at the center of this study. All three members of my committee patiently waded through drafts of chapters and provided me appropriately targeted comments and critiques to improve the study at every step. I could never have completed the study without their excellent leadership and academic insights.

Most importantly, I owe thanks for the foundations and core support for my efforts to my family. First to my parents for instilling in me the thirst for knowledge and education that made pursuing a doctorate such a natural choice. Second, and most prominently, I owe tremendous gratitude to my wife, Kathleen Gorak. Kathleen has been my most ardent supporter throughout the painstaking effort to complete this study in my "spare" time (which more appropriately can be understood as time I was not available to Kathleen and our daughters, Corinne and Olivia, during numerous weekends, holidays, and vacations). I love Kathleen, Corinne, and Olivia dearly and appreciate the tremendous sacrifices they've made to support me in this endeavor.

Richard A. Lacquement Jr.

Abbreviations

AEF Air Expeditionary Forces

BRAC Base Realignment and Closing

BUR Bottom Up Review

C4ISR Command, control, communication, and coordination (C4), Intelligence, Surveillance and Reconnaissance

CDI Center for Defense Information

CENTCOM U.S. Central Command

CINC Commander in Chief (of a combatant command)

CJCS Chairman, Joint Chiefs of Staff

CORM Commission on Roles and Missions of the Armed Forces of the United States

CRS Congressional Research Service

CSBA Center for Strategic and Budgetary Assessments

DoD Department of Defense

EUCOM U.S. European Command

FM Field Manual

FY Fiscal Year (in U.S. government, FY is from 1 Oct until 30 Sept)

GAO General Accounting Office

GDP Gross Domestic Product

HASC House Armed Services Committee

IBCT Interim Brigade Combat Team

ICBM Intercontinental Ballistic Missile

IDA Institute for Defense Analysis

IFOR Implementation Force (Bosnia)

INF Intermediate Nuclear Force

IW Information Warfare

JCS Joint Chiefs of Staff

JFCOM U.S. Joint Forces Command (Formerly Atlantic Command or ACOM)

JSF Joint Strike Fighter

JSTARS Joint Surveillance, and Target Attack Radar System

KFOR Kosovo Force

MOOTW Military Operations Other Than War

MRC Major Regional Contingency

MTW Major Theater War

NATO North Atlantic Treaty Organization

NBC Nuclear, Biological, and Chemical

NDP National Defense Panel

NG National Guard

NMD National Missile Defense

NMS National Military Strategy

NSS National Security Strategy

O&M Operations and Maintenance

OPMS Officer Professional Management System

OSD Office of the Secretary of Defense

PA&E Program, Analysis, and Evaluation

PACOM U.S. Pacific Command

PDA Project for Defense Alternatives

PME Professional Military Education

PPBS Planning, Programming and Budgeting System

QDR Quadrennial Defense Review

RDT&E Research, Development, Test and Evaluation

RMA Revolutions in Military Affairs

SASC Senate Armed Services Committee

SFOR Stabilization Force (Bosnia)

SLBM Submarine Launched Ballistic Missile

SOCOM Special Operations Command

SOF Special Operations Forces

SOUTHCOM U.S. Southern Command

SSBN Strategic Ballistic Missile Submarine (Nuclear)

SSC Smaller-Scale Contingency

STRATCOM U.S. Strategic Command

TRANSCOM U.S. Transportation Command

U.N. United Nations

UAV Unmanned Aerial Vehicle

WMD Weapons of Mass Destruction

Our Strategy for this new era recognizes the opportunities and challenges before us, and includes among its principles:...reducing our defense burden as appropriate, while restructuring our forces for new challenges.
—President George Bush, August 1991[1]

The world remains a dangerous place, but the nature of those dangers has dramatically changed. Our military forces...must therefore, continually be redesigned....Our goal is to reshape our forces to provide us the capabilities we need to defend our continuing interests, deal with new problems and threats, and contribute to the promotion of democracy, prosperity, and security in a new world.
—President Bill Clinton, February 1993[2]

An effective response [to national security threats] requires a willingness to think anew about our security and about the way our government and our military are organized to defend against the threats of today. We should not assume that the bureaucratic structures of our foreign policy and national security apparatus, nor the force postures that were successful for waging the cold war, are the right ones for the threats we will face in the future.
—Senator Sam Nunn, September 27, 1996[3]

Today our military is still organized more for Cold War threats than for the challenges of a new century—for industrial age operations, rather than for information age battles. There is almost no relationship between our budget priorities and a strategic vision.... Now we must shape the future with new concepts, new strategies, new resolve.
—Governor George W. Bush, September 23, 1999[4]

The need for military transformation was clear before the conflict in Afghanistan, and before September the 11th ... in 1999, I spoke of keeping the peace by redefining war on our terms. The same recommendation was made in the strategic review [2001 QDR] that Secretary Rumsfeld briefed me on last August—a review that I fully endorse. What's different today is our sense of urgency—the need to build this future force while fighting the present war.
—President George W. Bush, December 11, 2001[5]

NOTES

1. President George Bush, *National Security Strategy of the United States,* (Washington D.C.: Government Printing Office, August 1991), 33.

2. President Bill Clinton, *A Vision for Change for America* (Washington, DC: Government Printing Office, 1993), 69.

3. Senator Sam Nunn, Senate floor speech, "Terrorism Meets Proliferation: Convergence of Threats in the Post–Cold War Era," *Congressional Record,* September 28, 1996, p. S11759.

4. Texas Governor George W. Bush, "A Period of Consequences," Speech given at The Citadel, South Carolina, 23 September 1999.

5. President George W. Bush, "President Speaks on War Effort to Citadel Cadets," Text of presidential statement, Charleston, S.C., 11 December 2001. Available from http://www.whitehouse.gov/news/releases/2001/12/20011211–6.html; Internet; accessed 12 December 2001.

Chapter 1

Introduction

> It is valuable to remember how different the world is today than it was during the Cold War. "From the end of World War II and the onset of ... the Cold War" the hostility of the two great powers was the central factor in international life, threatening mass destruction, dominating global politics and affecting the lives, attitudes and even nightmares of people everywhere.[1]

Throughout the Cold War, the United States based much of its international behavior and national defense on opposition to the Soviet Union. In 1985, Mikhail Gorbachev became the Soviet leader and set in motion the changes that would end Soviet involvement in Afghanistan, unravel the Warsaw Pact, bring down the Berlin Wall, and dissolve the Soviet Union itself. The Soviet Union's demise was a welcome change for the United States. It was a change that demanded major American policy adaptations.

In 1989, General Colin Powell noted an old saw, "What will all the preachers do when the Devil is dead?" as he spoke to an audience of army leaders about the declining Soviet threat.[2] Like hellfire and brimstone preachers of the old saw, American military and civilian leaders would face a similarly difficult question without a hostile U.S.S.R. With so much energy and attention devoted to countering the Soviet Union militarily, the role and structure of American armed forces required reevaluation in the absence of that clear foe and great simplifier. In Powell's memoirs, "When You've Lost Your Best Enemy"[3] is the title of the chapter in which he describes the first major post–Cold War plan to adjust American armed forces—the Base Force. With his efforts to create the Base Force, Powell set in motion the first in a series of efforts by American leaders to figure out how to respond to the devil's death and adapt the military capabilities of the United States to a new era.[4]

Since the Base Force plan, there have been four other significant attempts to step back from the routine defense policy process and figure out how to adapt American military capabilities to the challenges of the new era. In the first year of the Clinton administration, Secretary of Defense Les Aspin led the Bottom Up Review that published its report in October 1993.[5] In 1995, an independent

Commission on Roles and Missions of the Armed Forces presented its recommendations for reformulation of U.S. defense policy and for changes to American military capabilities.[6] In 1997, the Department of Defense and an outside panel of experts (the National Defense Panel) presented the results of their efforts to rethink U.S. defense policy and military capabilities.[7] In September 2001, the new Bush administration published its quadrennial review of defense policy.[8] The four latter efforts to reformulate U.S. defense policy have generally followed the path set forth by the Base Force. From 1989 until 2001, policymakers agreed on substantial reductions in the size of American armed forces to account for the end of the Cold War but decided not to require significant changes in basic force structure or doctrine. Hence, the current American armed forces are a smaller but fundamentally similar version of what they were during the Cold War. The devil may be dead, but the sermon is the same. The central purpose of this study is to describe, explain, and evaluate this result.

The preponderance of the research for this study took place prior to 11 September 2001 and focused on the years from 1990 to 2001. The period was characterized primarily as peacetime. On 11 September 2001, the major terrorist attacks on the United States dramatically challenged U.S. national security. The United States subsequently conducted combat operations in Afghanistan in the first phase of a larger war against global terrorism.[9] The events of 11 September 2001 renewed attention to U.S. military capabilities. This may mark the opening of a new window of opportunity to address fundamental issues of force structure and doctrine for future American military capabilities. The report of the 2001 Quadrennial Defense Review released in late September 2001 does not include major force structure or doctrinal changes but does declare, in strong terms, support for transformation of the armed forces.[10]

SUMMARY OF FINDINGS

The end of the Cold War presented a window of opportunity for dramatic policy change with respect to the force structure and the doctrine of the American armed forces. The changes in the international environment as well as various changes in the domestic political environment conditioned the opportunity for policy change. During this period, several alternative approaches were advocated for the force structure and doctrine of the armed forces to reflect these opportunities. Nonetheless, after five attempts to reformulate defense policy concerning fundamental military capabilities, the resulting military capabilities are generally the same as during the Cold War, albeit smaller. "The Cold War is over, but to a too great extent the structure and strategies appropriate to that era of bipolar, super power stand-off continue to govern our armed services."[11]

The explanation for this lack of restructuring is relatively simple and somewhat unsurprising: The military leadership of the U.S. armed forces—army, navy, marines, and air force—have been united in their support for incremental reduction while avoiding dramatic changes that might damage the highly capable force they built in the closing stages of the Cold War. In the window of opportunity for policy change represented by the dramatic alteration of the international environment surrounding the collapse of the Soviet Union, the military was able to set the agenda for change and establish the trajectory for force structure and doctrine. The military is a large, powerful, and popular institution that has successfully defended its preferred position. General Colin Powell, the extremely popular and highly respected Chairman of the Joint Chiefs of Staff, was the main architect of the initial plan, the Base Force, which has been modified only slightly over the years since it was first presented in 1990. The military has established and defended a strong bureaucratic position. This position represents a conceptual status quo easily traced to the patterns established during the Cold War.

More surprising, however, was the diminishing challenge to the military's preferences from other political actors involved in national security policy. This acceptance of the military's conceptual status quo persists even as the Cold War recedes into history. The military leadership's preferences were accepted by civilian leaders in the executive branch and Congress. Part of this acceptance of the military's preferences was the result of the lower salience that defense issues held for the public in general, at least until September 2001. From the end of the Cold War until 2001, the general public showed little interest in defense issues and defense was not a central issue in elections. Furthermore, the military's popularity and respect make it a difficult institution for any civilian leader to challenge publicly. In addition, presidential leadership in examining the fundamental capabilities of the armed forces was minimal. This was particularly true during the Clinton administration. The Clinton administration was widely perceived as having low credibility on military issues based on the President's lack of military service (highlighted during the election campaign in 1992) and his early difficulties with military policy concerning the issue of gays in the military. The policy reviews that have taken place since the end of the Cold War have been dominated by the military. The result is the continued promulgation of a cautious military plan for modest adaptation of the armed forces.

EVALUATION

There is strong support among members of the defense establishment, particularly the uniformed military leadership, for current defense policies. The strength and the success of the military's preferences are evident in the defense policy-making story that emerges from this study.

My own opinion, presented in more detail in chapter 10, "Evaluation and Recommendations," is that the preference for sustaining the fundamentally similar force structure and doctrine of the Cold War era is inappropriate. This policy poorly serves the long-term security interests of the United States. The United States should make better policy choices now regarding force structure and doctrine. These decisions are important for the security interests of the United States and for the international community as a whole. The United States has a responsibility to be prepared to fight potential regional foes; however, the United States should regard the end of the Cold War as an opportunity to reshape its armed forces so that the United States can more effectively shape the future international environment and respond to new security threats. This includes greater efforts to respond to the revolution in military affairs (RMA),[12] greater emphasis on the demands of peace operations,[13] and some modest adaptations to improve homeland security.

The ability to confront remaining regional foes is still important but does not preclude the American ability to better meet the transformation requirements of the RMA, the challenges of peace operations, and the imperatives of homeland security. Prompt efforts to address tensions within and among states have been a major concern since the end of the Cold War. The use of properly configured armed forces holds the possibility of preventing more dangerous and destabilizing challenges from arising. Peace operations are an important part of U.S. national security strategy and the United States should better adapt its military capabilities to support such missions. If, however, in spite of the United States and other countries' best efforts, major military challengers to the United States and its allies arise, the military capabilities of such opponents are likely to differ substantially from those of the past. Hence, the ability to sustain a peaceful international environment or defend against future military challenges will rely on the timely identification and assimilation of technological advances in military capabilities (the revolution in military affairs). The United States must be prepared to meet the potential challenges that technological advances pose to the nature of future warfare. Given the long lead times to identify, develop, and produce such capabilities, defense policy must provide the support for the innovation, testing, and evaluation that can anticipate and address a myriad of potential threats. Conversely, continued emphasis on the expensive upgrade of weapons, organizations, and doctrine based on the conceptual continuity with Cold War patterns inhibits American ability to prepare for future challenges. The dramatic attacks on the United States in September 2001 require review and adjustment of military capabilities to improve homeland security. In sum, continued reliance on military capabilities that are merely smaller but similar versions of Cold War forces could jeopardize U.S. security.

STRUCTURE OF THE STUDY

Force structure and doctrine. Military capabilities are composed of two main elements: force structure and doctrine. Chapter 2, "Context for Adapting Military Capabilities: National Strategy, Defense Budgets, and

Alternative Policy Options," presents a brief overview of the importance of force structure and doctrine to national security policy. Force structure is primarily the material and personnel that comprise the armed forces and the manner in which they are organized. Doctrine is the set of ideas that define how these assets will be employed and includes the rationale for organizational structures.[14] These capabilities cannot be changed easily or quickly. The ability to provide military capabilities to meet present requirements effectively as well as to anticipate the capabilities that will be required to address future challenges effectively is an extremely important responsibility of the country's national leaders. Chapter 2 also reviews national security strategy and aggregate defense-spending trends since the end of the Cold War that provide the context for decisions about military capabilities. The chapter concludes by looking at the major defense policy alternatives that have been identified and debated concerning the nature of future military capabilities.

What happened? The focus of chapter 3, "Trends in Military Capabilities Since the Cold War," is the description of changes and continuity in force structure and doctrine since the end of the Cold War. Chapter 3 includes presentation and analysis of a variety of force-structure and doctrine indicators. The analysis of change and continuity in these indicators supports the assessment that today's American armed forces are smaller but similar in capabilities to those of the Cold War.

How did it happen? American military capabilities are the result of the defense policymaking process. The decisions concerning military capabilities are not always explicit. Some results come from implicit decisions not to challenge the continuation of existing capabilities or not to consider new capabilities. Whether caused by the essence or absence of decision, the resulting capabilities, nonetheless, reflect government-policy choices. To explain the political forces that shaped force structure and doctrine, this study analyzes five major defense-policy reviews that have occurred since the end of the Cold War: the 1990 Base Force, the 1993 Bottom Up Review (BUR), the 1995 Commission on Roles and Missions (CORM), the 1997 Quadrennial Defense Review (QDR), and the 2001 QDR. The five reviews are presented and analyzed separately in chapters 4–8. Each of these efforts to reformulate defense policy influenced American military capabilities. All five attempts to reformulate defense policy are part of the same general effort by civilian and military leaders to grapple with the challenges of a changing international security environment and issues concerning the appropriate size and shape of the American military capabilities needed to support national objectives. Each chapter looks at the historical context—international and domestic—within which the particular review took place, the key defense issues and associated advocates for alternative approaches, the process of the particular effort, the policy result and an analysis of the outcome.

Why did it happen the way it did? Chapter 9, "Explaining Decisions about Military Capabilities Since the End of the Cold War," explains, in general, why the outcome occurred the way it did. It summarizes the characteristics of defense-policy decision making derived from the five major policy reformulation efforts described in chapters 4–8.

Why does it matter? Chapter 10, "Evaluation and Recommendations," provides an evaluation of defense-policy decisions about military capabilities since the end of the Cold War. The chapter also provides some policy suggestions to improve the adaptation of U.S. military capabilities to differing demands of the post–Cold War era. Chapter 10 also presents a brief conclusion to the study.

The overall conclusion of this study is that there are substantially different security challenges and opportunities for the United States that require substantially different forces and doctrine. We need forces that are not smaller versions of those designed to defend against the Soviet Union. We need force structure and doctrine that can meet the demands of the remaining regional foes, enhance homeland security, support stability operations that can help avert future wars, and vigorously explore the possibilities of future war that may challenge the United States.

NOTES

1. Don Oberdorfer, *The Turn: From the Cold War to a New Era: The United States and the Soviet Union, 1983–1990* (New York: Poseidon Press, 1991), 11.

2. Gen. Colin L. Powell, "National Security Challenges in the 1990s: 'The Future Just Ain't What it Used to Be,'" *Army* 39, no. 7 (July 1989) 12. The article was based on a speech Powell delivered to army leaders at a seminar on 16 May 1989.

3. Colin Powell with Joseph E. Persico, *My American Journey* (New York: Random House, 1995), 435.

4. Lorna S. Jaffe, *The Development of the Base Force, 1989–1992* (Washington, D.C.: Office of the Chairman of the Joint Chiefs of Staff, July 1993).

5. Les Aspin (Secretary of Defense), *Report on the Bottom Up Review,* October 1993 (Hereafter referred to as BUR).

6. Commission on Roles and Missions of the Armed Forces, *Directions for Defense: Report of the Commission on Roles and Missions of the Armed Forces,* Washington, D.C.: Government Printing Office, May 1995. (Hereafter referred to as CORM).

7. Department of Defense, *Report of the Quadrennial Defense Review,* (Washington, D.C.: Department of Defense, May 1997) and National Defense Panel, *Transforming Defense: National Security in the 21st Century,* Washington, D.C.: Government Printing Office, December 1997. (Hereafter referred to as 1997 QDR and NDP).

8. Department of Defense, *Report of the Quadrennial Defense Review,* Washington, D.C.: Department of Defense, September 30, 2001 (Hereafter referred to as 2001 QDR).

9. George W. Bush, "Address to Joint Session of Congress and the American People," Text of presidential statement. Washington, D.C. 20 September 2001, available from http://www.whitehouse.gov/news/releases/2001/09/20010920–8.html; Internet; accessed 12 March 2002.

10. 2001 QDR, 29–47.

11. Executive Office of the President of the United States, *A Blueprint for New Beginnings: A Responsible Budget for America's Priorities,* Washington, D.C.: Government Printing Office, 2001, 53.

12. The most common definition of the current revolution in military affairs relates it to the technological advances in computers and digitization. Many refer to this revolution in military affairs in conjunction with changes associated with a general move of society from the industrial age to the information age. For a detailed discussion of this transformation, see Alan and Heidi Toffler, *The Third Wave* (New York: Bantam, 1980). Within U.S. military circles, the analog is called information warfare or IW, JCS Publication, *Information Warfare.* For an excellent overview of the arguments concerning the revolution in military affairs, see Colin S. Gray, *The American Revolution in Military Affairs: An Interim Assessment.* Number 28. Camberley, Great Britain: The Strategic and Combat Studies Institute, 1997; Eliot Cohen, "A Revolution in Warfare," *Foreign Affairs* 75, no. 2 (March/April 1996): 37–54; Joseph S. Nye and William A. Owens, "America's Information Edge," *Foreign Affairs* 75, No. 2, (March/April 1996), 20–36; Edward N. Luttwak, "A Post-Heroic Military Policy," *Foreign Affairs* 75, No. 4 (July/August 1996), 33–44.

13. A variety of terms have been tried over the past several years to capture the missions other than war, such as peacekeeping, peace enforcement, humanitarian assistance, noncombatant evacuation, disaster relief, drug interdiction, and so on. In U.S. military joint publications, these missions are generally referred to using the term Military Operations other than war (MOOTW). I have used the general term *peace operations* to encompass all of these missions. Also see United States Department of the Army, *Field Manual 100–23: Peace Operations,* Washington D.C.: U.S. Government Printing Office, 1994.

14. Some descriptions of military capabilities list training and logistical support as separate elements of military capabilities. This study subsumes training and readiness support as instrumental in reinforcing the link between the primary elements of doctrine and force structure.

Chapter 2

Context for Adapting Military Capabilities: National Strategy, Defense Budgets, and Alternative Policy Options

> The fact that the fixed programs (equipment, personnel, and routines that exist at the particular time) exhaust the range of buttons that leaders can push is not always perceived by the leaders. But in every case it is critical for an understanding of what is actually done.
>
> —Graham Allison[1]

OVERVIEW

This study seeks to understand how the U.S. government chose to shape its military capabilities since the end of the Cold War. This understanding is important because such choices constrain options for the employment of military capabilities to support national objectives. The U.S. government, however, is not a coherent, unitary actor. The government's decisions represent the political resultant of individuals and organizations that participate in the efforts to formulate policy on specific issues. Legislative requirements (laws), executive branch orders, and organizational interpretations all help account for the shape military capabilities assume. Furthermore, whereas a realist's analysis of security might stress the overriding importance of the international balance of power in shaping defense capabilities, the absence of the need to balance against a particular foe throws into starker relief the disagreements concerning appropriate military ends and means within the government.

Much of the civil-military relations literature focuses on how civilian and military leaders interact, usually in times of crisis, to decide whether and how to use armed forces.[2] These decisions represent dramatic moments in history. They provide hints of the strengths and weaknesses of the individuals, institutions, and processes that serve critical national values. When armed forces are called upon in a crisis, however, their capacity to act has been significantly determined by earlier decisions or absence of decisions on the part of civilian or military leaders.

Organizational outputs structure the situation within the narrow constraints of which leaders must make their decisions about an issue. Outputs raise the problem, provide the information, and take the initial steps that color the face of the issue that is turned to the leaders.[3]

Since organizational outputs—in this case military capabilities—structure the choices leaders make, it is important to understand how such outputs are created. Creating and maintaining the military capabilities that will be available to serve national interests in time of crisis is a critical task of national government.

In the short-response time, come-as-you-are nature of most international crisis situations, the employment of the armed forces places critical importance on existing forces and their existing organizational routines (SOPs, doctrine, and so on). The structure and doctrine of armed forces establish how they operate. States bear the consequences of their military's performance—the most significant consequences are those affecting a state's existence.[4] Significant change or innovation of armed forces is difficult in the middle of a crisis or war. The time required to implement major innovation successfully is generally long, making preparations during peace the most important factor in influencing performance in war.[5] A similar operating imperative also influences the effectiveness of armed forces performing short-notice deployments for peace operations. It is also difficult to achieve ends successfully without properly designed means.[6] These factors highlight the importance that routine decisions in the absence of crisis can have on the capabilities available when a crisis arises.[7]

For the armed forces, force structure and doctrine represent two critical characteristics that define the military capabilities upon which leaders can draw. Force structure reflects doctrinal decisions and assumptions about mission execution. It represents a specific mix of personnel, equipment, organizational structure, and assumptions about operational effectiveness. Force structure constrains options for employing the military. For example, the inability of active forces to sustain themselves for long deployment required the call up of National Guard and Reserve forces in Desert Storm. Doctrine provides the conceptual framework that relates military means to desired ends. "Military doctrine presents fundamental principles that guide the employment of forces ...doctrine deals with the fundamental issue of how best to employ the national military power to achieve strategic ends."[8] Doctrine operationalizes a theory of military action.[9] It is the driving force behind training and preparation for military operations by units at the tactical and operational levels.

The next chapter provides a description of trends in military capabilities since the end of the Cold War. To put these trends in context, this chapter provides a description of American national security-strategy and defense-budget trends since the end of the Cold War. In general, there have been dramatic changes in national security strategy and overall resource allocation. Such changes in the general context for decisions concerning appropriate military capabilities provide a backdrop against which modest adaptation of military capabilities stands out as a puzzle.

NATIONAL STRATEGY

The end of the Cold War represented a fundamental change in the international strategic environment. American policy reflected this change in the national security strategies promulgated by the presidents. This section illustrates the significant changes in strategy by comparing recent post–Cold War strategy with Cold War era strategy.[10]

Fundamentally, Cold War and post–Cold War documents are similar in their strong internationalist approach. They sustain support for an active international role for the United States. Additionally, the strategies maintain an important role for the military. However, different security challenges define the international contexts of the strategies. The collapse of the Soviet Union removed the single most important impetus of Cold War era security strategy. Recent strategy statements focused on regional adversaries.

The most significant change in U.S. policy since the end of the Cold War is the end of the strategy of containment. The imperative for containing the Soviet Union's direct threat to American survival has not been replaced by any similarly overwhelming security threat. Hence, containment has not been replaced by any one, clearly articulated strategy that reflects a broad consensus.

The transition from the Cold War to the post–Cold War world has been one from strategic urgency to strategic uncertainty. The very term "post–Cold War world" testifies to an inability to characterize that world in terms other than what it is not.[11]

Presidents Bush and Clinton made attempts to put their stamp on the era and find concise ways to express the overall American national strategy. For President Bush, the phrase was a "New World Order."[12] For President Clinton, national strategy was initially tagged as "Engagement and Enlargement,"[13] later reduced to "Engagement."[14] To date, the administration of George W. Bush has yet to articulate a new overarching strategy but appears to have largely accepted the engagement approach bequeathed by President Clinton.[15] The way engagement occurs leaves much room for debate and allows a spectrum of choice between engagement on narrowly defined, vital national interests relating directly to the survival of the United States (extremely selective engagement) to a broad willingness to use U.S. capabilities to promulgate principles of universal and limitless value (a more liberal, activist agenda for engagement in any corner of the world where key principles are challenged).[16] One interesting aspect of the change in the international environment is that although the world may be safer for the United States due to the end of the tense global superpower standoff, the policy challenges of the post–Cold War era are more complicated and uncertain. The attacks of

September 2001 illustrate that the lack of a state peer competitor does not equal an absence of significant threats to basic American security and well-being. Technological advancement and increasing global interdependence generate vulnerabilities that augment the potential weapons and capabilities of the weak. Terrorism and guerrilla warfare traditionally associated with the militarily weak are more devastating and hence more threatening. Weapons and techniques of mass destruction[17] pose daunting asymmetric challenges to the United States.

Current American policy reflects the middle road of engagement. It is selective engagement in areas of vital and important U.S. interests and a principled promulgation of important American values (for example, democracy, free market economics, and human rights) as long as costs are not very great. The general themes of American foreign policy were expressed by President George W. Bush as follows in his 2001 inaugural address:

America remains engaged in the world by history and by choice, shaping a balance of power that favors freedom. We will defend our allies and our interests. We will show purpose without arrogance. We will meet aggression and bad faith with resolve and strength. And to all nations, we will speak for the values that gave our nation birth.[18]

Strategic Military Requirements

We can identify fundamental differences between the Cold War era and the post–Cold War era by comparing the strategic military requirements the armed forces are directed to execute. At the center of the differences between the strategies during and after the Cold War are the different expectations concerning the source of security challenges. President Reagan's last national strategy report sums up the focus of the Cold War:

The United States' most basic national security interest would be endangered if a hostile state or group of states were to dominate the Eurasian landmass—that area of the globe often referred to as the world's heartland. We fought two world wars to prevent this from occurring. And, since 1945, we have sought to prevent the Soviet Union from capitalizing on its geostrategic advantage to dominate its neighbors in Western Europe, Asia, and the Middle East and thereby fundamentally alter the global balance of power to our disadvantage.

The national strategy to achieve this objective has been containment, in the broadest sense of that term.[19]

Consequently, the emphasis for American armed forces was the global confrontation with the Soviet Union. Military focus was on the maintenance of the capacity for response, throughout the world, along a spectrum from strategic nuclear to conventional forces. This policy was known as "flexible response."[20]

Recent statements of national security strategy do not focus on a clear foe, such as the Soviet Union. Instead, as the 2001 quadrennial defense-review report notes, the defining element is an absence of definition: uncertainty.

An assessment of the global-security environment involves a great deal of uncertainty about the potential sources of military threats, the conduct of war in the future, and the form that threats and attacks against the Nation will take. History has shown that rapid and unexpected changes, such as the collapse of the Soviet Union, can transform the geopolitical landscape. It also has demonstrated that new military technologies can revolutionize the form of military competition and the nature of armed conflict in ways that render military forces and doctrines of great powers obsolescent.[21]

With no one foe upon which to focus, the role of the U.S. armed forces is also more complex. The national security strategy envisions not only the preparation for war and the ability to defeat foes in different regions, but also the military's continued role in smaller-scale contingencies in peacetime.[22] From the most recent National Security Strategy, smaller-scale contingencies (SSC) are defined as operations that,

Encompass the full range of military operations short of major theater warfare, including peacekeeping operations, enforcing embargoes and no-fly zones, evacuating U.S. citizens, reinforcing key allies, neutralizing NBC weapons facilities, supporting counter-drug operations, protecting freedom of navigation in international waters, providing disaster relief and humanitarian assistance, coping with mass migration, and engaging in information operations.[23]

Table 2.1 summarizes and compares the strategic military requirements from the Reagan National Security Strategy at the end of the Cold War and the strategic military requirements from the most recent national security strategy.[24]

Table 2.1
American Strategic Military Requirements

Cold War (NSS January 1988)[1] CONTAINMENT	Current (2001 QDR)[2] ENGAGEMENT
FOCUS: Global containment and prepare for global war • Strategic Deterrence • Forward Defense (and conventional deterrence) • Mobilization and Reinforcement	*FOCUS:* Homeland Defense and preparation for major regional wars • Homeland Defense • Strategic Power Projection • Smaller-Scale Contingency Operations • Counterproliferation • Forward Deterrence

1. Numerous documents support this description of U.S. strategic military requirements. These elements of strategic military requirements are normally embodied as the defense policy aspects of national strategy. These descriptions are taken from NSS 1988.
2. As of June 2002, the most recent national strategy report submitted to Congress was the final report from the Clinton administration in December 2000. The 2001 QDR report contains the new Bush administration's statement of national security strategy which was generally consistent with the last Clinton report.

Cold War Military Requirements

Strategic deterrence. This requirement represented the fundamental concern for the strategic nuclear balance, including creation and deployment of forces to maintain a strong nuclear triad and the efforts to establish arms-control and arms-reduction agreements with the Soviet Union. Strategic deterrence also included extended nuclear deterrence to support NATO allies and Japan.

Forward defense. This requirement was reflected in the forward deployed elements of U.S. armed forces to support containment and deter aggression, including forces deployed on the territory of allies, especially in Europe and Korea,[25] and forces deployed at sea throughout the world. Forward defense also included the planned reinforcement of conventional forces with theater and tactical nuclear weapons. "The overall size, capabilities, and characteristics of the U.S. armed forces are strongly influenced by the need to maintain such presence."[26]

Mobilization and reinforcement. This requirement was a critical underpinning of U.S. strategy for global war. It was reflected in the missions of many active-duty forces and even more clearly in the missions of federal reserve and National Guard forces. These forces formed the strategic reserve that could mobilize and deploy to reinforce forward defense forces.[27] Mobilization also included emphasis on the maintenance of a broad industrial base to sustain military capacity.

Post–Cold War Military Requirements

Since the Cold War, the strategy is best captured by the term "Engagement." The main aspects of engagement that bear on the capacities of the armed forces are those to *shape* the international environment, *respond* to crises, and *prepare* for future threats.[28] The military role now has five main components: Homeland defense, smaller-scale contingency operations, counterproliferation, power projection, and regional deterrence.[29]

Homeland defense. As the 2001 Quadrennial Defense Review was in its final stages of preparation, the 11 September 2001 terrorist attacks on the World Trade Center and Pentagon cast the entire defense debate in a new light. Setting aside contentious issues of force structure and doctrinal change, the 2001 QDR instead emphasized the need for defense of the United States homeland clearly challenged by the terrorists' boldness and success. The confidence in the seeming invulnerability provided by the country's two-ocean cushion was seriously shaken. For the George W. Bush administration, homeland defense also includes the effort to develop and deploy ballistic missile-defense systems.[30]

Strategic power projection. This requirement reflects increased emphasis on the capacity to deploy conventional military forces rapidly from the United States to respond to a spectrum of potential crises around the world. In the absence a single, clear adversary, the ability to deploy forces to a myriad of potential danger points demands greater flexibility in basing and equipment prepositioning. The importance of power projection is also a function of the fact that the remaining armed forces are now mainly based within the United States. During the post–Cold War force reductions, overseas forces were deactivated at a higher rate than those in the United States. The personnel and equipment from many units were also moved back to the continental United States. Forces in the United States now often provide the bulk of the forces for contingency deployments in times of crisis. Increased reliance on forces based within the United States also places greater emphasis on the means of deployment to move those forces to the place in the world where they are needed, which has increased the importance of airlift and sealift assets. Additionally, potential adversaries are likely to increase efforts to deny U.S. and allied forces access to the bases and ports necessary to support large-scale force deployments. Therefore, part of strategic power projection includes efforts to overcome access-denial attempts and to create capabilities that will speed the deployment of robust combat capabilities to wherever they are needed.

Smaller-scale contingencies or peace operations. This requirement is a new area of emphasis since the Cold War that reflects increased concern with a wide range of crises and opportunities, short of war, for which the armed forces can play useful roles. These roles include support for broadly defined interests of international security, including humanitarian assistance, conflict prevention, support for democracy, peacekeeping, peace enforcement, noncombatant evacuations, military-to-military contacts, combined exercises with foreign troops, and so on. The George W. Bush administration placed a much lower emphasis on participation in such missions; however, pressure to sustain existing missions and the likely follow-up military operations related to the global war on terrorism highlight the continued need for U.S. forces to conduct such operations well. The 2001 QDR report for the first time explicitly recognizes the need to account for smaller-scale contingencies as one of the elements that defines the size of the U.S. armed forces.[31]

Counterproliferation. This requirement is the effort to prevent the spread of materials and technology related to the creation of weapons of mass destruction (WMD) and to mitigate or prevent the effectiveness of such weapons if used. WMD include nuclear, chemical, and biological weapons. Counterproliferation includes efforts to prevent the spread of WMD among states and nonstate actors, such as terrorist groups, as well as efforts to defeat the use of nuclear weapons and other WMD. Counterproliferation concerns also extend to long-range ballistic missiles as a delivery means for such weapons. For the military, counterproliferation provides the rationale for continuing to maintain an arsenal, albeit much smaller, of American strategic nuclear weapons. These weapons continue to provide deterrence against the use of WMD by potential adversaries. Counter-proliferation has also been the main rationale behind the pursuit of theater and national missile-defense systems.

Forward deterrence. This requirement refers to the central military task to be prepared to fight and defeat "attacks against U.S. allies and friends in any two theaters of operation in overlapping timeframes."[32] This includes "maintaining regionally tailored forces forward stationed and deployed in Europe, Northeast Asia, the East Asian littoral, and the Middle East/Southwest."[33] The 2001 QDR no longer claims to be able to execute two near simultaneous regional wars across the full spectrum of military operations. Instead, U.S. policy now supports the ability to fight one war to include occupation of an enemy's capital and territory while being able to halt the aggression of a second foe without decisive ground operations to occupy the opponent's territory or capital.[34] With the exception of the Korean peninsula, where front lines with a Communist threat remain, the purpose of forward-deployed American armed forces differs from the Cold War when most forces were deployed with a mission to defend nearby geographic boundaries. Instead, such forces are now available for rapid response throughout the local region to meet remaining threats to allies and to American interests. These forces are still available for the defense of allies, as they were during the Cold War, but with fewer direct threats, the utility of these forces is more valuable for the shortened logistical supply lines and deployment distances they provide to other world danger areas.[35]

The change from containment to engagement is best understood as the response to the collapse of the Soviet Union. Furthermore, the strategic military requirements have changed from focusing on potential global conflict with the Soviet Union to dealing with a myriad of diverse regional security challenges in the post–Cold War era. The most salient changes for the military in this respect are the emphasis on homeland defense and the identification of peace operations as critical missions for the armed forces in shaping the international environment. Side by side with the new emphasis on peace operations is a continuing recognition of the need for U.S. armed forces to remain prepared for combat. However, in the post–Cold War era, the war-fighting focus is on the ability to fight and win two major theater wars. While the emphasis on peace operations is a major change in the post–Cold War era, the emphasis on fighting wars, albeit at the regional rather than global level, reflects basic continuity with the dominant military missions of the Cold War era.

AGGREGATE DEFENSE SPENDING

The change in the fundamental national security strategy has also driven a basic reassessment of the appropriate level of defense spending. There were decreases in real (inflation adjusted) defense spending every year between 1985 and 1999. Overall, from 1985 to 1999, defense spending was reduced by approximately one third. In early 1999, after increasing criticism of inadequate defense spending to meet competing modernization needs, readiness needs, and the demands of continued U.S. presence in Bosnia, President Clinton proposed the first real increase in defense spending since 1985.[36] The intent of the increase in defense spending was to provide more resources for personnel and readiness (particularly changes to pay and retirement systems) and to provide more resources for procurement and modernization.[37] The adjusted level of defense spending would sustain defense at approximately 3 percent of gross domestic product (GDP). Since 1999, President Clinton and his successor, President Bush, have supported annual increases in funding for defense (in real terms). In the wake of the September 2001 attacks, increased defense spending is certain. In January 2002, President Bush proposed increases of over $48 billion for the fiscal year (FY03) defense budget and increases of over $400 billion in the aggregate through 2007.[38] Figures 2.1 and 2.2 help put defense budget changes in perspective. In general, the significant trends since the Cold War can be summed up by the real reduction in the defense budget as a proportion of GDP and as a proportion of the federal budget.

Figure 2.1
Defense Budget as Percent of Gross Domestic Product (GDP)[1]

1. Data from the Executive Office of the President of the United States, *The Budget For Fiscal Year 2000, Historical Tables,* Washington D.C.: Government Printing Office, 1999, Table 8.4, "Outlays By Budget Enforcement Act Category as Percentages of GDP: 1962–2004," 120 and from Rumsfeld, "2003 Defense Budget Testimony." (Rumsfeld testimony used for 2003 data.)

Figure 2.2
Defense Budget as Percent of Federal Outlays[1]

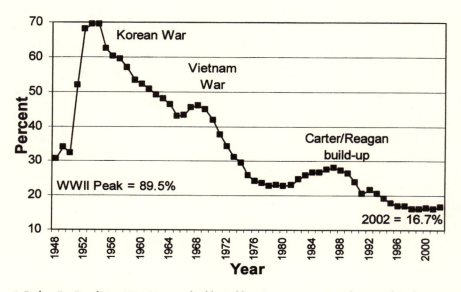

1. *Budget For Fiscal Year 2000, Historical Tables,* Table 8.3, "Percentage Distribution Of Outlays By Budget Enforcement Act Category: 1962–2004," 119.

The demise of the Soviet Union brought calls for a "peace dividend." This prominent, popular demand, echoed by elected officials, induced the defining change in the military—the reduction of national resources devoted to defense. Public demands for a peace dividend were reflected in public opinion polls.[39] By 1990, the idea that the defense budget must yield a peace dividend for the country was a common refrain in public statements and official testimony of many leaders throughout the government.

These pressures resulted in a major reduction in the size of the defense budget. In real terms, the defense budget declined by approximately 34 percent between the peak of the Reagan defense build up in 1985 and 1999.[40] In broader historical terms, however, the decline is not very great compared to other eras of peace before World War II. Compared to average spending throughout the Cold War (to include the Korean and Vietnam Wars), aggregate defense spending declined by only approximately 13 percent.[41] Additionally, current peacetime defense spending remains well above the levels of spending associated with national demobilization between major wars. The recent war posture the United States assumed to fight terrorism will reinforce recent efforts to increase defense spending in real terms.

Defense Spending as a Percent of GDP

Over the years, various analyses have attempted to assess how much of America's resources are enough for defense. One prominent standard has been the proportion of the GDP devoted to defense. Defense spending as a percent of GDP recently reached a post–World War II low. This drop also represents an approximately 50 percent reduction in defense spending as a proportion of GDP from the peak of the Reagan defense build up. If passed in its entirety, the Bush administration's proposed FY03 defense budget increase to $379 billion would represent a rise to 3.3 percent of GDP.[42] Figure 2.1 also demonstrates the general trend of defense spending becoming a progressively smaller proportion of national economic output over time (except during wars and the Reagan build up). That is, even when defense spending held relatively steady, the defense budget declined further as a proportion of GDP due to the increased rate of economic growth of the national economy.

Defense Spending as a Percent of Federal Spending

As with defense spending as a proportion of GDP, the defense budget as a share of federal spending has also shown a decline that reflects both the continued real reduction in military spending coupled with the increased federal spending for other budget categories. Note that the slope of the decline for defense spending as a percent of overall government spending is even steeper than the decline relative to GDP.[43]

In a general trend that can be traced back to the early 1960s, discretionary outlays of the federal budget have decreased as a proportion of the overall budget while mandatory spending has steadily increased as a proportion of outlays. Mandatory spending includes Social Security; means-tested entitlements, such as Medicare, Medicaid, Food Stamps, Head Start; and interest on the national debt. Since 1962, discretionary spending, including defense, has dropped from over two thirds of federal outlays to less than one third. In the same period, Social Security, other means-tested entitlements, and interest on the national debt have all increased substantially as a proportion of outlays. Within discretionary spending, defense and domestic spending now represent roughly equal proportions, which is a change from typical Cold War distributions that favored defense.[44]

OPTIONS FOR MILITARY CAPABILITIES

The fact that there has been little change in military capabilities other than reduction is not due to lack of alternatives. Since the end of the Cold War, several proposals for major changes to military capabilities relate to the major changes in the international-security environment. Many of these proposals were addressed in military professional journals, and some are still actively debated. Nonetheless, the fact remains that few of the proposals have been the basis for anything other than continued study and debate.

This is not to say that there is no interest in trying to change defense policy. Since the end of the Cold War, leaders in the government and many analysts in the larger defense-interested community have pressed for significant change in the U.S. military. Among the Washington think tanks and advocacy groups, the Brookings Institution,[45] Center for Defense Information (CDI),[46] Center for Strategic and Budgetary Assessments (CSBA, formerly the Defense Budget Project),[47] and RAND[48] have been prominent advocates for change. However, the general nature of the challenges posed by these groups is better understood as a debate among experts rather than as the vanguard of broader public movements. Similarly, Congress has had a handful of defense-minded members who have been active in pursuing major changes. These included Representatives Les Aspin and Ron Dellums, and Senators Sam Nunn, Joseph Lieberman, Dan Coats, and John McCain.

With the end of the Cold War, policymakers were confronted with the need to fundamentally reevaluate defense policy and the military capabilities that should support it. While the Soviet Union still existed, some argued strongly that the changes in Eastern Europe and the Soviet Union were reversible and, therefore, the United States should not act unilaterally to decrease military capabilities. In other words, there was a 'do nothing' option that would be reflected in sustained levels of defense spending and sustainment of all existing forces. As long as the Soviet Union existed, the potential for renewed Cold War tension remained a possibility.[49]

With the collapse of the U.S.S.R. and the end of the Cold War, the choice to do nothing and simply sustain the existing policy course was not a realistic option. The result is that from the end of the Cold War, the need for change has not been in dispute. Rather, the issue has been what changes should be undertaken.

In the debates since the end of the Cold War, a myriad of approaches have been considered for defense policy, and there are endless numbers of combinations and permutations of possible force packages and doctrinal changes. Overall, however, the various changes proposed can be summarized by three main options: demobilization, restructuring, and reduction.

Demobilization

Demobilization represents the most common historical response for changes to military capabilities following major wars. Until World War II, the general pattern was the existence of a small standing military force backed by militia or reserve forces that could be mobilized for war or major crisis. When the United States went to war, a call up of reserve forces occurred. After the war ended, the forces were demobilized with most service members going back to the civilian sector and the active force once again reduced to a small residual size to handle remaining security missions and serve as the foundation for future mobilizations.

Following World War II, the United States did begin to demobilize, as it had after all previous major wars. A force of over 12 million personnel (1945) was soon reduced to a little under 1.5 million (1950).[50] Those forces still remaining were predominantly engaged in occupation duty in Japan and Germany. Commensurate with their occupation duties, there was also a significant drop off in combat readiness.

As the conflict between the Soviet Union and the United States became more serious, the United States decided to maintain a large standing military force to support the strategy of containment. The Korean War in 1950 put an end to the post–World War II demobilization and firmly established the pattern of defense policy for the Cold War that relied on the maintenance of a substantial active military force ready for war with the Soviet Union or other communist forces. In that sense, the Cold War can be regarded as another in the series of American wars for which the government called into being a substantial standing force to address the crisis at hand.

With the end of the Cold War, many argued that it was possible to institute the sort of demobilization that had traditionally occurred.

When the Cold War ended, America did not demobilize, as it had after previous great conflicts. True, the awesome U.S. military arsenal was reduced in size, but it remains configured and equipped to confront a war of maximum scale.[51]

The general outlines of demobilization would include the massive reduction of active military forces with primary reliance on ready reserves (federal reserves and state National Guard forces) that can mobilize in response to future military needs.[52]

Some Democratic Congress members proposed what amounted to a demobilization of the active force in line with historical precedents following other major wars in U.S. history. The concern was the tremendous size of the peacetime defense budget and the effect on other priorities. This alternative proposed a radical reduction in the active force with responsibility transferred to National Guard and reserve forces that could be activated and mobilized in a crisis.[53] Commensurate with demobilization of the military forces themselves were proposed reductions to the military industrial base. Questions of whether to close production facilities, bases, and other parts of the military support and infrastructure created important stakes for elected leaders with military communities and defense-industry sites.

Variation on the demobilization alternative included attempts to reduce dramatically U.S. military involvement overseas due to fewer direct military threats to the United States and its vital interests and the less critical nature of those threats. This demobilization variation is a natural outcome of a policy of extremely selective engagement in the international arena.

Another variation on demobilization is for the United States to demobilize most of the current forces while placing greater emphasis on collective action with other like-minded states to address the military threats that remain. Again, a robust reserve force would be maintained for possible activation in the event that a new major power threat emerges in the future.[54]

One reason that is often advanced to support demobilization is the need to emphasize the long-run economic health of the country—a critical element of national security. When not confronted with a clear need for standing forces, this approach holds that it is more fiscally sound to rely on the reserves. A prominent advocate of this approach was Representative Ron Dellums (D-CA).

Contrary to those who worry that we spend too little on defense, I believe that our current level of spending—far in excess of our most robust potential adversary—is excessive and represents a long-term threat to our national economy and to the integrity of the national treasury and, therefore, to our national security.[55]

Because of the massive budget savings that would be realized from demobilization, it was also a popular option among groups with budget priorities that competed with defense (for example, important domestic programs, such as Welfare).

Since September 2001, there has been no evidence of any support for demobilization. The United States is at war. It is unlikely that there will be renewed pressure for demobilization until the war against global terrorism is complete.

Restructuring

Restructuring is defined by the radical reorganization and reorientation of existing military capabilities or the creation of new capabilities. There are many ways to consider restructuring the existing armed forces. Common threads of restructuring proposals are a departure from patterns of Cold War defense policy regarding force structure and doctrine and an effort to match military capabilities more closely with perceptions of future demands. Assumptions about service roles and missions, the organization of the military services, and doctrine are subject to question and potential change. Restructuring changes can be understood as alternatives to Cold War era business as usual. Prominent advocates for restructuring include former Senator Nunn, Senator Lieberman, and the members of the National Defense Panel. All three presidents of the post–Cold War era also suggested that American armed forces should be radically restructured or transformed. Actual changes to Cold War developed force structure and doctrine have been minimal to date. However, recent developments suggest that efforts to transform the armed forces are beginning to gain broader support both inside and outside the military services.

Restructuring changes can effect the fundamental division of labor among the military services or between active and reserve components. Such changes include proposals to ignore long-standing agreements on relative equity among services and instead emphasize efforts to pursue changes in one service at the expense of another service. Implicit in many restructuring proposals is the possibility for trade-offs across services. For example, one approach is to increase support for precision air-power capabilities to attack enemy targets with less emphasis on the use of ground forces to close with and destroy the enemy. An example of this sort of restructuring change is the creation of the air force as a separate service after World War II and the disproportionate emphasis on nuclear delivery missions at the expense of the army and navy.

Such changes may also be characterized by proposals to change the doctrine and force structure of one or more of the services without necessarily affecting the other services. Recently, such efforts to radically reorganize the individual services have been described as transformation efforts. For example, army efforts to restructure divisions with different types of equipment, navy interest in the arsenal ship, and marine Hunter Warrior experiments represent internal service initiatives that could alter the basic structure of their respective services (each of these initiatives is discussed in more detail later). Transformation is now the buzzword of choice. All the services have claimed to be undertaking transformation efforts. The degree to which such efforts might radically change force structure is still a matter of debate. Such changes have yet to be implemented, although realistic evidence suggests that the services are seriously exploring force-structure alternatives that may well lead to major reorganization of entire services within the next ten to fifteen years.

Proposals that would lead to major restructuring stem from three main challenges: the high-tech revolution in military affairs, peace operations, and, most recently, homeland security. First and most prominent are many proposals that focus on the assimilation of new technology and tactics appropriate to the revolution in military affairs (RMA). Second are proposals to create or reorient existing forces for peace operations. Most recently, the events of September 2001 have opened a debate about the fundamental structure of the U.S. national-security establishment with regards to homeland security. A subset of this debate is the role and structure of the U.S. armed forces in support of homeland security.

Revolution in military affairs. At the high end of the conflict spectrum, the RMA is generally associated with advances in computer and information systems that have substantially altered the technological foundations of war. The RMA is characterized by a variety of high-technology features, such as the increased use of information, robotics, precision-guided weapons, and precise, real-time reconnaissance tied to attack platforms that place few if any lives at risk. Advocates of restructuring based on the RMA perceive the imperatives of change and adaptation as an effort to avoid fighting the last war and risk being surpassed by an innovative peer competitor that incorporates the technology into fundamentally different organizations and tactics. Responding to this revolution calls for more than just generational upgrade of existing programs employed by existing organizations. To be effective, RMA advocates believe that the United States must explore new ways of fighting with newly designed forces. The most prominent advocates of this approach include the National Defense Panel (NDP). The NDP's statement for change can be found in its 1997 report.[56] President George W. Bush also endorsed the importance of the RMA as the driving force behind a new way of warfare. In December 2001, he declared the transformation of the military as the first priority in America's efforts to improve its security following the terrorists attacks of September 2001. He cited the combat operations in Afghanistan as an illustration of a new approach to warfare based on high-tech weaponry and innovative doctrine related to the RMA.[57]

Peace operations. Since the end of the Cold War, peace operations have been a common and an important part of U.S. national-security efforts. To recognize and better respond to these demands, one innovative approach would be to create military forces more specifically configured and prepared for peace operations. These forces would perform missions similar to many that have been undertaken by U.S. forces throughout its history. Missions, such as security and pacification of the American West in the 1800s, and long-term stability missions in Haiti, Nicaragua, and the Philippines in the first half of the 1900s, are a common occurrence between major wars. Proposals include the creation of separate peace-operation forces distinct from other parts of the military force structure.[58] Such specifically configured forces are in contrast with the historical U.S. tendency to rely on traditional military units to perform these missions as a temporary diversion from primary war-fighting tasks. A variation on this approach is to make peace operations the primary mission for some forces that would also train for war, which is the reverse of the current tendency for forces trained for war to execute peace operations as a lesser included mission.

An example of the argument in favor of creating some forces trained primarily for peace operations is provided by Don Snider in his article "Let the Debate Begin."[59] He draws on the constabulary-force concept advanced by Morris Janowitz in his 1960 book *The Professional Soldier*.[60] The argument in favor of creating forces specifically for peace operations draws on the experience of the Canadians, Scandinavians, and other countries that have been active in peace operations in recent decades and who have adapted special training programs and created forces that are often used as part of U.N. and other peace operations. For the U.S. military, the creation of peace operation forces could accomplish two main purposes. First, forces configured for peace operations could include the specialized personnel for those missions and therefore avoid the stress on the current force that occurs when low-density skills of the current combat force are overtaxed due to the greater need for such specialties in peace operations (for example, military police, intelligence, electronic early warning aircraft monitoring, and so on). Second, the remainder of the force would, therefore, be able to devote its time and resources to preparation for war without the distraction of missions that are distinctly different from the primary mission to fight and win our nation's wars.

Another version of this approach to better restructure armed forces to accommodate peace operations includes suggestions to simply increase the size or quantity of units, such as civil affairs, military police, and so on, that tend to be in high demand for peace operations.[61] Without segmenting these elements off from the regular armed forces, the structure could include more robust capabilities that recognize the increased demands of peace operations.

During his run for the presidency, George W. Bush campaigned against the use of the military for peace operations and criticized the use of U.S. armed forces for such missions by the previous administration. Following the September 2001 attacks, he reiterated his opposition to the use of the military for such missions.

When the Cold War ended, some predicted that the era of direct threats to our nation was over. Some thought our military would be used overseas—not to win wars, but mainly to police and pacify, to control crowds and contain ethnic conflict. They were wrong.[62]

Nonetheless, even as the United States fights abroad to defeat global terrorist networks, the situation in Afghanistan has shown the continuing need for armed forces to help establish stability and local security. Other nations have already begun to provide forces to assist in peacekeeping, and there have been calls for the United States to contribute armed forces to assist with this mission.[63] Furthermore, previous commitments to support peace operations in Haiti, Bosnia, and Kosovo are unlikely to end soon.

Homeland defense. Since the end of the nineteenth century when the United States effectively secured its frontier, the dominant focus of the U.S. military establishment has been threats from abroad. Hence, the military forces have focused on the ability to fight other great power military forces. The size and shape of the active military in particular has been governed by the security threats the United States perceived from other states. Similarly, the National Guard (the former militias) and other reserves were reconfigured for rapid mobilization and deployment to augment the active force in fighting great power competitors. The events of September 2001 elicited calls for a fundamental reassessment of U.S. organization for homeland security. As President Bush stated on 11 December 2001,

The enemy who appeared on September 11th seeks to evade our strength and constantly searches for our weaknesses. So America is required once again to change the way our military thinks and fights.[64]

The structure, roles, and missions of several agencies are part of the homeland security debate. The border patrol, customs service, immigration and naturalization service, FBI and Coast Guard are prominent organizations with traditional roles that support homeland security. But, with National Guard units assigned to airport security and increased concern about weapons of mass destruction, there have been calls for greater effort on behalf of our war-fighting forces—active and reserve—to become more involved in homeland defense tasks.[65] One proposal includes the creation of a new unified command for homeland defense.[66] Even before 11 September, some studies recognized the potential tensions between the demands for forces to assist in critical homeland-security tasks and the roles those same forces would be expected to perform in war. As with peace operations, homeland-security missions have been lesser-included missions of the forces structured for the major theater war strategy.[67] Therefore, to devote units to homeland defense requires reassessment of the risks created with regard to their previous missions.

Reduction

Reduction accepts the basic premise that the United States must maintain large standing forces to address residual threats in the wake of the Cold War (major theater wars) and hedge against the uncertainty of the international environment. Adaptation of military forces focuses on reducing the size of the force while maintaining the same basic organization, mix of units, personnel specialties, equipment and doctrine. Other than size, there are no significant changes to the roles and missions of the military services or to the proportion of resources dedicated to the remaining forces.

The most prominent support for this approach comes from the uniformed military leadership The most common argument for not significantly changing existing force structure and doctrine is, in essence, 'if it ain't broke, don't fix it.' There is considerable logic to this for a force that has been successful in war and has averted any significant problems in peace operations.[68]

In comparing the three general approaches to change, it is worth noting that although all three approaches are distinct, they are not mutually exclusive. Demobilization can be thought of a more radical form of reduction that also includes reorientation from reliance on active forces to reliance on the ready reserves. Furthermore, both reduction and demobilization could certainly take place simultaneously with efforts to alter service roles and missions or even create new forces. Most advocates of restructuring for either the RMA or peace operations do not advocate greater defense spending or larger armed forces, just that the remaining armed forces be structured to address more appropriately the challenges of the post–Cold War era.

Very few individuals have advocated radical demobilization (similar to demobilizations before 1950). Both on the right and left of the political spectrum, continued belief in the need for the ready capability to intervene abroad remains strong. This is true for conservative, realist advocates, who cite security-related interests, as well as for liberal advocates, who support intervention on behalf of liberal values, such as democracy promotion or humanitarian assistance. However, with regard to other political interests, members of the political left, including prominent members of the Democratic Party, have suggested greater reductions in defense spending as a means to free resources for competing government efforts. The likelihood of additional reductions in the military was significantly reduced after Republicans gained control of Congress.

During the 2000 Presidential election, both candidates (Gore and Bush) proposed increased defense spending. In fact, Democratic Party candidate Gore proposed greater increases in defense spending than Republican candidate Bush.[69] The events of 11 September 2001 and the subsequent war against global terrorism have reinforced and accelerated the support for additional defense spending. Additionally, the war against global terrorism ended, at least temporarily, efforts to further reduce the size of the armed forces.[70]

NOTES

1. Graham Allison and Philip Zelikow, *Essence of Decision: Explaining the Cuban Missile Crisis* (New York: Addison, Wesley Longman, 1999), 164.

2. Some of the most prominent works include Allison and Zelikow's, Richard Betts, *Soldiers, Statesmen, and Cold War Crises* (New York: Columbia University Press, 1991) (1977). Yuen Foong Khong, *Analogies at War: Korea, Munich, Dien Bien Phu, and the Vietnam Decisions of 1965* (Princeton: Princeton University Press, 1992). David Petraeus, "The American Military and the Lessons of Vietnam: A Study of Military Influence and the Use of Force in the Post-Vietnam Era." Ph.D. diss., Princeton University, 1987. Peter M. Dawkins, "The United States Army and the "Other" War in Vietnam: A Study of the Complexity of Implementing Organizational Change," Ph.D. diss, Princeton University, 1979, and Bob Woodward, *The Commanders* (New York: Simon and Schuster, 1991).

3. Allison and Zelikow, *Essence of Decision*, 164.

4. Barry R. Posen, *The Sources of Military Doctrine: France, Britain, and Germany Between the World Wars* (Ithaca: Cornell University Press, 1984).

5. Stephen P. Rosen, *Winning the Next War: Innovation and the Modern Military* (Ithaca: Cornell University Press, 1991), 253.

6. This point is well illustrated by Allison, Andrew F. Krepinevich, Jr., *The Army and Vietnam* (Baltimore: The Johns Hopkins University Press, 1986), and John Nagl, "Learning to Eat Soup with a Knife: British and American Army Counterinsurgency Learning in Malaya and Vietnam," D.Phil. diss, Oxford University, 1997.

7. An illustration of this point was the deployment of U.S. Army Apache helicopters (known as Task Force Hawk) to support the air attacks against Yugoslavia during the crisis in Kosovo. Designed for use in support of attacking ground forces, it was difficult to adapt tactical methods of attack helicopter employment to support the differing demands of a precision air campaign that sought to minimize collateral damage and friendly casualties. In the end, the adaptation was not successfully accomplished in time for the Apaches to join the campaign. For an explanation of the difficulties encountered see Sean D. Naylor, "Sidelined: How America Won a War Without the Army," *Army Times*, 16 August 1999, 18–21.

8. Joint Chiefs of Staff, *Joint Warfare of the Armed Forces of the United States,* Washington, D.C.: Government Printing Office, 10 January 1995, I-3.

9. Posen, *The Sources of Military Doctrine,* 13–14.

10. The sources of these strategies are the reports submitted to Congress in accordance with the Defense Reorganization Act of 1986 (Goldwater-Nichols). The reports are submitted by the president to the Congress to address the national security strategy of the United States.

11. Earl Tilford, in the Foreword to Jeffrey Record, *The Creeping Irrelevance of U.S. Force Planning* (Carlisle, PA: Strategic Studies Institute, May 19, 1998), iii.

12. President George Bush, Report to Congress, *National Security Strategy of the United States* (Washington, D.C.: The White House, August 1991) (hereafter referred to as NSS 1991).

13. President William Clinton, Report to Congress, *A National Security Strategy of Engagement and Enlargement* (Washington, D.C.: The White House, May 1994) (hereafter referred to as NSS 1994).

14. President William Clinton, Report to Congress, *National Security Strategy for a New Century* (Washington, D.C.: The White House, October 1998) (hereafter referred to as NSS 1998).

15. As of June 2002, the Bush Administration has yet to publish a formal national security strategy document. The administration's general strategy is suggested by the 2001 QDR report and a variety of policy speeches. Department of Defense, *Quadrennial Defense Review Report* (hereafter referred to as 2001 QDR), 30 September 2001.

16. Barry R. Posen and Andrew L. Ross, "Competing Visions for U.S. Grand Strategy," *International Security* 21, No. 3 (Winter 1996/97), 5–53.

17. For example, the attacks of 11 September 2001 had mass destructive effects, although the means used were not traditionally understood weapons of mass destruction.

18. George W. Bush, "President George W. Bush's Inaugural Address," 20 January 2001, available from http://www.whitehouse.gov/news/inaugural-address.html; Internet; accessed 14 March 2002.

19. Ronald Reagan, Report to Congress, *National Security Strategy of the United States* (Washington, D.C.: The White House, January 1988) (hereafter referred to as NSS 1988), 1.

20. NSS 1988, 13.

21. 2001 QDR, 3.

22. Ibid, 21.

23. William J. Clinton (President of the United States), *A National Security Strategy for a Global Age,* Washington, D.C.: The White House, December 2000 (hereafter referred to as NSS 2000), 27.

24. The requirement for the president to submit a report to Congress setting out the national security strategy of the United States was contained in the Goldwater-Nichols Defense Department Reorganization Act of 1986 (Section 603).

25. Other forward-conventional defense deployments during the Cold War included forces in Panama, Vietnam, the Philippines, and Japan.

26. NSS 1988, 18.

27. The idea of the mobilization and deployment of strategic conventional reserves to forward areas was exemplified by events such as the annual REFORGER exercise in Europe (REturn of FORces to GERmany) and the annual TEAM SPIRIT exercise in Asia (reinforcement of the Korean peninsula).

28. NSS 2000, 1–3. Also described in the May 1997 report of the Quadrennial Defense Review, v.

29. The titles for these components summarize the military strategic requirements outlined by NSS 2000 and a variety of other defense documents, such as the 2001 QDR.

30. Donald H. Rumsfeld (Secretary of Defense), "2003 Defense Budget Testimony," Remarks as prepared for delivery to the House and Senate Armed Services Committees, 5 & 6 February 2002.

31. 2001 QDR, 18.

32. Ibid, 21.

33. Ibid, 20.

34. Ibid, 21.

35. This is most clearly true for Europe where the Cold War mission to provide forward defense along the front line at the Iron Curtain has disappeared with the collapse of the Soviet Union and its communist satellite states. The forces deployed there focus on working with new friends and potential allies from the former Soviet Bloc as well as serving as a pool of forward-deployed units more easily dispatched to situations in that corner of the world (for example, the current deployment to Bosnia and the deployment of a substantial segment of U.S. forces Europe to Operations Desert Shield/Storm).

36. Real defense spending did increase in 1991 due to the Gulf War (not as part of the defense budget plan). Source, *The Budget For Fiscal Year 2000, Historical Tables*.

37. Steven Lee Myers, "Administration to Propose Largest Increase in Military Spending Since the Mid-1980s." *New York Times* (2 January 1999), available from http://www.nytimes.com/yr/mo/day/news/washpol/military-budget.html; Internet; accessed 2 January 1999.

38. Rumsfeld, "2003 Defense Budget Testimony."

39. For example, see Chicago Council of Foreign Relations analysis of support for defense spending, 1974 to 1999. The surveys note that the preference for cutbacks in defense spending have been greater than for expanded defense spending among both the public and leaders since the mid-1980s. Furthermore, leaders have more strongly supported cutbacks than the public (contained in chapter 5, "Military Relationships" in *American Public Opinion and American Foreign Policy 1995*, available from http://www.ccfr.org/publications/opinion/chap5.html; Internet; accessed 18 January 1999.

40. Using 1985 peak outlays of $409.4 billion and 2000 outlays (est.) of $270.3 billion from the FY 2000 budget historical tables (figures expressed in constant, FY 2000 dollars). OMB, *FY 2000 budget*, Washington, D.C.: GPO, 1999.

41. Using 1947–1989 average defense spending of $313.6 billion and projected budget of $270 billion for FY2000 (figures expressed in constant, FY 2000 dollars).

42. Rumsfeld, "2003 Defense Budget Testimony."

43. The trend is toward lower government discretionary spending overall with the increases in the federal budget due primarily to entitlement programs.

44. From historical tables, *Budget of the United States Government,* Fiscal Year 1999, Table 8.3, "Percentage Distribution of Outlays by Budget Enforcement Act Category: 1962–2003," Internet, http://www.access.gpo.gov/su_docs/budget99/hist_wk4.html, accessed, 2 January 1999.

45. At the Brookings Institution, noteworthy advocates for change include Michael O'Hanlon and Lawrence Korb (who recently moved to the Council on Foreign Relations). Their primary arguments have been for a smaller force that is sized for one major regional contingency and some residual capacity, less emphasis on recapitalization of the current force (and more emphasis on long-range modernization), more reliance on multinational operations, and greater emphasis on peace operations as a preventive measure. Michael O'Hanlon, *Defense Planning for the Late 1990s: Beyond the Desert Storm Framework* (Washington, D.C.: The Brookings Institution, 1995).

46. The Center for Defense Information is a defense watchdog group staffed by many former military officers, including the director, Vice Admiral (ret.) John Shanahan. Their focus is on reduced defense spending with emphasis on the less threatening nature of the post–Cold War international environment and the absence of any threat comparable to the former Soviet Union. For representative arguments, see Statement of Vice Admiral John J. Shanahan, USN (Ret), Director, Center for Defense Information, Before the National Defense Panel Public Hearing April 29, 1997 (text from http://www.cdi.org/issues/qdr/shanpan.html, accessed 19 January 1998).

47. The most prominent critic at CSBA is the director, Dr. Andrew Krepinevich who was also a member of the 1997 National Defense Panel that conducted an independent evaluation of the 1997 QDR. Krepinevich is a vocal advocate for greater emphasis on the RMA and the need to put more resources into modernization now to prepare for the future. For a representative statement, see Andrew Krepinevich, *Restructuring for a New Era: Framing the Roles and Missions Debate* (Washington, D.C.: The Defense Budget Project, April 1995).

48. At RAND, the prominent advocates of change are those associated with Project Air Force. As one might expect, their emphasis is on the RMA and its potential for increased air-power effectiveness. A representative statement of this approach is Christopher Bowie, Fred Frostic, Kevin Lewis, John Lund, David Ochmanek, and Philip Propper, *The New Calculus: Analyzing Airpower's Changing Role in Joint Theater Campaigns* (Santa Monica, CA: RAND, 1993).

49. For example, former Secretary of Defense Caspar Weinberger, as demonstrated in the forward to his book, *Fighting For Peace: Seven Critical Years in the Pentagon* (New York: Warner Books Inc., 1990).

50. Office of Management and Budget, *Historical Tables: Budget of the United States Government, Fiscal Year 1996*, Washington, D.C.: Government Printing Office, 1995, 245.

51. William Greider, *Fortress America: The American Military and the Consequences of Peace* (New York: PublicAffairs, 1998), viii.

52. An example of approach along these lines is fourth of the force options that then House Armed Services committee Chairman Les Aspin proposed in 1992, "An Approach

to Sizing American Conventional Forces for the Post-Soviet Era: Four Illustrative Options," February 25, 1992. (Hereafter, Aspin, "Four Illustrative Options.")

53. Ronald V. Dellums, *Envisioning a New National Security Strategy*, March 10, 1997. Committee Reproduction.

54. For example, see Carl Conetta and Charles Knight, "Defense Sufficiency and Cooperation: A U.S. Military Posture for the Post–Cold War Era," Project on Defense Alternatives, 12 March 1998. Available from http://www.comw.org/pda/opdfin.html; Internet; accessed 19 March 2000.

55. Dellums, *Envisioning a New National Security Strategy*.

56. National Defense Panel, *Transforming Defense: National Security in the 21st Century*, Washington, D.C.: Government Printing Office, December 1997. See also Andrew F. Krepinevich, *Restructuring for a New Era:* and Michael E. O'Hanlon, "Modernizing and Transforming U.S. Forces: Alternative Paths to the Force of Tomorrow," Chapter 11, 293–318 in Michele A. Flournoy, ed. *Strategy-Driven Choices for America's Security* (Washington, D.C.: National Defense University Press, 2001).

57. President George W. Bush, *President Speaks on War Effort to Citadel Cadets*, text of presidential statement, Charleston, S.C., 11 December 2001. Available from http://www.whitehouse.gov/news/releases/2001/12/20011211-6.html; Internet; accessed 12 Dec 2001.

58. For an example of this force restructuring, see Daniel Smith, Marcus Corbin, and Christopher Hellman, *Reforging the Sword: Forces for a 21st Century Security Strategy* (Washington, D.C.: Center for Defense Information, 2001), available from http://www.cdi.org/mrp/reforging-full.pdf; Internet; accessed 9 March 2002.

59. Don Snider, "Let the Debate Begin: The Case for a Constabulary Force," *Army* (June 1998): 14–16.

60. Morris Janowitz, *The Professional Soldier* (New York: The Free Press, 1960).

61. An example of this is John J. Spinelli, "Peacetime Operations: Reducing Friction," Chapter 10, 262–291 in Michele A. Flournoy, ed. *Strategy-Driven Choices for America's Security* (Washington, D.C.: National Defense University Press, 2001).

62. President Bush speech at Citadel, 11 December 2001.

63. Mark Landler, "Biden Wants U.S. Troops to Join Peace Force," *New York Times*, January 13, 2002, 12.

64. President Bush speech at Citadel, 11 December 2001.

65. Bryan Bender, "National Guard Faces Drastic Overhaul," *Boston Globe*, November 20, 2001, 12.

66. Bradley Graham, "Military Favors a Homeland Command," *Washington Post*, November 21, 2001, p. 1.

67. Michele A. Flournoy, Kenneth F. McKenzie, Jr., and John J. Spinelli, "Identifying Force Structure Issues: Sifting the Screen," Chapter 8, 217–233 in Michele A. Flournoy, ed. *Strategy-Driven Choices for America's Security* (Washington, D.C.: National Defense University Press, 2001).

68. However, some have argued that the mission in Somalia was undermined by the U.S. armed forces when they adopted essentially combat operations more central to their training to deal with one of the Somali clans. Similarly, available weapons and

tactics significantly affected the manner in which the NATO air war against Serbia took place. (In particular, the inability to adapt a unit or Apache helicopters to participate in the campaign highlights the effects of inappropriately configured forces.)

69. Stuart A. Ibberson, "Candidates Offer Differing Views on Future of Military," *Journal of Aerospace and Defense Industry News*, 3 November 2000, available from http://www.aerotechnews.com/starc/2000/110300/Bush_Gore.html; Internet; accessed 13 March 2002.

70. Jonathan Weisman, "Cuts Get Cut From Pentagon Budget," *USA Today*, January 8, 2002, 4.

Chapter 3

Trends in Military Capabilities since the Cold War

> We are convinced that the challenges of the twenty-first century will be
> quantitatively and qualitatively different from those of the Cold War and
> require fundamental change to our national-security institutions, military
> strategy, and defense posture by 2020.
> —National Defense Panel, December 1997[1]

OVERVIEW

The changes in the national-security strategy and the political decisions on the
appropriate aggregate level of the defense budget provide the general context
for selecting or creating the military capabilities for the country. The previous
chapter demonstrated that the national-security strategy and aggregate defense spending have changed significantly since the end of the Cold War.
The next sections explore how military capabilities have been affected by these
constraints.

This chapter describes key elements of force structure and doctrine in terms
of change and continuity relative to Cold War capabilities. Although the trends
include some indicators of change in American military capabilities, they are
small in comparison to the substantial continuity in the fundamental character
of the U.S. armed forces. The character of these forces remains essentially
grounded in the Cold War era. There is nothing inherently good or bad about
either change or continuity. I argue, however, that the predominant continuity
that has defined military capabilities since the end of the Cold War is a negative
outcome. It inhibits effective preparation for future military challenges related
to the revolution in military affairs, and it imposes significant inefficiencies and
maladaptations on preparations for peace operations.

A variety of measures indicate the nature of change and continuity in military forces since the end of the Cold War. Where variables can be clearly quan-
tified (for example, personnel, equipment, units, and budget) the statistical
analyses provided are mainly simple comparisons over time. The justification
for focusing on such simple statistical measures is that these are precisely the

measures that are discussed and deliberated upon by defense policymakers themselves. The measures presented in this chapter frequently recur in the briefing charts, memoranda, press reports, and official reports of defense policymakers.

The measures of military capabilities discussed in the aggregate in this chapter are indicators of the political decision-making process that will be discussed in greater detail later. Chapters 4–8 provide a brief history and analysis of the policymaking process to substantiate the suggestive association between the various measures in this chapter and the dominance of continuity versus significant change to military capabilities.

For capabilities as vast as those of the U.S. armed forces, generalizations concerning reduction versus restructuring are unsustainable without some caveats. This chapter is divided into four sections that present evidence of change and continuity (see Table 3.1 for a summary). The first section identifies indications of restructuring changes, which, albeit few and small, *do* represent a fundamental shift from the past. The second section provides evidence of reductions that reflect changes in degree but not in the fundamental balance or essential nature of military capabilities. These are the reduction efforts brought about by the end of the Cold War that, nevertheless, preserve capabilities in the same general form designed for the Cold War. The third section addresses the tremendous continuity with the past that is the dominant characteristic of U.S. military capabilities since the Cold War. This chapter concludes with a brief summary and analysis of service strategic doctrines and vision. In this area, the evidence of change or continuity is ambiguous. There is strong evidence of continuity in each service as well as substantial rhetoric in support of change or transformation. The rhetoric of future change is promising. The realty of actual achievements seems dominated by the logic of the past.

Table 3.1
Force Structure—Change and Continuity

CHANGE		CONTINUITY
Restructure	Reduction	
• **Special Operations Forces** • **Airlift and Sealift** • **Reserves** • **Nuclear Forces** • **Army IBCTs**	• **Conventional Forces** • **Personnel** • **Production**	• **Service Roles and Missions** • **Shape of the Armed Forces (by service and key service elements)** • **Selection of Future Weapons** • **Shape of the Defense Budget** — **By Service** — **By Appropriation Category**
AMBIGUOUS: Strategic Doctrine and Vision		

CHANGE: RESTRUCTURING

Although I argue that the dominant characterization of the post–Cold War period is one of substantial continuity, it is not an all-encompassing description that captures every measure of defense capabilities. Some elements of the defense establishment's force structure and doctrine do seem to reflect significant change in response to the end of the Cold War. Taken together, however, such changes in force structure and doctrine represent a small portion of defense capabilities and are dwarfed by the much more substantial elements that have been maintained with striking consistency.[2]

Restructuring in the context of this study refers to dramatic or innovative change in force structure or doctrine. Changes of this magnitude can be understood using the criteria Stephen Rosen defined with respect to innovation. Rosen defines military innovation as

a change in one of the primary combat arms of a service in the way it fights or alternatively, as the creation of a new combat arm.... A major innovation involves a change in the concepts of operation of that combat arm ... A major innovation also involves a change in the relation of that combat arm to other combat arms and a downgrading or abandoning of older concepts of operation and possibly of a formerly dominant weapon. Changes in the formal doctrine of a military organization that leave the essential working of that organization unaltered do not count as an innovation by this definition.[3]

The armed forces of the United States have undergone an overall reduction of approximately one third since 1988. In line with Rosen's definition, the changes that would represent restructuring of U.S. armed forces should include the creation of new organizations, the substantial reorientation of existing organizations, or a significant relative change of emphasis or priority on elements of the current structure relative to one another. Additionally, to represent restructuring, formal changes in doctrine must be accompanied by changes to the essential workings of the armed forces, or significant portions thereof. A good historical example of restructuring is the creation of the U.S. Air Force after World War II. With the advent of the Cold War and the nuclear RMA, the structure of the U.S. armed forces and related defense budget shares were weighted disproportionately in favor of the air force at the expense of the other services (army and navy).[4]

Few new organizations have been created within the military establishment, and there are only some minor signs that existing organizations have undertaken major reorganization (for example, different size units, new configurations of existing subunits, and so on).[5] Changes in formal doctrine do acknowledge the different strategic demands of the new era but have had little influence on the essential workings of the armed services. The few changes that appear to represent restructuring are ones of relative emphasis. That is, changes in relative force structure and budget that deviate from the overall one-third reduction of U.S. forces.

Among the various suggestive measures related to force structure and doctrine, the ones that reflect restructuring of U.S. military capabilities include the increased emphasis on Special Operations Forces, airlift and sealift assets, and reserve forces. In an opposite manner, the disproportionately greater cut in budget shares for nuclear forces reflects significant restructuring. The one major example of a new organization being created within the armed services is the creation of the interim-brigade combat teams in the army since 1999. Although currently representing less than 5 percent of the army's brigades, the creation of these new formations and the plan to create several more within the next five years does represent a major restructuring effort within the army.

Special Operations Forces

Although only a small fraction of total military forces, special forces in all the services have been preserved at Cold War levels or increased. The budget allocation for Special Operations Forces is one of only two DoD programs, out of eleven, for which funding has *increased* since the end of the Cold War. (The other program that increased is airlift and sealift—see next section.)[6]

In an institutional change undertaken in 1987, Special Operations Command (SOCOM) was created as a unified command with the unique characteristic of having control over its own budget.[7] For budget purposes, SOCOM functions essentially like a fifth military service with a separate set of congressional authorizations and appropriations.[8] SOCOM has responsibility for a variety of missions. The specialness of special forces is relative to the more traditional war-fighting roles of the armed forces. From the most highly trained, lethal commando forces to civil-affairs units, special forces provide a variety of capabilities to support national-security policy.

Special Operations Forces have a dual heritage. They are one of the nation's key penetration and strike [unconventional warfare] forces, able to respond to specialized contingencies across the conflict spectrum with stealth, speed, and precision. They are also warrior-diplomats capable of influencing, advising, training, and conducting operations with foreign forces, officials, and populations.[9]

Special forces often provides military trainers to help other states improve their defense capabilities and can provide a variety of country and region-specific skills (language, cultural, and so on) to serve various policy goals around the world.

In the wake of the Cold War, the increased emphasis on and volume of military-to-military contacts with other states increased the demands on special-operations forces. With high strategic mobility, high-caliber training, and low incremental costs, special forces have been valuable tools for post–Cold War foreign relations. In 1997, for example, Special Operations Forces deployed on 3,061 training or operational missions to 144 countries.[10] Recent combat operations in Afghanistan highlight the diverse and extremely valuable role that special operations forces can perform.

The diverse capabilities of SOCOM provide an excellent set from which policymakers can draw on short notice. SOCOM is the most broadly capable command, which makes it ideally suited for the complexity and uncertainty of the post–Cold War era. With fewer clear foes and general uncertainty about the nature of future war, the diverse skills of special forces seem a natural hedge. Nonetheless, personnel assigned to special-operations forces represent less than 5 percent of the total population of any service.

The increased emphasis on special forces *does* seem to be a response to the differing demands for armed forces often associated with low-intensity conflict or operations other than war. Therefore, it does represent a restructuring of the military in size relative to other parts of the armed forces—in that these same forces existed during the Cold War but now comprise a significantly larger, albeit still modest, proportion of the total force.

Airlift and Sealift

Another major challenge created by the end of the Cold War and the new national strategy was the increased need for strategic power-projection capabilities. The primary theater of operations is less certain. The possible deployment locations are many and spread around the globe. There is strong justification to increase sealift and airlift to carry personnel, supplies, and equipment to a variety of global locations rapidly.

The Gulf War and the demands of deploying the 500,000-person force, including armored combat units, clearly demonstrated the need for the heavy sealift and airlift capacity. The national military strategy acknowledges how critical these assets are for the rapid deployment of necessary forces to support the two major theater wars that have been the cornerstone of force-sizing calculations since the Bottom Up Review.[11]

To describe this change in airlift and sealift as the result of the Cold War is not completely accurate. The plan to purchase more cargo aircraft (especially the C-17) and faster resupply ships began in the latter stages of the Cold War. During the Cold War, these efforts were driven by the requirements of U.S. Central Command (CENTCOM) with missions in the Persian Gulf region. The creation of CENTCOM occurred in the late 1970s as a result of oil shocks and the Iranian Revolution. With no forces forward deployed in the Persian Gulf area (other than naval units rotating through), airlift and sealift assets were critical to the ability to deploy rapidly a more substantial force into the region in the event of a crisis. Additionally, the effort to upgrade the cargo aircraft fleet was a function of recapitalization needs to refit and replace aging cargo planes approaching the end of their service lives.[12]

Nevertheless, the increase in the need for power-projection support since the end of the Cold War has led to the sealift and airlift program being spared the same cuts as the other programs. In fact, spending for airlift and sealift has increased by more than any other program since 1988, in both relative and absolute terms.[13]

Ready Reserves

Another area reflecting restructuring of the armed forces is with respect to the ready-reserve forces.[14] The most significant aspect of restructuring is the significantly smaller decrease in the overall number of personnel in the National Guard and reserves relative to the active forces.

An important continuity exists in the National Guard in that combat formations have retained their basic structure and a doctrinal focus on fighting wars with emphasis on combat-arms formations. The same is not true of the federally controlled reserve-force structure. In particular, the largest reserve force, the Army Reserve, has been almost completely restructured to do away with combat and combat support units in favor of combat-service support (logistical) units.

Within the army, the move of many logistical functions into the reserves was a deliberate response to draw-down pressures. In this case, the army chose to keep a higher proportion of combat and combat-support units on active duty, while moving more service-support functions into reserve forces. This also had the intended consequence of making it very difficult for civilian political leaders to execute extensive military operations without a call up of at least part of the reserves.[15] The emphasis was on making federal-reserve forces complementary to the active force. Although active military leadership proposed similar shifts in the National Guard's force structure to complement active forces, the National Guard has effectively resisted this significant shift and instead retained the supplementary war-fighting character that defined its role during the Cold War.

In the wake of the September 2001 attacks, increased emphasis has been placed on the need for homeland defense. As policymakers work on plans to address these new challenges, it appears likely that there will be major changes to the ready reserve—in particular the National Guard—to better support such missions within the United States. Currently, however, there have been no changes to the structure of reserve units to address specifically this new emphasis on homeland defense.

In budget terms, this shift in emphasis is represented by the much slower rate of reduction of the reserve-forces program. Whereas general-purpose forces were reduced almost 43 percent, reserve forces were reduced only 16 percent. Furthermore, when measured as a share of the total budget devoted to particular programs, the National Guard and reserve program share of the budget rose by 2 percent compared to a 4 percent reduction for general-purpose forces.[16] This budget share reflects the greater political difficulty for reducing reserve forces, especially National Guard units, where service members are concentrated in specific and easily identified districts.[17] Also, Congress has shown strong political support for the logic of historical demobilization that emphasizes war-fighting forces in the reserves for possible contingencies in the future and a decreased emphasis on standing military forces in the absence of a major threat to American national security.

Nuclear Forces

The nuclear forces of the United States have been massively reduced and substantially restructured. This process began in the latter stages of the Cold War. This restructuring reflects the dramatic change in the role envisioned for these weapons. Table 3.2 highlights this change.

During the Cold War, reliance on nuclear weapons was a critical component of military strategy. In the early Cold War years, policies, such as massive retaliation, reflected a heavy reliance on nuclear weapons. Nuclear forces were a critical component of the West's ability to offset a substantial Soviet and Warsaw Pact advantage in conventional forces. By the end of the Cold War, nuclear

Table 3.2
Nuclear Force Levels[1]

NUCLEAR FORCES	1988	2001	% CHANGE (1988-2001)
SSBN	43	18	-58.14%
SLBM	528	432	-18.18%
Trident D-5	192	432	
Poseidon C-3	336		
ICBM	1,000	550	-45.00%
Minuteman	954	500	
Peacekeeper	46	50	
HEAVY BOMBERS	324	154	-52.47%
B-1B	90	56	
B-52G/H	234	82	
B-2A		16	
INF MISSILE BATTALIONS[2]	12	0	-100.00%
Pershing BN	4	0	
Lance BN	8	0	

1. 1988 Strategic force data from Appendix D, "Force Structure Tables" in Les Aspin, Annual Report to the President and Congress. Washington, D.C.-U.S. Government Printing Office, January 1994. 1999 strategic force data from Appendix D, "Force Structure Tables" in William Cohen, Annual Report to the President and the Congress. Washington, D.C.-U.S. Government Printing Office, 1999. Available from http://www.dtic.mil/execsec/adr1999; Internet accessed 12 April 1999.
2. INF stands for Intermediate-range Nuclear Force.

weapons were less central to American defense strategy overall but were still critical as a capability at the most violent end of the flexible response ladder. In defense policy debate, however, nuclear weapons continued to garner the lion's share of coverage and popular attention.

Although nuclear weapons are still in the U.S. arsenal, their role is no longer viewed as a backstop to inadequate conventional military capabilities. When addressed, the continued utility of nuclear weapons is generally recognized as a means to deter the use of nuclear weapons and weapons of mass destruction by other international actors.

Nuclear weapons serve as a hedge against an uncertain future, a guarantee of our security commitments to allies and a disincentive to those who would contemplate developing or otherwise acquiring their own nuclear weapons.[18]

The removal of tactical nuclear weapons from the military services is a further example of the separation that has been achieved between conventional military forces and nuclear weapons. In the navy and air force, there have been substantial reductions in the units that have nuclear missions. In the army, exclusively nuclear units were disbanded completely and dual-use (conventional and nuclear) units were reoriented towards solely conventional military tasks. Increasingly compartmentalized strategic forces, represented by the remaining nuclear missile submarines, the strategic missile forces (MX and Minuteman), and the long-range heavy bombers assigned to nuclear delivery missions perform the remaining nuclear missions.

Army Interim Brigade Combat Teams (IBCTs)

In 1999, General Eric Shinseki became the Army Chief of Staff. In one of his first acts, he explained that his priority effort would be to improve the strategic mobility of the army. The total effort would be a thirty-year transformation plan to create new weapons systems and formations that would be capable of decisive combat operations as well if not better than the present force but with substantially better strategic mobility.[19] As the first step in the process, General Shinseki directed the use of available technology to create interim brigade combat teams (IBCT). The IBCTs represent entirely new army formations that differ from the various light and heavy forces of the Cold War era. They are maneuver units with medium-armored vehicles at their core. These units retain much of the strategic mobility of current light infantry forces but will have greater mobility, firepower, and flexibility. The IBCTs are not as powerful or survivable as the current heavy-armored forces that form the army's core. The legacy forces—those forces designed and created during the Cold War—still define the force structure of the army and will for many years to come. Nonetheless, the new IBCTs will increase in proportion as units in the legacy force are reorganized as IBCTs. At the same time, research and development efforts for the army focus on the development of new systems to replace the heavy armored forces of the Cold War era with new capabilities generated by the technological advancements associated with the revolution in military affairs.

CHANGE: REDUCTION

The single dominant element of the change in defense since 1988 was the 34 percent real reduction in the defense budget. The one-third real reduction in overall defense spending was mirrored closely by several other measures of reduction. This one-third reduction carried over proportionally to several elements of conventional forces and reduction in overall active duty personnel.

Conventional Forces

The reduction in the size of conventional military forces has been generally commensurate with the overall one-third reduction in defense since 1988. Table 3.3 highlights key elements of force reductions. By most measures, conventional forces shared similar cuts across the board by service and by many of the major sub-elements of the services. The one significant exception to this is the much smaller reduction of the Marine Corps.

Table 3.3
Key Conventional Force Reductions[1]

Forces	1988	2001	% Change (88-01)
Army divisions and division equivalents[2]	37	25	-32.4%
Navy carriers	15	12	-20%
Other Navy surface combatants & attack subs	508	317	-37.6%
Marine divisions	4	4	0%
Attack and fighter squadrons (all services)[3]	232	147	-36.6%

1. Aspin, *Annual Report* (January 1994) and Cohen, *Annual Report* (2001) from Appendix D, force structure tables. All figures include the totals of active and reserve forces.
2. Division equivalents equal separate brigades divided by three plus the number of divisions.
3. Includes attack and fighter squadrons from the Air Force (from 122 in 1988 to 87 in 1999 = −28.7%), Navy (from 77 to 39 = −49.4%), and the Marines (from 33 to 25 = −24.2%).

In the marines and navy, the reduction in core elements (marine divisions and navy carriers) has been more modest. For the marines, the maintenance of four divisions (three active, one reserve) represents no decline from Cold War levels. There have been, however, modest reductions in some component elements of the marine divisions, such as fewer total battalions. The navy has been able to retain twelve aircraft carriers—a loss of only three (20 percent) from Cold War levels. In other areas, the naval reductions have been greater with the overall number of combatant ships besides carriers (for example, attack submarines, battleships, cruisers, frigates, and destroyers) reduced by almost 44 percent.

These general measures of force structure (divisions, carriers, and squadrons) continue to be the main yardstick the services use to define their capabilities. In and of themselves, these are superficial metrics. Potentially, a division, squadron, or other unit could be completely reorganized and retrained to perform different functions. However, this has not generally happened. The exceptions are the creation of the IBCTs (mentioned early in the chapter) and the association of air force units as part of air expeditionary forces (AEFs). For the air force, this is not a major restructuring of squadrons or of the functions performed by the various aircraft. Rather, the AEF is a mechanism to manage the deployment and availability of a mixed package of air-force aircraft on a rotational basis that does not unduly overstress one segment of the force due to shifting worldwide requirements.

Personnel

Since the end of the Cold War, the number of personnel on active duty was reduced by almost 35 percent (see Table 3.4 and Figure 3.1). This is in line with the one-third draw down in the defense budget. The cuts in active-duty personnel were shared almost evenly across the military services with the exception of the more modest decrease in the personnel strength of the Marine Corps.

In contrast to the active forces, the number of reserve soldiers decreased by only 25 percent. This reinforces the analysis of relative restructuring of the ready-reserve forces addressed early in this chapter. This disparity is even greater regarding the state-supported National Guard. Much of this is due to the greater political influence that the National Guard is able to wield on behalf of its members through active lobbying and the much closer affiliation of National Guard soldiers and units with particular districts and states.[20]

Nevertheless, active-duty forces dominate the military. This is unlike the peacetime history of U.S. armed forces before World War II when militia and other reserve forces far outnumbered the much smaller standing elements of the armed forces. Currently, active forces comprise over 61 percent of the total force with reserves comprising the rest (National Guard 20 percent; federal reserves 19 percent). Although there has been a shift in relative emphasis to the ready reserves since the end of the Cold War, the current American

Table 3.4
Personnel Reductions[1]

FORCES	1988	2000	% Change
Active Total	**2,138,200**	**1,384,500**	**-35.25%**
Army	771,800	482,200	-37.52%
Navy	592,600	373,300	-37.01%
Marines	197,400	173,300	-12.21%
Air Force	576,400	355,700	-38.29%
Ready Reserve Total	**1,158,400**	**864,600**	**-25.36%**
National Guard	*570,400*	*459,400*	*-19.46%*
Army	455,200	353,000	-22.45%
Air Force	115,200	106,400	-7.64%
Reserves	*588,000*	*405,200*	*-31.09%*
Army	312,800	206,900	-33.86%
Navy	149,500	86,300	-42.27%
Marines	43,600	39,700	-8.94%
Air Force	82,100	72,300	-11.94%

1. Personnel figures from Cohen, *Annual Report* (March 1999), Personnel Tables, C-1.

military posture is still dominated by the standing forces of the four military services.

Production

There is tremendous continuity in the types of weapons that the military is planning to produce in the future (see continuity section under "Selection of Future Weapons"). However, there have been reductions in the production plans for major weapon systems relative to initial acquisition plans. Examples of such reductions include the Seawolf submarine, the B-2 bomber, and AEGIS cruiser. During the 1997 and 2001 QDR, although there was discussion of possibly terminating programs, no major production programs were ended.[21] For several programs, however, the final production target was reduced. The most dramatic example of this was the continuation of three major tactical aircraft programs, all at reduced levels and with extended production runs (to spread costs over a greater period of time), rather than the elimination of any programs. In the 1997 QDR, this included decreased total production of the F-22 from 438 to 339 aircraft and a change in maximum production rate from

Figure 3.1
Active Military Personnel Strength by Service

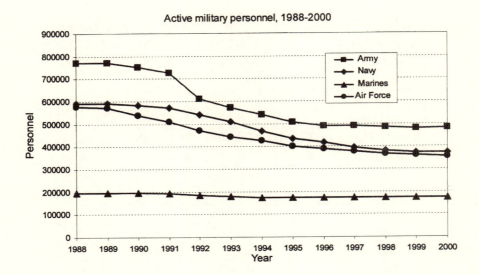

forty-eight per year to thirty-six per year. Similarly, the F/A-18E/F was cut back from a maximum production of sixty per year to forty-eight per year. The joint strike fighter total buy was only cut by 126 aircraft (from 2,978 to 2,852) with the achievement of maximum yearly production (194 per year) moved back from 2010 to 2012.[22] The preservation of all three fighter/attack aircraft came despite many calls from Congress and many defense policy groups for the elimination of one or two, if not all three programs.[23] Other examples of production reductions associated with the QDR process include the changed total program objective for the V-22 Osprey tilt rotor aircraft from 425 to 360 and reduction of Joint Surveillance, and Target Attack Radar System (JSTARS) from nineteen to thirteen.[24]

CONTINUITY

There are several indicators of how the military maintained tremendous continuity in the transition to the post–Cold War era. Fundamentally, the structure and core competencies of the military and its component services have remained the same. The Base Force, BUR, CORM, and QDRs have all maintained the same basic force mixture of army and marine combat units, navy combatant ships and air force aircraft. Doctrines for all services remain fundamentally the same except for modest doctrinal additions for stability operations (but no new units specifically structured for such missions). Similarly, modernization plans call for improvements on the same basic weapon systems that defined the military services in the recent past (for example, new carriers and attack submarines for the navy; new fighters for the air force, navy, and marines; and new attack helicopters and artillery for the army). Several consistent trends in the defense budget support this continuity.

Service Roles and Missions

The clearest indication of the substantial continuity in the military from the Cold War era to the present is lack of any major change in the roles and missions of the armed forces. Title 10 of the U.S. Code, which governs the statutory roles and missions of the armed services, remained unchanged during the period,[25] despite calls by many civilian leaders and defense analysts for a reassessment of the fundamental structure of U.S. armed forces.[26] (See Figure 3.2 for a brief summary of Title 10 service functions) The calls to reassess the roles and missions of the military were related to the collapse of the Soviet Union (the prime determinant of the size and shape of the force during the Cold War) and the assumption that the threats and capabilities of the future will differ from the model used for Soviet containment. The most direct effort to address roles and missions was the 1995 Commission on Roles and Missions (CORM) of the armed services. The commission ultimately decided not to recommend any major changes to roles and missions and instead chose to focus on improving support for unified commanders.[27] Chapter 6 provides a more detailed description of the commission's work. None of the other major efforts at defense-policy reformulation included specific recommendations for changes in service roles and missions.

Shape of the Military

At the most simplistic level, the continued existence of the four military services and the absence of any revision to their Title 10 missions represents continuity from the Cold War era. The focal point of each of the services was also unchanged. In each service the core competency is associated with the same elements of combat power that characterized the Cold War years: Combat divisions in the army (particularly armored divisions), marine expeditionary forces, aircraft carriers in the navy, and fighter and bomber squadrons in the air force are still the main units of measure. But this says little about change, because these same units are capable of a variety of activities. Structure is a suggestive but not a definitive indicator of the roles the forces can play in support of U.S. policy. What has happened, however, is that these organizational focal points have not changed significantly except

Figure 3.2
Service Functions[1]

ARMY: It shall be organized, trained, and equipped primarily for prompt and sustained combat incident to operations on land.[2]

NAVY: The Navy shall be organized, trained, and equipped primarily for prompt and sustained combat incident to operations at sea.[3]

MARINE CORPS: The Marine Corps shall be organized, trained, and equipped to provide fleet marine forces of combined arms, together with supporting air components, for service with the fleet in the seizure or defense of advanced naval bases and for the conduct of such land operations as may be essential to the prosecution of a naval campaign. In addition, the Marine Corps. . . shall perform such other duties as the President may direct.[4]

AIR FORCE: It shall be organized, trained, and equipped primarily for prompt and sustained offensive and defensive air operations.[5]

---

1. Title 10, United States Code.
2. Ibid., Subtitle B, Part I, Chapter 307, Sec. 3062 (b).
3. Ibid., Subtitle C, Part I, Chapter 507, Sec. 5062 (a).
4. Ibid., Subtitle C, Part I Chapter 507, Sec. 5063 (a). The Marine Corps is also unique in that law in this same section of Title 10 dictates its structure of three combat divisions.
5. Ibid., Subtitle D, Part I, Chapter 807, Sec. 8062 (c).

in quantity. Naval aircraft carrier task forces, marine and army divisions, and air-force squadrons retain the same general shape they did in the Cold War with the same key weapons and other equipment providing the essential capabilities of the force in the hands of personnel training in the same methods and routines. As subsequent sections demonstrate, this smaller force maintains strong continuity with the structure and functions it had during the Cold War.

The proportion of the force represented by each service has remained consistent over time.[28] One minor divergence from this pattern is the success of the marines in their relative growth in personnel strength at the expense of the other services since the end of World War II. The marines followed the army's pattern of Korean and Vietnam War increases in troop strength without the same dramatic reductions following each war. While the marines are still the smallest service, they have increased their size relative to the other services since the Cold War (from 9 percent to 12 percent of the total active force). Figure 3.3 highlights the changes from 1988–2000.

Figure 3.3
Personnel Percent of Total Active Force by Service

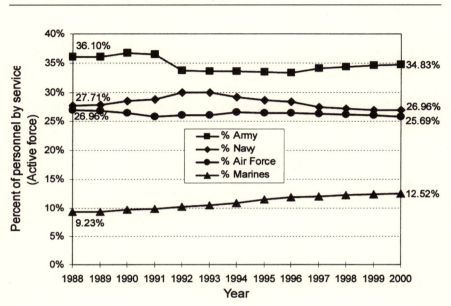

Selection of Future Weapons

Most of the current procurement plans were developed towards the end of the Cold War when the global threat of the Soviet Union was the dominant planning factor. As the National Defense University's 1996 Strategic Assessment noted:

the major items in the fiscal year 1996–2000 procurement program were originally intended for high-intensity conflict against the Soviet Union and Warsaw Pact .... Given that major equipment typically lasts decades (and major procurement programs, from conception to deployment, take a decade or more), the major equipment items in the U.S. armed forces will continue for some time to be items conceived and designed for use against the Soviet Union.[29]

Furthermore, the services continue to push for the same weapons designed for high-intensity warfare with the Soviets and even to push for follow-on systems that are designed to address the same high-end threats.

The basic problem, congressional critics and some defense analysts say, is that even in a time of uncontested U.S. military superiority, the Pentagon continues to develop ever more sophisticated and expensive weapons for large conventional battles instead of devoting greater resources to new missions, such as peacekeeping, and new threats ... [30]

This tendency to maintain current production plans and to have modernization plans that keep military production lines open is strongly reinforced by Congress. When it comes to procurement:

The Congress is incapable of making hard choices in defense. Because of members' predisposition toward accommodation, stopping an ongoing program is virtually impossible.... The more common congressional decision is to preserve programs, even those unwanted by the military services and the Secretary of Defense.... Confronted with a need to cut defense spending, the Congress's response inevitably is to spread the pain across the board. Instead of canceling a single weapons program, dozens of them are slowed.[31]

This trend has been noticeable since the end of the Cold War. A recent example is the desire by the air force to discontinue production of the B2 bomber[32] and the efforts to end production of C-130 aircraft.[33] There is also evidence of production reductions and slowdowns as mentioned earlier.

Other concerns raised by the continued purchase of Cold War-related systems and their generational successors are that such procurement plans may induce other states to begin competing with the United States in an arms race and that these plans represent a significant allocation of budget resources to replace weapons systems that have not been matched by any adversary.

... we should avoid buying new systems that maintain the United States and the world on a treadmill of weapons development. Pressing ahead with such invites an arms race that we would be well advised to avoid.... In addition, we must avoid making purchases of systems that are excessive, redundant, and are designed to replace systems that currently work perfectly well because they are far superior to anything that they confront in a potential theater and will continue to do so into the mid-term future.[34]

In each service, the modernization and procurement programs have as their highest priority the replacement or upgrade of the same main weapons with which they have been closely associated for at least the past fifty years. In the navy, the focus of modernization is on the purchase of one more Nimitz-class nuclear aircraft carriers and the design of a new follow-on carrier.[35] Similarly, the Seawolf submarine and plans for a follow on to it are examples of the evolutionary development of attack submarines.[36] For navy and marine air capabilities, the most expensive modernization program is the upgrade of the F-18 fighter/bomber.[37] For the army, the most prominent modernization programs are for upgrade of the M1 tank,[38] upgrade of the Apache attack helicopter, procurement of the Crusader self-propelled howitzer, and procurement of the Comanche attack helicopter.[39] For the air force, focus is on the acquisition of the F-22 fighter and the follow-on Joint Strike Fighter (JSF).[40] All these programs are evolutionary improvements in dominant weapon systems that are familiar to the main combat units.

The plans to pursue modernization along existing lines has not gone unchallenged. But such challenges have been generally unsuccessful. In 1999, there were renewed efforts to eliminate one of the three major attack aircraft programs. Although the House of Representatives did remove funding for the F-22 from the defense appropriation bill, funding for the aircraft was restored during conference committee with the Senate and was included in the final bill President Clinton signed into law.[41] There are indications that some programs were targeted for elimination in the early stages of the 2001 QDR process. Congressional and military leaders successfully resisted and there were no weapon program cuts in the final report published after the terrorist attacks.[42]

Shape of the Defense Budget

By service. There is continuity in the share of the defense budget allocated to each of the three military departments (the marines' budget is part of the navy's). As one report noted, "The relative portions of the Pentagon budget assigned to the army, navy, and air force have not varied more than 2 percent over the past twenty-five years."[43] This is not an accident. This is very much a source of explicit concern of the services within the Pentagon. When new budgets are formulated and reconciled, one of the items likely to draw the strongest response from any of the services is a shift in these relative shares of the budget.[44] A change in these shares is a zero sum game whereby the change in percent of budget allocated to any service must necessarily equal the change in the sum of the budget share given or taken from the other services. These shares have remained remarkably stable since the end of the Vietnam War.[45] (See Figure 3.4)

By category. Looking at the trends in the structure of the defense budget by category, there is continuity in the proportion of the defense budget devoted to personnel, operations and maintenance, and research, development, test and evaluation (RDT&E). All three of these categories exhibited very little volatility over the years. (See Figure 3.5.) The only major category of the defense budget that does seem to exhibit some change over time is procurement. With regard to procurement, the 1990s was characterized as a procurement holiday, which was a function of the robust acquisitions of the Carter/Reagan buildup in the 1980s as well as the reduction in overall force structure. In recent years, the percent allocated to procurement has risen to a level more in line with long-term trends. This outcome reflects contracts for production of new systems as well as for procurement to upgrade existing equipment.

Each of these categories encompasses a variety of purposes and priorities that are hard to discern at the macro level and are merely suggestive about overall defense priorities; however, the trends in these categories do imply some important conclusions about the strategic behavior behind defense decision making. In particular, spending on personnel,[46] and operations and maintenance[47] can be read as upkeep of the current force (short or near-term readiness). Spending on procurement includes recapitalization of current forces and acquisition and modernization in the near to mid term (out to ten years). Research, development, test and evaluation spending can be understood as mainly supporting long-run modernization objectives.

Figure 3.4
Defense Budget Authority Share by Service[1]

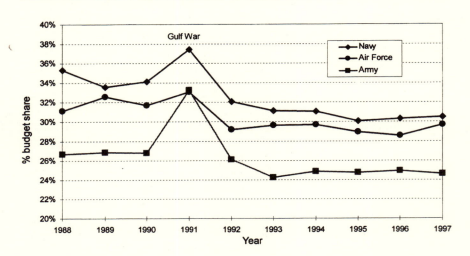

1. This chart does not include the share of the budget dedicated to defense-wide activities. This accounts for the percentages not adding up to 100. Furthermore, this explains the relative increase in all three service shares of the budget during the Gulf War (defense-wide share was negative due to foreign contributions) and for the fact that the share for all three services declined, proportionately, at the expense of an increase in defense-wide. This decline is due to the shift in health care costs from the services to defense-wide accounts. Office of the Under Secretary of Defense (Comptroller), National Defense Budget Estimates for FY2000 (Washington D.C., March 1999), Table 6-10, "Department of Defense Budget Authority by Service," 122–123.

In the post–Cold War years, the most important trends are the increase in the relative importance of operations and maintenance (with relative levels higher than any point since the Korean War) and the procurement holiday. The procurement holiday can be attributed to enjoying the fruits of the Reagan build up and the end of the Cold War, which reduced the overall demand for new procurement as older equipment was retired without increasing demands for new purchases. Large pools of equipment created or programmed by the end of the Cold War have provided systems to meet the needs of the reduced force. The aging of the equipment over time, however, requires that the older equipment be replaced or upgraded to meet current needs. This accounts for much of the recent interest and emphasis on recapitalization of military forces to account for the wasting value and effectiveness of older systems.

The generally consistent level of spending dedicated to research, development, test and evaluation, indicates that there has been no appreciable increase in the dedication of resources to explore alternatives for the future. Given the degree of uncertainty that is widely acknowledged regarding the post–Cold

Figure 3.5
DoD Budget Authority by Appropriations Category

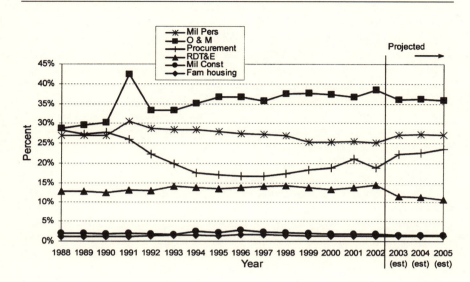

War era, increased emphasis on research and development would seem to be a natural way to try to understand and hedge against a myriad of future possibilities. The consistent portion devoted to research, development, test and evaluation does not indicate any greater emphasis on exploration and experimentation above that allocated during the Cold War.

AMBIGUOUS

Service Strategic Doctrine and Vision[48]

Within each service, there have been some changes in strategic doctrine and future vision. Nevertheless, in each service the dominant characteristic has been the continuity that these statements reflect with respect to strategic doctrine and vision for the services. All the services have adopted strong rhetoric in favor of transformation and have suggested conceptual changes that could result in substantial transformation and adaptation of the various services. With few exceptions, however, this rhetoric produced few and minor changes to the structure and training of the armed services.[49] The primary doctrinal publications of each service retain the character established during the Cold War, and the vision statements that each service produced reflect similarly fundamental continuity.

Unsurprisingly, for all the armed services, the focus remains on fighting wars. The central doctrinal statements have remained essentially the same,[50] including the focus on the two major theater wars as a central-force sizing tool. Each service laid out a vision of how its war-fighting roles and other capabilities fit the new strategic environment. The remarkable outcome is that existing force structures from the Cold War era have been doctrinally justified as sufficient to meet the different strategic demands of the post–Cold War era. In other words, doctrine and strategic vision have been a means for services to explain how the forces they already possess, with their existing organizational structures, are capable of meeting the strategic demands of the revised national security strategy and national military strategy. The RMA and peace operations are acknowledged as important challenges, but the related solutions are addressed using the current force in its familiar form. In the case of the RMA, technological advancements are envisioned primarily as force enhancements to the current structure (an appliqué approach). Peace operations are lesser-included missions for forces optimized to fight wars.

Strategic doctrine is comprised of the "rules or principles about the best way military power can be forged to pursue strategic objectives."[51] Strategic doctrine looks at the military component of the national security strategy. Since the end of the Cold War, each service has promulgated a vision statement of how it sees itself operating in the future that represents strong continuity with the past. The Army statement of this vision is *Soldiers on Point for the Nation.*[52] The Navy statement is *Forward ... from the Sea*[53] and is complemented by the Marines *Operational Maneuver from the Sea.*[54] The Air Force statement is *Global Engagement: A Vision for the 21st Century Air Force.*[55]

Addressing the efforts of the military to think about the post–Cold War era, Carl Builder noted,

The military has once again built up large vested interests in traditional weaponry—intended to defeat their opposite number in kind, to fight and win wars—to the neglect of other capabilities (such as special operations forces) that might be more directly and adroitly applied to the nation's highest or ultimate objectives.

In order to retain and modernize traditional arms, our military institutions have ... become mostly rooted in the idea that weapons should be conceived to defeat their opposite numbers in a major regional conflict....[56]

What is clear through an analysis of the major statements of strategic doctrine that each of the services have published since the end of the Cold War is the tremendous degree of continuity to central operational and tactical missions the services established during the Cold War and the lack of significant change to account for the differences in the international security environment that have been reflected in similar changes in the national security strategy the services support.

Chapter 10 contains a more detailed analysis of the potential implications of this continuity compared to the demands for dramatic change in military forces suggested by the revolution in military affairs (RMA) and compared to the demands of peace operations.

Army: Decisive Victory (1994) and Force XXI (1995)[57] and Soldiers on Point for the Nation (1999)[58]

The army was initially the slowest of all the services to try to redefine itself for the post–Cold War era. The army's argument for relevance is rooted in a historical claim to being the decisive force in war—fighting force on force against enemy ground forces. All three statements of the army's vision for the future focus on maintaining the "trained and ready force" for warfighting. The army's primary justification for its force structure and doctrine has been the need to be prepared for the two major theater wars at the heart of national security strategy.

Although these army documents acknowledge peace operations and the other challenges that differ from those during the Cold War, these are clearly regarded as distractions from the primary mission of force-on-force ground combat. The most recent vision statement (1999) does, however, place greater emphasis on the need for versatile army forces that can easily execute missions throughout the spectrum of conflict (from peace operations through war fighting). The first two emphasize the technological enhancement of war-fighting capabilities within the existing army structure, centered on combat divisions and suggest no major doctrinal innovations. After taking over as Army Chief of Staff in 1999, General Eric Shinseki unveiled a plan that *could* dramatically re-structure the army (see section on Army IBCTs earlier in this chapter).[59] General Shinseki began a process to explore alternative, brigade-size units with wheeled vehicles that would "retain today's light force deployability while pro-viding it the lethality and mobility for decisive outcomes that our heavy forces currently enjoy."[60] The intent would be to create forces that have rapid strate-gic mobility as well as potent firepower. Two brigades have already been con-verted, and four more are projected for conversion before 2005. General Shinseki's vision also presents a thirty-year concept that would completely transform the entire army. By 2032, the entire army would become what is re-ferred to as the objective force. This future force based on technologies and or-ganizational concepts yet to be determined would displace the army's current configuration, to include the interim brigades (hence their description as in-terim until the objective force can be created). The legacy force from the Cold War era and the IBCTs are responsible for near-term security (to shape the international environment and respond to crises). The objective force of the fu-ture is a developmental concept for design and experimentation. Its shape is yet to be determined pending the assessment of available and feasible capabilities.[61]

Following the end of the Cold War, the number of army forces overseas was drastically reduced. The largest reduction occurred in Europe, where troop strength was reduced from over 250,000 to well under 100,000. Remaining army forces were primarily stationed within the United States with the mission to deploy overseas in the event of a crisis. Given deployment requirements and lead times, the army therefore placed emphasis on the need for strategic mobility (airlift and sealift) and prepositioned equipment. General Shinseki's effort to form and evaluate quickly the interim brigade combat teams is driven by the need to make the army more strategically mobile.

Navy and Marines: . . . From the Sea[62] (1992) and Forward . . . From the Sea[63] (1994) Operational Maneuver From the Sea[64] (1997)

As the implementing doctrinal document for these vision statements, *NDP 1, Naval Warfare* notes

Clearly, the uses of military force are being redirected toward regional contingencies and political persuasion, moving away from the prospect of all-or-nothing global war with another superpower. Nevertheless, a significant theme of this publication is that our naval services' fundamental missions have not changed.[65]

Following the Gulf War and the collapse of the Soviet Union, the navy and marines moved quickly to provide statements of their future utility in the context of the new international environment. The emphasis of these statements was on the ability of existing forces to provide rapid global deployment to potential tension points. The tensions and uncertainties of the post–Cold War world and the need to be able to reach areas of the globe without U.S. bases, support increased reliance on sea-based power projection. For the marines, there is little shift from its historical role as a small-war force capable of global deployment. The marine's general role has been expeditionary and the post–Cold War era did not substantially alter that role. For the navy, the shift in emphasis was from the ability to maintain command of the sea and to keep open sea lines of communications to the ability to reach and project power in the coastal littorals of the world. For the navy, the shift was from a priority on deep or 'blue water' tasks to tasks in the coastal littorals or 'brown waters' of the world.

The most important change that these documents reflect is a shift from the Cold War emphasis on maritime engagement against the forces of the Soviet navy (a predominantly open-ocean or 'blue-water' mission) to the emphasis on the ability of the navy to reach the coastal littorals of the world and provide presence and power projection over the shore. The marine supplement to this, *Operational Maneuver From the Sea*,[66] continues traditional focus on amphibious operations as a critical aspect of power projection. It emphasizes improvement of existing operations by coupling "maneuver doctrine with technological advances in speed, mobility, firepower, communications, and navigation to achieve a seamless transition from ship to shore and the rapid movement inland to exploit enemy weaknesses."[67] For the marines, this engenders little real change of mission and is more significant in the prominence that it now plays in overall naval operations. Although the means of amphibious projection to shore have changed little, the purposes for which the marines envision the use of this capability are broader. The marines emphasize their service's flexibility to execute a variety of missions from high-intensity war fighting to military operations other than war. In this sense, the marines have been forthcoming in their willingness to accept non-war-fighting missions and to establish themselves as the crisis-response unit of choice for everything from humanitarian disasters to high-intensity, combined arms combat.[68] Over the past 100 years, the marines have also been very active in a variety of missions other than war and are more open to the requirement to conduct such operations. Acknowledging and accepting such missions has not, however, led to any change of force structure. The marines have tried a variety of experimental approaches (for example, the Hunter Warrior program[69]) but have yet to acknowledge or implement any major changes to force structure and doctrine based on these efforts.

Without a peer challenger, the navy has taken greater interest in the global power projection missions of its aircraft carriers and the marines as the missions that best justify the maintenance of their existing forces. Similarly, the navy has closely embraced the value of "presence" and the powerful contribution that on-station naval forces, especially aircraft carriers, can make to showing the flag.

Within navy circles, there have been some significant ideas that could substantially restructure the service or create fundamentally new capabilities. Two examples of this are the arsenal ship concept and street fighter. The arsenal ship idea was to create several very large, stealth ships with a small crew but a large number of long-range precision-guided missiles. Street fighter is the idea of building numerous smaller ships that could fight closer to shore. A large number of these smaller craft would reduce the current vulnerabilities of the larger, lucrative targets represented by the current naval combatants. Similarly, these smaller vessels would retain greater freedom of maneuver and access within restricted waters closer to land. Both the arsenal ship and street fighter concepts require the creation of significantly different new platforms and operational concepts. The arsenal ship concept has been shelved. After stiff opposition, the navy has provided funding for prototype street fighter vessels.

One concept for change within the navy that has received a lot of attention and general support is the incremental effort to improve the integration of existing platforms through network-centric warfare (NCW). At its heart is the application of RMA principles related to the velocity and availability of information technology. As a realization of the greater power of automation and the networking of complex systems, network-centric warfare is a powerful conceptual advance. Network-centric warfare fits the appliqué description of change in that advanced technology is being grafted on to the existing platforms and force structure. The result is improvement of the existing force structure through technological enhancements of communications and electronics that facilitate rapid integration of systems. This is an evolutionary approach to change that incorporates advances in information technology to increase the effectiveness of existing and planned weapons systems.

The Marine Corps clearly states that it sees no need to transform significantly to meet the diverse challenges of the new era. "As we confront the uncertain world of the 21st Century, the Marine Corps' strategic and expeditionary posture remains sound."[70] In essence, the marines have been an expeditionary force for the better part of the past century, and its key focus in the post–Cold War era simply reinforces the value of this expeditionary character. The one significant change to marine structure is the attempt to acquire the V-22 Osprey to improve marine ship-to-shore assault capabilities. The V-22 and other technological enhancements help the marines reduce their dependence on seizing and holding a particular beachhead. Instead, with increased aerial maneuverability, the marines could vertically envelope enemy forces on the coast. The marines could strike at operational objectives well inland without having to first conduct a potentially risky attack against prepared coastal defenses.

Air Force: Global Reach—Global Power (1990) and Global Engagement: A Vision for the 21st Century Air Force (1995).[71]

The Air Force is the service that has most strongly embraced the revolution in military affairs and its potential to integrate exceptionally capable sensors with long-range platforms and precision munitions. The Air Force perceives that increased responsiveness to information and enhanced accuracy may have fundamentally changed air power from a supporting capability to one of decisive results. Related to this is the fact that the air force has also taken the lead in the development and consideration of space as a dimension of warfare. Currently, space is used mainly as the source of intelligence and as the critical infrastructure for global information systems.

The Air Force's vision of the future is little different from its historical aspiration for the ability to dominate conflicts through air power. The Air Force roots its arguments in the advantages of precision technology and advanced aircraft to provide rapid global reach and the power to influence decisively events from the air. In its most ambitious form, the ability for rapid power projection by air with devastating destructive power holds the possibility of decisive action with little risk to American lives.

For the air force, as with the army, the most important change in emphasis from the Cold War came from the lack of a clear geographical focal point and the associated forward deployment of forces for that area (the central NATO front in Europe). For the air force, the response to decreased need for forward-deployed forces in a particular theater gave way to emphasis on the ability of U.S. Air Force elements, including those stationed in the United States, to reach any spot on the globe in a relatively short period of time.[72] Furthermore, to more evenly distribute the impact of extended operational deployments since the end of the Cold War, the air force created Air Expeditionary forces (AEFs) that associate packages of aircraft (fighter, bomber, support, and so on) for immediate deployment around the world and for rotation of units engaged in extended operations. Even if air force aircraft are not physically stationed in a particular theater, they are never far away if needed to support vital U.S. or allied interests. Furthermore, the ability to operate from allied or other friendly bases reduces the vulnerability inherent in naval or ground forces that need to operate from locations closer to the threat.

There is also a striking element of continuity concerning the belief the air force espouses that air power alone may yet hold the answer to decisive victory.

New technology and new operational concepts already offer an alternative to the kind of military operation that pits large numbers of young Americans against an adversary in brute, force-on-force conflicts. This new way of war leverages technologically superior U.S. military capabilities to achieve national objectives. It is a strategy of asymmetric force that applies U.S. advantages to strike directly at an adversary's ability to wage war. It offers potentially decisive capabilities to the Joint Force Commander to dominate the conduct of an adversary's operations across the spectrum of conflict.[73]

More than the other services, the air force has mapped out its role by emphasizing high-tech, precision-guided munitions and long stand-off range delivery systems that will reduce the chances of casualties.

In 1999 in Kosovo, the Air Force made its strongest case yet for air-power dominance. After a 78-day air campaign, the use of air power alone appears to have convinced Yugoslavia to concede to NATO demands and withdraw from Kosovo to allow the NATO force to enter.[74] Similarly, recent events in Afghanistan reinforced the arguments of air-power enthusiasts. This strengthens the air force claim that improvements in technology, particularly those related to precision attacks against targets, increase the value of the air force to achieve national-security objectives while reducing risks to American lives.

The Air Force is the service that has most closely embraced the revolution in military affairs. The Air Force interprets this mainly in terms of technological advancement in precision attack of enemy targets by aerial platforms. However, even in this sense the air force has placed greatest emphasis on upgrade or generational replacement of manned fighters that perpetuate existing service structure. Missing from a consistent argument for long-range precision attack is an emphasis on more robust development programs.

SUMMARY

By a variety of measures, continuity of the force structure and doctrine of U.S. armed forces, albeit at a reduced size, is more significant than the changes that have occurred. This is not just a coincidence. It is the political outcome of a defense policymaking process that has favored the status quo and has had great difficulty in trying to adapt American military capabilities to meet the different security challenges of the post–Cold War era.

NOTES

1. National Defense Panel cover letter to Secretary of Defense William Cohen, *Transforming Defense: National Security in the 21st Century*. Washington, D.C.: Government Printing Office, December 1997.

2. For force structure, the smaller relative changes are measured in terms of budget, equipment, and personnel compared to the other elements of force structure. The measurement of change in doctrine is more subjective. Although there are many instances of new documents or new portions of existing documents that do address differing challenges of the post–Cold War era, the relative significance of words on paper is also assessed against the behavior of the forces to which the doctrine applies. Hence, the assessment of doctrinal change is a function of both words (publications) and deeds (demonstrated changes to the manner in which forces operate that reflect doctrinal adaptation).

3. Stephen P. Rosen, *Winning the Next War: Innovation and the Modern Military* (Ithaca: Cornell University Press, 1991), 7–8.

4. For a good description of this early Cold War restructuring and its rationale, see John Lewis Gaddis, *Strategies of Containment* (Oxford: Oxford University Press, 1982), 148–71.

5. At the operational level, the regional and functional commands have been retained, although the boundaries and some of the responsibilities of specific commands have shifted. The command responsible for the forces within the continental United States (Joint Forces Command) has also received the mission of conducting testing and evaluation of new forces designs and doctrine. However, there are no forces designated specifically to pursue this mission.

6. *National Defense Budget Estimates for FY2000*, Table 6–5, "Department of Defense TOA by Program," 91.

7. An excellent summary of the Nunn-Cohen Amendment to the 1986 Defense Reorganization Act establishing SOCOM is contained in Susan Marquis, *Unconventional Warfare: Rebuilding U.S. Special Operations Forces* (Washington, D.C. Brookings Institution Press, 1997), 144–147. Unlike SOCOM, other unified commands do not have separate budgets—the military services provide the resources.

8. Special Operations Command is made up of special forces units from the army (Rangers, Special Forces, Special Operations aviation, Civil Affairs, and Psychological operations units), navy (SEAL teams) and air force (special aviation elements). The marines do not have any significant forces in SOCOM.

9. William S. Cohen (Secretary of Defense), *Annual Report to the President and the Congress*, Washington, D.C.: U.S. Government Printing Office, 1998, 51.

10. Ibid, 54.

11. Les Aspin (Secretary of Defense), *Report on the Bottom Up Review*, October 1993, iii. (Hereafter referred to as BUR.)

12. C-141 aircraft acquired in the 1960s are the most significant of these concerns.

13. Comparison of program data, *National Defense Budget Estimates for FY2000*, Table 6–5, "Department of Defense TOA by Program," 91.

14. There are two types of ready–reserve forces. There are the federally controlled reserves associated with each of the military services that are under the direct control and management of the federal government in both peace and war. The second major part of the ready reserves are the forces of the National Guard (of which there are only army and air force units) that are under the control of state governments in peace but under the federal government during war and certain other national emergencies when they are explicitly called to national service by the federal government.

15. This was a conscious effort dating back to General Creighton Abrams and other Vietnam War era leaders who saw President Johnson's ability to sidestep a reserve callout as a fundamental flaw that broke a key connection between the military and the rest of American society. For an account of Abrams' efforts, see Lewis Sorley, *Thunderbolt: General Creighton Abrams and the Army of His Times* (New York: Simon & Schuster, 1992).

16. Comparison of program data, *National Defense Budget Estimates for FY2000*, Table 6–5, "Department of Defense TOA by Program," 91.

17. One statement of this difficulty is Powell's memoirs where he outlines how he and Secretary Cheney were unable to institute planned reductions in the reserve forces due to successful political opposition from congressional supporters of reserve forces. Colin Powell with Joseph E. Persico, *My American Journey* (New York: Random House, 1995), 550.

18. William J. Clinton (President of the United States), *A National Security Strategy For a New Century* (Washington, D.C.: The White House, October 1998), 12. (Hereafter NSS 1998.)

19. Department of the Army, *The Army Vision*, Wasington, D.C., October 1999.

20. Sean D. Naylor, "Cohen Delays QDR-Mandated Cuts in Guard, Reserve." *Army Times* 3 January 2000, 8.

21. In 2002, after the QDR, Secretary Rumsfeld canceled the Crusader howitzer program. As of this writing, there is still a small chance the program could be resurrected by Congress. However, the program does not appear to have much chance.

22. William S. Cohen, *Report of the Quadrennial Defense Review* (Washington, D.C.: Department of Defense, May 1997), 45–46. (Hereafter referred to as 1997 QDR.)

23. Patrick Sloyan, "Top Brass Has Budget Jitters," *Queens Newsday*, 29 January 1997, 17.

24. 1997 QDR, 44, 46.

25. A complete, up-to-date copy of the U.S. Code, Title 10 is available from http://www4.law.cornell.edu/uscode/10/; Internet; accessed 12 April 1999.

26. See Senator Sam Nunn, "The Defense Department Must Thoroughly Overhaul the Services' Roles and Missions." *Vital Speeches* 20 (1 August 1992): 717–24. Another very good analysis of alternative ways to think about roles and missions is Andrew Krepinevich, *Restructuring for a New Era: Framing the Roles and Missions Debate* (Washington, D.C.: Defense Budget Project, April 1995).

27. Commission on Roles and Missions of the Armed Forces. *Directions for Defense: Report of the Commission on Roles and Missions of the Armed Forces*. Washington, D.C.: Government Printing Office, May 1995, ES-1 to ES-9. (Hereafter referred to as CORM.)

28. There have been changes to the relative proportions of the active forces represented by each service during times of war or major conflict since World War II. During the Korean and Vietnam Wars, the size of the army and marines increased relative to the navy and air force.

29. National Defense University, *Strategic Assessment 1996: Instruments of U.S. Power*, Hans A. Binnendijk, ed. (Washington, D.C.: National Defense University, Institute for National Strategic Studies), 184.

30. Bradley Graham, "The Pentagon's Budget Battle: Defense Spending Is out of Step with Modern Threats, Critics Say," *Washington Post National Weekly Edition*, 6 September 1999, 6–7.

31. Barry Blechman, *The Politics of National Security: Congress and U.S. Defense Policy* (New York: Oxford University Press, 1990), 55–56.

32. Tony Capaccio, "Nine More B-2s Carry $20 Billion Price Tag," *Defense Week*, 16 June 1997, 1.

33. Michelle Cottle, "High on the Hog," *New York Times Magazine*, November 22, 1998, 58–59.

34. Ronald V. Dellums, "Envisioning a New National Security Strategy," March 10, 1997. Committee reproduction.

35. 1997 QDR, 47.

36. In an article interview with Chief of Naval Operations Jay Johnson concerning the navy's plans for the future, emphasis is on the procurement of the last Nimitz-class aircraft carrier (funding for which is proposed in the FY 98 budget) and the design of the "next-generation aircraft carrier." For the aircraft carrier modernization and the new attack submarine, the intent is to use the familiar platforms as the shell for increasingly more sophisticated technology-insertion approaches. The article also mentions the arsenal ship demonstration program (a stealthy, lightly manned surface ship that will carry hundreds of advanced land-attack weapons); however, "Johnson bluntly refuses to answer any questions on whether the navy will proceed beyond a demonstrator into a fielded system." Barbara Starr, "Interview," *Jane's Defense Weekly*, March 19, 1997, 32. Since that time, the arsenal ship has been canceled, see Greg Schneider, "Navy Scuttles Arsenal Ship," *Baltimore Sun* 25 October 1997, 1, 14C.

37. 1997 QDR, 45.

38. Matthew Cox, "M1A2 Upgrades Mean More Lethal Tanks," *Army Times*, 20 September 1999, 8.

39. Supported by Secretary of Defense Cohen, testimony before the House of Representatives Committee on National Security, 12 February 1997. See also, DoD, Program Acquisition Costs by Weapon System, February 1999, 1 (Apache Longbow upgrade), 2 (Comanche procurement), 42 (M1A2 Abrams Tank upgrade), and 44 (Crusader artillery system procurement).

40. Ibid., 16 (F-22 acquisition) and 19 (Joint Strike Fighter development).

41. The effort to restore funding for the F-22 included a major lobbying effort by the plane's builders (Lockheed-Martin), as well as the leaders of all of the military services. Alan Fram, "Congressional Leadership Wants Money for F-22," *Leaf-Chronicle*, 21 September 1999, B5. One interesting vignette associated with restoration of F22 funding

was that the Chief of Staff of the Army, General Shinseki, was pressured by the other chiefs of staff and the Chairman of the Joint Chiefs of Staff to support restoration of the funds for the F-22 despite Shinseki's personal reservations and initial opposition, Sean D. Naylor. "Shinseki Pressured to Support F-22: Army Chief of Staff Faced Firestorm for not Backing Beleaguered Fighter," *Army Times*, 20 September 1999, 8.

42. The one exception to this trend is the recent effort by Secretary of Defense Rumsfeld to end the Crusader howitzer program. Although Congress may yet restore funding, as of late 2002, Secretary Rumsfeld appears to have successfully ended the Crusader program. This occurred after the 2001 QDR.

43. Richard J. Sherlock, "New Realities, Old Pentagon Thinking," *Wall Street Journal*, 24 April 1997, 1, 18.

44. Colonel Tom Davis, Colloquium, Department of Social Sciences, U.S.M.A., 13 March 1997.

45. Before that time the army's share increased substantially during both the Korean and Vietnam wars. In addition, the air force share of the budget was very high relative to the other two services throughout the 1950s—a time noted for massive retaliation strategy and the buildup of the bomber and ICBM strategic nuclear force. (Data drawn from National Defense Budget Estimates for FY 1997.) The sharp one-year change in 1991 is accounted for by the crediting of foreign contributions to the Gulf-War effort to the defense-wide account, and the commensurate relative increase of the services spending these sums for the Gulf War.

46. Personnel costs include both active duty and retired pay in addition to pay for reservists and National Guard when in federal service or undergoing periodic training mandated by federal requirements.

47. Operations and maintenance includes the costs of current operations, such as fuel, spare parts and other consumables, short run contracts, and other expenses associated with current operations.

48. By doctrine, this chapter addresses primarily the strategic doctrine for each of the services that translates national goals into service guidance. This focus is to differentiate between the operational and tactical doctrines of the services that dictate specific procedures and actions for military units.

49. For a similar assessment, see Thomas G. Mahnken, "Transforming the U.S. Armed Forces: Rhetoric or Reality?" *Naval War College Review* 54, no. 3 (Summer 2001): 85–99.

50. For the primary operational doctrine statements of each service see the following: U.S. Army, Field Manual 3–0, *Operations*, June 2001. U.S. Navy *Naval Doctrine Publication (NDP) 1, Naval Warfare*, March 1994. U.S. Marine Corps Fleet Marine Field Manual -1 (FMFM-1), *Warfighting*, June 1997 U.S. Air Force, Air Force Manual 1–1, *Basic Aerospace Doctrine for the United States Air Force*, March 1992. The general points of the service manuals are reiterated in the Joint service publications on doctrine, of which the most prominent is Joint Pub 1, *Joint Warfare of the Armed Forces of the United States*, 10 January 1995.

51. Carl H. Builder, "Keeping the Strategic Flame," *Joint Forces Quarterly* no. 14 (Winter 96–97): 81.

52. General Eric K Shinseki and Louis Caldera, "The Army Vision: Soldiers on Point for the Nation ... Persuasive in Peace, Invincible in War," October 1999, available from http://www.army.mil/armyvision/vision.htm; Internet; accessed 9 January 2000.

53. Sean O'Keefe (Secretary of the Navy), Frank B. Kelso II (Chief of Naval Operations), and C.E. Mundy Jr. (Commandant of the Marine Corps), ... *From the Sea: Preparing the Naval Service for the 21st Century* (Washington, D.C.: Navy News Service, 30 September 1992), available from http://www.chinfo.navy.mil/navpalib/policy/fromsea/fromsea.txt; Internet, accessed 19 March 1997.

54. C.C. Krulak (Commandant of the Marine Corps), *Operational Maneuver From the Sea: A Concept for the Projection of Naval Power Ashore*, 1997.

55. United States Department of the Air Force, *Global Engagement: A Vision for the 21st Century Air Force*. Washington, D.C.: 1997.

56. Builder, "Keeping the Strategic Flame," 83.

57. Gordon R. Sullivan (Chief of Staff, Army) and Togo D. West, Jr. (Secretary of the Army), *Decisive Victory, America's Power Projection Army* (Washington, D.C.: Department of the Army, October 1994). Sullivan and West, *America's Army of the 21st Century: Force XXI*, 1995.

58. Shinseki and Caldera, "Soldiers on Point for the Nation."

59. See Sean D. Naylor, "Radical Changes: Gen. Shinseki Unveils his 21st-Century Plans," *Army Times* 25 October 1999, 8, 10; and Sean D. Naylor, "Fast & Furious: Shinseki's Breakneck Battle Plan for All-Wheeled Brigades," *Army Times* 22 November 1999, 14–15.

60. Shinseki and Caldera. In the army, light units are those composed predominantly of light infantry, airborne, or air assault maneuver units; whereas heavy units are those composed of predominantly armored or mechanized maneuver forces (with tanks and armored fighting vehicles at the core).

61. U.S. Army, Concepts for the Objective Force, United States Army White Paper, undated, available from http://www.objectiveforce.army.mil/oftf/pages/briefing.html, Internet, accessed 25 May 2002.

62. O'Keefe, Kelso and Mundy, ... *From the Sea*.

63. John H. Dalton (Secretary of the Navy), J.M. Boorda (Chief of Naval Operations), and Carl E. Mundy Jr. (Commandant of the Marine Corps), *Forward ... From the Sea* (Washington, D.C.: Navy News Service, 9 November 1994) (revised, March 1997), available from http://www.chinfo.navy.mil/navpalib/policy/fromsea/forward.txt; Internet; accessed 19 March 1997.

64. Krulak, *Operational Maneuver From the Sea*. Also, see Krulak, "Operational Maneuver from the Sea." *Joint Forces Quarterly* no. 21 (Spring 99): 78–86.

65. Department of the Navy, *NDP1, Naval Warfare*, iv.

66. Krulak, *Operational Maneuver From the Sea*.

67. C.C. Krulak, Commandant's Planning Guidance, July 1995, paragraph 6.c.(3)(b). Text from http://ismo-www1.mqg.usmc.mil/cwl-main/html/cwlcpg.htm, Internet; accessed 19 March 1997.

68. Contrast this with the U.S. Army's resistance to similar missions. Although both services acknowledge the possibility, even likelihood of such missions, the army empha-

sizes such missions as a distraction from its focus on war fighting instead of as an integral, albeit subordinate, mission (the marine approach).

69. The Sea Dragon Program is a "... a five-year experimentation plan (FYEP) ... a process of concept development and experimentation that builds on the existing strengths of the naval services within a joint war-fighting framework ... [the] goal is to improve the capabilities of naval expeditionary forces across the conflict spectrum." Krulak, "Operational Maneuver from the Sea," *Joint Force Quarterly,* 86.

70. U.S. Marine Corps, *Concepts and Issues 2001: Forging the Future Marine Corps,* Washington, D.C., 2001, p. 2.

71. Department of the Air Force, *Global Engagement: A Vision for the 21st Century Air Force,* 1995. Text from http://www.af-future.hq.af.mil/21/indext.html; Internet; accessed 19 March 1997.

72. An example of this is the use of B2 bombers to strike targets in Kosovo in 1999 after flying from their base in Missouri.

73. Air Force, *Global Engagement,* from the first paragraph of section entitled "Today's Air Force."

74. Threats of ground action may have helped convince Yugoslavian leaders to concede when they did. For example, see Dana Priest, "The Battle That Never Was: Did NATO's Threat to Send Ground Troops Bring Milosevic to the Table?" *Washington Post National Weekly Edition,* 27 September 1999, 6–7.

Chapter 4

The Base Force (1990)

What will it take for the United States to remain a superpower after the Cold War is over in terms of U.S. military capabilities, forces, and alliance relationships? What will the United States need to be able to do in the world, and how should our military capabilities contribute to that?
—General Colin Powell, 1993[1]

OVERVIEW

The Base Force plan was the first effort to adapt military capabilities to the end of the Cold War. The Chairman of the Joint Chiefs of Staff (CJCS), General Colin Powell, developed the initial ideas for the Base Force during the thaw in relations with the Soviet Union that began in the late 1980s. It reflected what Powell thought would be appropriate changes to the size of the United States armed forces to reasonably respond to reduced tensions with the Soviet Union. The dramatic evidence of declining conflict represented by the fall of the Berlin Wall and the dissolution of the Warsaw Treaty Organization helped spur the plan forward. Powell anticipated the popular pressure for a "peace dividend" and thought the Base Force was a sufficient response to this pressure that would forestall more radical change. Powell presented the Base Force plan to Secretary of Defense Cheney and President Bush, who then adopted it as administration policy. President Bush officially unveiled the plan during a speech delivered in Aspen, Colorado on 2 August 1990—by coincidence, the same day that Iraq invaded Kuwait.[2] The central elements of the Base Force were enacted as part of the FY92 defense budget (submitted in January 1991). Congress approved the plan for implementation to take place between 1990 and 1997. It became the template for the largest draw down of American armed forces since the end of World War II. The plan entailed a 25 percent reduction in the size of the U.S. armed forces and a change in defense policy orientation from global conflict with the Soviet Union to regional challenges.

HISTORICAL CONTEXT

International Environment

On 7 December 1988, Soviet President Mikhail Gorbachev promised the unilateral reduction of 500,000 Soviet troops in a speech before the United Nations.[3] The promise was applauded the world over, but greeted with skepticism by many in the U.S. government. Many officials, including President Reagan and President-elect Bush, had spent years dealing with the Soviet threat and had developed deep distrust of the Soviets.[4] A similar period of reduced tensions in the early 1970s had been followed by a time of increased tensions that included the Soviet invasion of Afghanistan, Soviet support for anti-Western forces in Africa, and increased Soviet involvement in Central America, particularly Nicaragua. Cautious optimism about the positive course of the Soviet Union under Gorbachev's leadership was tempered with concerns about potential Soviet backsliding. Such concerns continued to linger well into Bush's presidency.

The events between Gorbachev's speech to the United Nations and the eventual dissolution of the Soviet Union in December 1991 represent the closing act of the Cold War. In the United States, the period was one of increasing public optimism about the security of the United States and the resurgence of domestic priorities as the dominant issues in American politics. Even the Gulf War had little impact on the increasing popular optimism concerning security. The cooperative great power effort that opposed Iraq, including the support of the Soviet Union, reinforced the sense of diminished global confrontation.

Domestic Political Environment

Ronald Reagan stepped down as President and George Bush was inaugurated on 20 January 1989. Bush successfully defeated Democratic party candidate, Michael Dukakis, in what turned out to be the last presidential election campaign of the Cold War. Part of the Republican strategy was to portray Dukakis and the Democrats as weak on defense and to portray Bush as the champion of the successful Reagan policy to confront the Soviet Union. "Peace through strength" was the slogan for strong national defense as the means to implement the well-established Cold War policy of global containment.

As the improving international environment made security issues seem less important, fiscal issues related to the huge budget and trade deficits of the Reagan era rose to the top of the domestic political agenda. A prominent pillar of the Bush presidential campaign had been the promise that there would be "No new taxes." In the absence of higher taxes, the ability to narrow the deficits would have to come through austerity measures for other programs. One target for budget savings was the defense budget, which had increased dramatically during the Reagan administration. Several procurement scandals of the mid-1980s generated negative attention for the defense budget and suggested it would be a source for greater savings through the elimination of "waste, fraud, and abuse." When Bush took office, the defense-budget authority had already undergone real reductions every year since 1985.[5]

Since the height of the Reagan defense build up in 1985, the public expressed support for decreased defense spending. Between 1985 and 1989, Gallup polls reported that at least 40 percent of the public felt defense spending was too high compared to no more than 15 percent, who though it was too low.[6] In 1989, as President Bush was beginning his term in office, 84 percent of the public thought that defense spending was about right or too high.[7]

DEFENSE ISSUES AND ADVOCATES

As tension with the Soviets decreased and pressure for reductions in defense increased, General Colin Powell began to explore ways to adjust American defense posture.

The objectives of Powell and others working on the Base Force were simple. The plan was a budget-focused exercise to get in front of and, if possible, control pressures for reduced defense spending as tensions with the Soviet Union subsided. The fact that the Soviet Union still existed is a critical point. Some analysts contended that the Cold War ended in 1989 (when the Soviet Union turned inward and allowed its Warsaw Pact allies to choose their own futures). Nonetheless, the huge Soviet war machine still remained a concern for defense planners. As General Powell judged in 1989, the Russian bear was benign, but it was not dead.[8]

Powell was not the only one who began to think about the need to readjust forces and reduce defense spending to respond to the changing international environment. Analysts on the Joint Staff recognized the disconnect between projected declines in future budgets and the maintenance of the large Cold War era force structure. In a series of "Quiet Studies"[9] Joint-Staff budget analysts laid out contingencies for reduced military force structure to accommodate reduced defense budgets.[10] Powell's vision was a good fit with these studies.[11] Powell and many others on the Joint Staff also believed that lessening tension with the Soviet Union did not solve all U.S. security concerns. Numerous regional threats around the world presented important security concerns for the United States even after the Soviet threat disappeared.

The Gulf War clearly illustrated military leaders' concerns about remaining regional threats. With predominantly Soviet type equipment and operating using basic Soviet tactical doctrine, the Iraqi military's operations appeared to validate the utility of U.S. military force structure and doctrine outside of the Cold War context for which they were originally intended. One devil may have died but similar, albeit lesser, devils seem to have survived.

In Congress, Senator Sam Nunn increased pressure on DoD to adjust to the end of the Cold War. In a series of four speeches in March and April 1990 about

"Defense Blanks," Nunn criticized the lack of change from Cold War defense policy relative to the dramatic changes in the Soviet threat. The change in threat included the dissolution of the Warsaw Pact and the ongoing liberal transformation of regimes in Central and Eastern Europe. The bottom line to Senator Nunn was that the rationale for Cold War defense policy was no longer sound.[12] Powell acknowledged the pressure from Senator Nunn and made the first public presentation of the Base Force concept the day after Nunn's first speech in March 1990.[13]

A more conservative approach to defense also existed. Many still doubted Gorbachev's vow to change the Soviet Union and continued to regard his efforts as a deliberate attempt to lull the West into passivity. Even after the cooperation evident between the Soviet Union and United States leading up to the Gulf War, prominent figures, such as former Secretary of Defense Weinberger and leaders at the CIA, continued to caution about resurgent belligerence from the Soviets.[14] Such advocates decried the downturn in defense spending authority that began in 1985 and urged real increases in defense spending even as the Warsaw Pact and Soviet Union crumbled. Some of the same analysts, to include Weinberger, highlighted the June 1989 Tiananmen Square massacre in shifting attention from the Soviet Union to the other large communist country in the world. Several military leaders also supported this conservative approach.[15]

PROCESS OF THE REVIEW

Unlike subsequent efforts to review and reformulate defense policy, the Base Force was not a formal process with a specified set of procedures and deadlines. Leaders, such as Powell and Cheney, understood the political forces for change and were concerned about bringing forth administration proposals to forestall other plans.

Colin Powell's individual effort stands out as the impetus behind defense-policy change at this time. Soon after returning to Washington as the Chairman of the Joint Chiefs of Staff in October 1989, Powell had the opportunity to act on his views of the declining Soviet threat and sketched out a vision of the future that would resize the U.S. military to deal with these changes.[16]

Powell drew on the Joint Staff and the analysis they had done to support his assessment. Powell decided first to brief his plan, which he originally titled, "View of the 1990s" to the secretary of defense and then the president before presenting it to the service chiefs and the commanders in chief (CINCs) of the unified commands. Powell presented his ideas to Secretary of Defense Cheney on 14 November 1989. Cheney agreed with the general idea of a plan for reduction but disagreed with many of the details of Powell's ideas, particularly the lesser emphasis on the global threat from the Soviet Union.[17] Nonetheless, with President Bush scheduled for a summit with Soviet President Gorbachev in early December, Cheney asked Powell to present his ideas to the president, which Powell did on 15 November 1989. Powell described the president's reaction as a yellow light to continue working on the ideas. President Bush would take the general ideas to Malta, with no hard numbers, and let Gorbachev know about the plan as a means of encouraging him to accelerate the redeployment of Soviet troops from Eastern Europe.[18]

The day after briefing the president, Powell briefed the chiefs of the military services on his plan.[19] The chiefs resisted the plan. Their initial response was against initiating any reduction without being forced to do so.[20] Powell countered resistance by noting that force reductions would be forthcoming regardless of the military's wishes and that it would be best for the military to control the process rather than leave it to Congress to make the cuts. Powell also made it clear that each of the services was going to have to accept at least some reductions as part of the draw down.

Powell knew that other military leaders believed that the change in the international environment warranted little change on the part of the U.S. military. As Powell stated, "Even though I thought the greatest challenge facing us was the controlled build-down of U.S. capabilities, the services offered plenty of evidence as to why they didn't need to do it."[21] However, Powell was

[d]etermined to have the Joint Chiefs drive the military strategy train.... I wanted to offer something our allies could rally around and give our critics something to shoot at rather than having military reorganization schemes shoved down our throats.[22]

In the months following the fall of the Berlin Wall, Powell spoke with each of the military chiefs and commanders in chief of the various unified commands to convince them of the need to support the Base Force as a 'hold the line' proposal to satisfy Congress and the public. To hold the line effectively would require the military leadership to provide a united front.

While he [Powell] regarded the civilian leadership as his principal audience, the chairman also hoped to win the support of the Service Chiefs. The Chiefs believed that he was usurping their force planning prerogatives by proceeding with his Base Force plan despite their objections.[23]

In the end, all of the service chiefs did line up behind the Base Force, albeit reluctantly in some cases. But it was not a plan about which the chiefs had much say, as one stated, "The planning for the defense build-down was a case of someone determining in advance what was needed and then seeing that the result was produced."[24]

Powell's vision of the strategy that the force would support was almost exclusively focused on regional threats with no major concern about a global threat. "We are tailoring the Base Force to regional interests. By that I mean we are bringing it down in a way so it is no longer oriented on fighting a global war with the Soviet Union."[25] With regard to this argument, Powell met resistance from Paul Wolfowitz and Secretary of Defense Dick Cheney, who were not ready to discount the possibility of a resurgent Russia.[26] With respect to the strategy, Powell's initiative to create the Base Force proposal coincided with an independent evaluation that Paul Wolfowitz did to assess the changing strategic environment. Powell's vision was less explicitly tied to particular international threats and was instead described in terms of the fundamental military capabilities the United States would need to maintain its role as a superpower. Powell referred to this as capabilities based planning in contrast to threat based planning.[27]

The primary analysis for force structure and doctrine came from the Joint Staff and was, as one participant put it, heavily couched in the terms of "considered military judgment,"[28] in particular, Powell's judgment—or, as Powell himself referred to it, "analysis by instinct" or "informed intuition."[29] In essence, it was a rationale based upon experience and judgment rather than detailed analysis.[30]

An essential aspect of the Base Force development process is the degree to which so few people were part of the deliberations. Other than Cheney and Powell, principal participants in the development of the draft plan included Paul Wolfowitz and a few military members of the Joint Staff.[31] Very few of the civilian offices of the Pentagon below the level of the secretary were involved in the Base Force process.

As Cheney considered the Base Force, he drew upon the analysis of the Office of the Secretary of Defense (OSD) Program, Analysis and Evaluation (PAE) office to try to understand similar reduction efforts in the past and how they had affected military effectiveness. PAE assisted the secretary of defense by providing a series of briefings that described similar draw downs in U.S. history.[32] These briefings highlighted to Secretary Cheney the difficulties that had occurred as a result of similar draw downs after World War II and Vietnam. Cheney wanted to avoid significant damage to the military and prevent major dissent directed against the administration from the military services.[33]

In March and April 1990, the concepts of the Base Force plan were presented to the American public in response to Senator Nunn's questions about the logic of defense policy in light of the new international environment. However, another factor governing the timing of the plan's release was the administration's effort to integrate it with the defense-budget process that would ultimately provide the primary mechanism for implementation.

RESULT

The central element of the Base Force was a call for a 25 percent reduction in force structure.[34] The original proposal included the reduction of army divisions from twenty-eight (eighteen active) to eighteen (twelve active); reduction of aircraft carriers from fifteen to twelve; total ships from 536 to 448; reduction of air force air wings from thirty-six to twenty-six. Overall, personnel strength would be reduced from 2.1 million to 1.6 million. Reserves would also be reduced in the same proportions as the active force. The original plan was to be implemented between 1991 and 1997.[35]

The service chiefs were not asked to provide any independent assessments of their views of the future and the forces likely to be required to meet the demands they expected. Powell's vision and assessment were the only ones in play among the military leaders. Relying on new powers the Chairman of the Joint Chiefs of Staff acquired in the 1986 Goldwater-Nichols Act, Powell knew that he could present his views without the consensus of the service chiefs. He nonetheless sought to line up their support.[36] Powell recognized that

[t]here was no way I could get group consensus. The chiefs also knew, however, that with the new Goldwater-Nichols authority, I did not need consensus. I could give my recommendations to the Secretary of Defense and the President on my own. Still, realistically, I knew that we had to shape the new military as a team.[37]

The next task was to sell the plan to Congress. To justify the plan, Powell declared to Congress that

The Base Force is what we believe is the minimum force needed for our enduring needs ... It has to be a force that is credible to our friends and to our foes ... I simply will not sit around and tolerate the hollow force situation ... No one should ever question the ability of the Armed Forces of the United States to do exactly what the President says they are going to do.[38]

The Base Force plan was used to guide the creation of the budget submission for FY92. The main portions of the plan were preserved in the legislative process.

The impact of the Base Force decisions took place immediately. Although the planned reductions were scheduled to take place over five years, the largest portion of the reductions took place within two years as military units were deactivated and personnel levels were reduced. Having accepted the Base Force reductions—sometimes grudgingly[39]—military leaders were very concerned about avoiding draw-down problems.[40] The program for personnel reductions was the central concern for military leaders during implementation. Done too rapidly and incorrectly, the removal of personnel could undermine the whole force as a poorly conceived reduction in force had after the Vietnam War.[41]

Implementation of the Base Force was put on hold by the Persian Gulf War but not shelved. Timetables for unit deactivation and personnel departures were quickly re-established in the months after the war.[42] Despite the efforts of Powell and the administration to get in front of and try to control the demands for a 'peace dividend,' many voices in Congress and the public lobbied for more reductions.[43]

Rather than treating the Base Force structure as the floor beneath which U.S. forces should not be allowed to fall, as Powell intended,[44] the Base Force numbers were regarded more as the ceiling for the forces that Congress would allow. When the Base Force plan was accepted, calls continued for additional cuts to provide more resources for domestic priorities. From the perspective of Powell and others trying to maintain a steady, measured draw down of the military over several years, the recent Gulf War was a valuable lesson that illustrated the continued international dangers even without the Soviet Union.[45]

Secretary of Defense Cheney tried to maintain a hard line on defense reductions. He sought to prevent additional cuts by emphasizing that the Base Force had already taken into account the diminishing threat occasioned by Soviet withdrawal from Eastern Europe and the collapse of the Warsaw Pact.[46] In a July 1991 exchange, Chairman of the House Budget Committee Leon Panetta, and Secretary of Defense Dick Cheney addressed the shape of the post–Cold War defense budgets:

CHAIRMAN PANETTA: "We have been given a unique opportunity, presented by the end of the Cold War. With the threat of a world war-sized confrontation receding, can we streamline the military even more? Can we find a real peace dividend to devote to our desperate needs here at home and to reduce the deficit? Surely if not now, when? ... yet there is a continuing push for new and better weapons systems, as if the changes in the world were only a dream ...

SECRETARY CHENEY: "Mr. Chairman, as difficult as I recognize the problems and pressures are with respect to the need for spending on various domestic problems, the day when we can continue to siphon resources away from defense in order to spend those dollars in other areas, I think has past."[47]

In addition to Panetta, many others in Congress and the public, while satisfied that the Base Force was a good first step, were not satisfied that it was the end of the post–Cold War military adjustment.

The diminished Soviet threat became even clearer in the next few months. In August 1991, Soviet President Gorbachev survived an unsuccessful coup attempt by disgruntled Communist hard-liners, including the head of the military. In December 1991, the Soviet Union dissolved. When this happened, the pressure for additional defense adaptation increased.[48] Most of the cold warriors who had insisted upon the possible resurgence of a belligerent Soviet Union were silenced. (Some simply pronounced new warnings about a resurgent Russia, albeit at some distant date.)

Powell recognized that this changed some of the assumptions upon which the Base Force had been predicated and could reopen consideration of the post–Cold War draw down. Powell had his staff work on a Base Force II to incorporate additional force reductions. These additional cuts were not based on any change in the missions or doctrine of the force. The impetus for considering a smaller force was the understanding by Powell and other military leaders that the international environment was more benign with the collapse of the Soviet Union than it was at the time that the original Base Force plan was created. Furthermore, these leaders believed that additional cuts would be necessary to respond to the political demands for lower defense spending generated by perceptions of this more benign environment. The bumper sticker version of the possible cuts was 10–10–10: ten active divisions (a further reduction of two), ten aircraft carriers (a further reduction of two), and ten active air wings (a further reduction of three).[49]

Secretary Cheney was aware of the Base Force II work but did not endorse it and chose not to forward it to President Bush.[50] He felt that the original Base Force plan was a solid concept. Therefore, the Base Force II plan was never publicized before the 1992 election. Cheney did not believe that announcing further cuts during the election campaign was prudent. In his opinion, the offer of additional cuts would simply be pocketed by the Democratic Congress and that Congress then would add more cuts later.[51] As Cheney left office as secretary of defense in January 1993, he published a brief document entitled, "Defense Strategy for the 1990s: The Regional Defense Strategy." In it, he acknowledged the move from containment to regional defense and advised against cutting the armed forces too far following the positive turn of events represented by the end of the Cold War.

Five years after our resounding global victory in World War II, we were nearly pushed off the Korean peninsula by a third rate power. We erred in the past when we failed to maintain needed force. And we paid dearly for our error.[52]

In this farewell message on defense policy, Cheney continued to hold the line against additional force cuts and efforts that he felt might create a hollow force.

SUMMARY AND ANALYSIS

The Base Force process was driven from the top down. Essentially, the main ideas were generated by Powell, briefed to Secretary of Defense Cheney and President Bush, and then sold to the services as a fait accompli. After initial resistance, the other military leaders agreed to support Powell's efforts, and the plan became the united military position. Citing the cautionary example of Task Force Smith in the opening stages of the Korean War,[53] defense leaders put forward the plan for a gradual draw down, while fighting to ensure that the remaining force received the resources and support to maintain high levels of combat readiness.

The Base Force was strictly a force-sizing plan. Referring to the chiefs' acquiescence to Powell's plan, Lorna Jaffe notes that the chiefs,

[h]aving reluctantly—and, they hoped, temporarily—accepted the need for force cuts, ...did not wish to restructure the forces that would remain....The Chiefs expressed reservations about the Chairman's view of the future and advocated proceeding with greater caution.[54]

There were no attempts to try to modify the structure or doctrine of any of the forces substantially. The Soviet Union still existed and was the continuing rationale for force structure and doctrine. Furthermore, Powell and many of the other military leaders were concerned about the immense difficulty of the draw down in and of itself and sought to avoid complicating the process any further. They were concerned about the danger of cutting too far too fast and thereby damaging the readiness and esprit of current forces, which many of these same leaders believed were associated with the unacceptable "hollow forces" of the post–Vietnam War era.[55] In other words, the military leaders had a plan and were united with a strong rationale for the plan.

The secretary of defense was also aware of the difficulties of previous draw downs and was concerned that the draw down take place in such a way that it did not break the force. The secretary of defense was interested in making sure that the military leadership supported the plans, so that it would not be a political issue that could hurt the Republicans.[56] In this regard, pushing for both reduction of military forces and substantial restructuring would require substantial political efforts to fight two battles on different fronts. Cheney and Powell decided to focus their political efforts on one front through support for the reduction plan.

One of the remarkable aspects of the Base Force process is the perseverance of General Powell in pushing the program through to adoption despite several events that might easily have been invoked to avoid or at least substantially curtail any major post–Cold War draw down. The Soviet Union itself continued to exist for most of the period and could have been used as an excuse for a much less dramatic draw down based on a wait-and-see approach (a justification that was in fact pursued by some of the services and, initially, by Cheney and Wolfowitz). The rise of antagonism with China following the Tiananmen Square massacre of June 1989 highlighted Communist resiliency in other quarters.

As the Soviet Union seemed to fade from the center stage of world politics, several other events served to demonstrate the continued utility of U.S. armed forces outside the efforts to contain the Soviet Union. Most prominent among these is the Gulf War against Iraq in 1990–1991. Recall also that events that had nothing to do with global communism, such as a coup attempt in the Philippines and the U.S. intervention in Panama (Operation Just Cause), took place in the early stages of the Powell chairmanship and within two months of the Berlin Wall's opening. Although these latter two operations were minor events on a military scale, they served to highlight the continued utility of armed forces aside from the Soviet threat.

Additionally, in the immediate aftermath of the Berlin Wall's opening, the path of the transitions taking place in Central and Eastern Europe was not clear. The potential for violence was a major concern for the United States and other NATO members. The logic of an immediate military draw down was not clear in light of the internal turmoil in several of countries bordering NATO members, the continued presence of Soviet troops in Eastern Europe, and the uncertainty as to how far the Soviets would allow their former allies to go in distancing themselves from communism in general and the USSR more specifically. To press forward with a plan for military reductions in the midst of this tumultuous international environment was not a simple matter. That a military leader would lead such an effort also contradicts prominent stereotypes of military conservatism.[57]

As national security advisor for President Reagan, General Powell was more aware than other military leaders of the changes taking place in the USSR. General Powell saw the dramatic impact that shifts in fundamental elements of world politics might have for the United States armed forces. His response was to seize the agenda and suggest a significant reduction of the military to adjust to this emerging reality. He was also astute enough to see that the other events in the world (Panama, Iraq, and so on) were not significant enough to offset fully the reduction in the Soviet threat. He thus resisted efforts to delay reducing the armed forces. Powell's efforts took the first and biggest step in changing the military establishment after the Cold War and set a path from which subsequent leaders chose not to deviate substantially. To the degree that much of what happened in subsequent years was path-dependent, it was Powell's path upon which others depended.

The Base Force turned out the way it did primarily through the efforts of Powell, supported by other military leaders. The other military leaders were initially reluctant supporters, but they did line up with Powell to provide a united front. The plan itself was meant to answer calls for change generated by reduced tensions with the Soviet Union. Powell's plan successfully responded to the public and congressional demands for a peace dividend. Nevertheless, the structure and strategic doctrine of the force were still predicated on the Soviet threat. The changes were, therefore, a matter of scale and not a major reorganization.

Citing the Base Force as the defense-policy response to the end of the Cold War and the collapse of the Soviet Union, the Bush administration and military leaders resisted additional pressure for major defense policy change. By the 1992 presidential election campaign, defense and foreign policy issues had dropped significantly as issues of popular concern. With little popular concern at home and with a peaceful ending to the Cold War, the window of opportunity for dramatic defense policy change seems to have closed following the acceptance of the Base Force approach.

NOTES

1. From Powell interview, February 1993, quoted in Don Snider, "A Comparative Study of Executive National Security Decision-Making During Periods of Fundamental Changes: The Beginning and End of the Cold War"(Ph.D. diss., University of Maryland, 1993. (Hereafter referred to as Snider dissertation), 93.

2. Colin Powell with Joseph E. Persico. *My American Journey* (New York: Random House, 1995.) For his account of the drafting of the outlines of the Base Force in November 1989 and his efforts to have it adopted, see chapter 17, particularly pages 435–40, 451–52, 454–55, and 457–58.

3. Ibid, 391.

4. The day Gorbachev spoke to the U.N., he met with President Reagan in New York City. Vice-President Bush and National Security Adviser Powell were also present. Bush had been elected a month earlier but was still a month away from inauguration.

5. Defense budget authority was reduced in real terms starting with the 1985 defense budget. Outlays measured in real terms continued to increase until 1987 (based on delayed payment of earlier procurement commitments). From 1987 on, defense outlays also decreased in real terms.

6. The remainder expressed the opinion that spending was "about right." Gallup poll data, presented in James Q. Wilson and John J DiIulio, *American Government* (Lexington, MA: D.C. Heath and Company, 1995), 615.

7. Americans Talk Security, "The Military Budget and Public Opinion," Press summary, February 16, 1989. Information included in William W. Kaufman and Lawrence J. Korb, *The 1990 Defense Budget* (Washington, D.C.: The Brookings Institution, 1989), 9.

8. Powell, "National Security Challenges in the 1990s: The Future Just Ain't What It Used to Be," *Army*, 39, no. 7 (July 1989): 12.

9. These studies, conducted by members of the J8 (Force Structure, Resource and Assessment Directorate) and their suggestion for a reduction of military forces to bring them in line with fiscal realities were briefed to Powell's predecessor, Admiral William Crowe, who decided not to push for any adjustments. Lorna S. Jaffe, *The Development of the Base Force, 1989–1992* (Washington, D.C.: Office of the Chairman of the Joint Chiefs of Staff, July 1993), 10.

10. Jaffe, *Development of the Base Force*, 9. Also, interview with military QDR participant.

11. Interview with military QDR participant.

12. Senator Sam Nunn floor speeches reprinted by CSIS, Nunn 1990: *A New Military Strategy* (Washington, D.C.: Center for Strategic and International Studies, 1990). The speeches were delivered on 22 and 29 March and 19 and 20 April 1990. Nunn referred to the problems he identified as the "blanks" in defense policy. Their significance in putting pressure on Secretary Cheney, General Powell, and others in the defense establishment is noted in Jaffe, *Development of the Base Force*, 28–30 and in Snider dissertation.

13. Jaffe, *Development of the Base Force*, 29.

14. Caspar Weinberger, *Fighting For Peace: Seven Critical Years in the Pentagon* (New York: Warner Books Inc., 1990). See particularly "Aftermath" included in the 1991 paperback edition, dated 31 January 1991, 433–444. Concerning CIA caution, see Melvin A. Goodman, "Who Does the CIA Think It's Fooling?" *Washington Post National Weekly* 3 January 2000, 22.

15. Jaffe, *Development of the Base Force*, 39–41.

16. As FORSCOM Commander, Powell had previewed his ideas in a speech before other army leaders in July 1989. In the speech, Powell noted that the Soviet threat had changed and that soon the army would have to change dramatically to respond. Powell, "National Security Challenges in the 1990s" 12–14.

17. Jaffe, *Development of the Base Force*, 18.

18. Powell, *My American Journey*, 441.

19. Powell acknowledges in retrospect that he should have informed the chiefs of what he was doing before he went to the president and that his briefing of 16 November blind-sided them. Ibid, 440.

20. Jaffe *Development of the Base Force,* 22, 38–45; Snider dissertation, 95.

21. Powell quoted in Snider dissertation, 89–90. From Snider's interview with Powell conducted February 1993.

22. Powell, *My American Journey,* 437.

23. Jaffe, *Development of the Base Force,* 27.

24. Quote attributed to one of the chiefs (name omitted) in Snider dissertation, 104. Snider's dissertation also contains a more detailed service-by-service description of participation in the coordination of the Base Force proposal. See particularly pages 96–104.

25. The Base Force concept is outlined in Colin Powell's testimony before Congress, House, Committee on Appropriations, *Department of Defense Appropriations for 1992: Part 8 Base Force Concept,* Hearings Before a Subcommittee of the Committee on Appropriations, 102nd Cong., 1st Sess., 21 September 1991, 1–77. This quote from page 13.

26. Interviews with senior DoD civilian officials.

27. Interview with senior DoD civilian official.

28. Ibid.

29. Powell, *My American Journey,* 436.

30. One senior DoD civilian official further noted that the considered judgment of the military was much more readily accepted by Secretary Cheney than by civilian leaders in OSD in the Clinton administration. In his opinion, Aspin, Deutch, Perry, and Warner, among others, were much more likely to push for detailed analysis and were less accepting of assertions of judgment and experience. Interview with senior DoD civilian official.

31. Jaffe, *Development of the Base Force,* 11–28.

32. Interview with senior DoD civilian official.

33. As a senior DoD civilian official put it, Cheney wanted to avoid hollow forces as well as anything like the earlier revolt of the admirals in the post–World War II draw down. Interview.

34. This 25 percent reduction referred specifically to force structure. The budget reduction for the Base Force was only about 10 percent.

35. Powell testimony, 21 September 1991. The committee print includes copies of General Powell's briefing slides. For analysis of the Base Force, see William W. Kaufmann, *Assessing the Base Force: How Much Is Too Much?* (Washington, D.C.: The Brookings Institution, 1992), and Dennis S. Ippolito, *Blunting the Sword: Budget Policy and the Future of Defense* (Washington, D.C.: National Defense University Press, 1994).

36. Before the 1986 Goldwater-Nichols Defense Reorganization Act, the chairman's role was that of spokesman for the consensus views of the service chiefs. The requirement for consensus among the chiefs before proffering recommendations or advice severely limited any ability of the chairman to lead the services based on his convictions about appropriate policy or actions and required him to act as facilitator in building consensus among the service leaders. Powell was able to exploit the Reorganization Act's designation of the chairman as the principle advisor to the Secretary of Defense and the

President by emphasizing his willingness to provide his own views, with support from the chiefs if possible, but in the face of dissension if necessary.

37. Powell, *My American Journey*, 439.

38. Powell, testimony, 21 September 1991, 13.

39. Jaffe, *Development of the Base Force*, 34.

40. Ibid., 40–41.

41. For a representative account of one of the service's efforts, see David McCormick, *The Downsized Warrior: America's Army in Transition* (New York: New York University Press, 1998). This was also substantiated by interview with a former senior military officer who worked on the Base Force plan.

42. This occurred with my unit from the Gulf War, the 1st Armored Division. Like soldiers in many other units that participated in the war, we knew before we left Germany, in December 1990, that our unit was on the chopping block. Less than a year after the war, the unit I had gone to war with no longer existed. This pattern was repeated all over Germany and in several locations in the United States.

43. Prominent examples in Congress include Senate Armed Services Chairman Sam Nunn, House Armed Services Committee Chairman Les Aspin, Budget Committee Chairman Leon Panetta, and Representative Ron Dellums.

44. Jaffe, *Development of the Base Force*, 39.

45. Interview with senior DoD civilian official.

46. Cheney's testimony, U.S. Congress, House, Committee on the Budget, Defense Policy in the Post–Cold War Era. Statement of Secretary of Defense Dick Cheney, 102d Cong., 1st Sess., 31 July 1991 (Washington, D.C.: U.S. Government Printing Office. 1991), 3–4.

47. Ibid., 1–4. Excerpted from the opening statements of Committee Chairman Panetta and Secretary Cheney.

48. Examples of vocal advocates for greater change in Congress were Senator Sam Nunn and Representatives Les Aspin and Ron Dellums.

49. Base Force II descriptions from interviews of a military member of the Joint Staff and a civilian member of Secretary Aspin's OSD staff.

50. Interview with senior DoD civilian official.

51. Ibid.

52. Secretary of Defense Dick Cheney, *Defense Strategy for the 1990s: The Regional Defense Strategy*, January 1993, 9.

53. Roy K. Flint, "Task Force Smith and the 24th Division: Delay and Withdrawal, 5–19 July 1950," in Charles E. Heller and William A. Stofft, eds., *America's First Battles: 1776–1965* (Lawrence, KS: University of Kansas Press, 1986).

54. Jaffe, *Development of the Base Force*, 34.

55. Interviews with senior military officers who participated in the process.

56. Interview with senior DoD civilian official.

57. See Samuel Huntington regarding his assessment of the military mind concerning the magnitude and immediacy of security threats, *The Soldier and the State: The Theory and Politics of Civil-Military Relations* (Cambridge: Harvard University Press, 1957), 66–67.

Chapter 5

The Bottom Up Review (1993)

It has become clear that the framework that guided our security policy during the Cold War is inadequate for the future. We must determine the characteristics of the new era, develop a new strategy, and restructure our armed forces and defense programs accordingly. We cannot, as we did for the past several decades, premise this year's forces, programs, and budgets on incremental shifts from last year's efforts. We must rebuild our defense strategy, forces and defense programs and budgets from the bottom up.
—Secretary of Defense Les Aspin, October 1993[1]

OVERVIEW

The dissolution of the Soviet Union in 1991 occurred after the American public had already written it off as a major threat. During the presidential election campaign of 1992, the concerns of the electorate focused on a domestic economy in recession. In the first post–Cold War election, defense was a lower priority. As the winning candidate suggested, and many post-election analysts agreed, the outcome was explained by, "The Economy, Stupid."[2]

After the Base Force had been presented and most of its major elements enacted, the debate concerning defense issues became a subset of the 1992 presidential election. Although General Powell was personally almost unassailable in the political arena, the Democrats initially tried to focus on the fact that the Base Force was largely a product of the pre–Gulf War years when the Soviet Union still existed.[3] During the election campaign, Chairman of the House Armed Services Committee Les Aspin proposed a series of alternative-force postures to stimulate debate about the future of U.S. military capabilities. Aspin and other Democrats also believed that levels of defense spending could be lowered further to extract savings for use in domestic programs.[4] Candidate Clinton, using Aspin's rationale, argued for further reduction in U.S. troops with commensurate budget savings. In November 1992, Clinton won the presidential election. Shortly thereafter, he designated Les Aspin as his pick for secretary of defense.

In the months following the inauguration, Secretary of Defense Aspin launched the effort he advocated in Congress and conducted the Bottom Up Review of defense. By the time the review was complete, the only major changes from the Base Force were a further increment of budget and personnel reductions, shared evenly across the services, that met the president's superficial campaign promises and little else. It also included a different formulation of the two-war strategy Powell had advocated by focusing on two specific regional threats: Iraq and North Korea. The BUR did little to alter Cold War era force structure and doctrine. Powell's successor as Chairman of the Joint Chiefs of Staff, General John Shalikashvili, acknowledged,

We found it necessary to focus almost exclusively on short and mid-range modifications to Cold War force structure. This process resulted in the Base Force and the Bottom-Up Review. The latter provided a 'sizing scenario' for designing force structure.[5]

HISTORICAL CONTEXT

International Environment

As the Cold War closed, a significant change in the international environment was the increased importance of the United Nations with regard to international security issues. For most of the Cold War, the U.N. was relegated to a secondary role on peace and security issues as the two superpowers dominated the management of global security affairs.

Although the Gulf War might be the most obvious example of cooperation between the two former superpower adversaries, the evidence of Cold War thaw and subsequent U.N. effectiveness was also apparent in peacekeeping efforts in El Salvador, Cambodia, and Angola. As the Bush administration completed its term, President Bush had committed U.S. troops to the U.N. mission in Somalia to help reopen supply lines and feed a staving population. As the obstacles created by superpower confrontation diminished, the opportunities for multilateral efforts on behalf of international peace and security apparently increased.

Significant security challenges remained. Among the unresolved international conflicts, Yugoslavia began to split apart violently. Fighting in Bosnia and Croatia was a recurring front-page feature. In the former Soviet Union, several disputes also deteriorated to armed conflict (for example, Georgia, Chechnya, and Abghzia). In Haiti, military leaders continued to defy the United Nations and prevent the return of the country's democratically elected leader, President Aristide. In Iraq, the aftermath of the Gulf War included the continued presence of coalition armed forces to enforce no-fly zones. U.N. inspectors also continued to work inside Iraq to achieve compliance with the accords that had ended the war in 1991. On the Korean peninsula, one of the few remaining Cold War era confrontations included continued forward deployment of American forces and efforts to prevent the proliferation of weapons of mass destruction to the highly insular communist North Korean regime. In short, the Cold War was over, but the world was by no mean free of dangerous conflicts and security challenges for the United States.

Domestic Political Environment

With the collapse of the Soviet Union and the end of the Gulf War, securing a substantial peace dividend from the defense budget was a prominent issue. The presidential campaign of 1992 had been a clear indication of the lack of general concern about foreign affairs and defense. The dominant issues were concerns about domestic well-being. For many, the defense budget was a promising source for funding to meet domestic concerns.

In the 1992 presidential campaign, neither President Bush nor candidate Clinton made a major issue of national security strategy and only marginal references to defense spending. The campaign had few concrete defense proposals other than Clinton's promise to cut defense by an additional $60 billion and 200,000 troops, derived from the force options Les Aspin had proposed a year earlier.[6] Additionally, echoing Senator Nunn, Governor Clinton called for a major effort to reshape and redesign the armed forces.[7] In the Pentagon, there was consideration of additional cuts beyond the Base Force; however, Secretary Cheney decided against using the potential savings from the Base Force II plans as part of the Bush administration's campaign position. Overall, candidate Clinton clearly preferred to steer away from defense issues, an area in which he was at a disadvantage relative to President Bush. President Bush did not emphasize defense in his campaign.[8] For the Democratic party leaders and candidate Clinton, defense issues were not the ones that would win the election. The important point was to be inoculated on defense so that it would not be an issue that would cost Democrats the election.[9] The general focus of the election was the weak American economy.

Another major factor in the domestic political arena concerning defense issues was the popularity and respect for General Powell and the continuity in military leadership he represented between presidential administrations. When President Clinton was inaugurated, General Powell still had nine months remaining in his term as Chairman of the Joint Chiefs of Staff. Powell's public statements concerning Bosnia as well as his sponsorship and support of the Base Force had already put him at odds with Clinton's campaign and many of the individuals that joined the new administration.

In the first week following inauguration, President Clinton chose to make the military's policy towards homosexuals his first major defense-related action. Politically, the move was a disaster on several fronts. The united opposition of the military chiefs, general public outcry, and the opposition of prominent members of his own party—most notably the Chairman of the Senate Armed Services Committee, Sam Nunn—caused Clinton to back down.[10] This opening event in his official relationship with the military added to perceptions of strains with the military first brought out during the campaign.

The election clearly demonstrated that defense and foreign policy were no longer major electoral issues as they had been during much of the Cold War. After the election, the defense issue that garnered the greatest public interest was "gays in the military."[11] Furthermore, the popularity of the military itself was high. As an institution, the military was the most highly regarded in the government.[12]

DEFENSE ISSUES AND ADVOCATES

The objectives that emerged for defense policy were predominantly focused upon how to reduce the defense budget given the end of the Cold War. At the same time, the end of the Cold War raised the question of what types of military forces were appropriate for the new era. The upsurge in U.N. peacekeeping missions, the technological surge of computerization, and the changing structure of the international system from bipolar confrontation to multilateral management presented the underlying contexts for a variety of alternative defense approaches.

The first approach was the one already presented by the military in its proposals for the Base Force—in essence, the do-nothing-new option. This plan was presented by military leaders in the closing stages of the Cold War and defended as the appropriate path even after the dissolution of the Soviet Union. General Powell defined this approach mainly in terms of the appropriate capabilities that the United States should maintain to protect its global interests. The capacity for using U.S. armed forces in simultaneous, regional conflicts provided redundancy and flexibility commensurate with the complex responsibilities of a superpower.

The rationale for armed forces boiled down to the considered military judgment of General Powell and his staff that the forces they recommended were the minimal baseline capabilities to serve broad national objectives. Many critics found this formulation unsatisfactory given the historical tendency of the United States to develop its armed forces to meet particular threats. A recent example of this was the explicit relationship between Cold War force structure and doctrine and the Soviet threat. Powell's attempt to define the level of forces in terms of capabilities was a way of responding to the absence of the Soviet threat without providing an explicit substitute threat for force sizing.

A widely circulated alternative approach to defense was Aspin's Force Option analysis. In the approach to the 1992 presidential election, then Representative Les Aspin, chairman of the House Armed Services committee, proposed a series of force options that drew on recent military operations as templates for a set of force packages that could meet various contingencies. Presidential candidate Bill Clinton adopted these force options and their suggested reductions in personnel and budget requirements.

In Congress, HASC Chairman Aspin's intent had been to capture a range of the proposals that reflected the diversity of opinions about possible future postures. The four options that he presented in early 1992 captured much of this thinking. In presenting the options, Aspin endorsed one that maintained a robust active force only slightly smaller than the Base Force but with increased emphasis on connecting such forces to specific threat contingencies—to include major regional war-fighting scenarios and peacekeeping operations.

PROCESS OF THE REVIEW

The process of formulating the Bottom Up Review cannot be fully understood without backing up to the latter stages of the Bush administration and the genesis of the plan with the House Armed Service Committee chairman Aspin and his staff. It was during the time following the Gulf War and the Congressional debates concerning the Base Force that Aspin began to formulate an alternative to Powell's approach. During the latter part of the Bush administration, Aspin and Chairman of the Senate Armed Services Committee Sam Nunn pressured for changes in the military.[13]

Leading up to the 1992 presidential elections, a concern for Aspin, Nunn, and the Democratic party was the creation of defense policy alternatives that could counter President Bush's plan without hobbling the Democratic presidential challenger.[14] The intent was to provide the Democratic challenger with plans that would prevent the candidate from being painted as insufficiently pro-defense—a major problem for recent Democratic presidential candidates. The most noteworthy of the Democratic pre-election defense plans were Les Aspin's 'Force Options' aimed at suggesting alternative force structures for implementation by 1997.[15] The force options were developed and staffed among Democrats in the Fall of 1991.[16] In February and March 1992, Aspin sent out the force options to defense leaders, experts, and analysts for comment. As Aspin noted,

The fundamental change in the world requires a fundamental re-examination of our force posture. It requires a bottom-up review of our forces.... Doing it from the top down, the subtraction method, will not supply us with the forces we need for the future ... our defense must be threat based.[17]

The heart of the force options were a set of building blocks that sought to capture recent military experience and translate the forces required for those operations into packages that would address existing threats to the United States. Underlying all the options were the foundations of defense based upon the following list:

- Strategic nuclear forces
- Defense forces for U.S. territories

- Overseas presence/residual Soviet threat
- Research and development/force modernization
- Training/operating tempo
- Special operation forces
- Industrial base[18]

The smallest of the packages, force option A, included a "Basic Desert Storm Equivalent," forces for a Provide Comfort-type operation[19] and lift/prepositioning. Force options B was option A plus the forces for an "Additional regional contingency/Korea" and additional lift/prepositioning. Option C was option B plus "Rotation base for Long-term deployments" and a "Panama-sized contingency." Option D was Option C plus another Provide Comfort, more strategic lift, and more robust contingency forces.[20]

As Aspin saw it, the force-option approach differed substantially from the Bush administration's approach. Figure 5.1 shows the comparison Aspin drew up.

The key point that Aspin emphasized was the last—that this would be a threat-based approach in contrast to the capabilities-based approach Powell advocated to support the implementation of the Base Force.

Aspin won the support of the Democratic caucus in Congress for the force options to be the centerpiece of the party's defense policy in the upcoming elections. The support of the Democratic caucus was essential as a means of

Figure 5.1
Underlying Philosophy for U.S. Military Forces in the New Era[1]

Secretary Cheney's Position[2] [Base Force]	A Better Methodology
Responds to one revolution (1989 breakup of the Warsaw Pact)	Responds to two revolutions (1991 breakup of the U.S.S.R.)
Defense by subtraction	Bottom-up review of forces
Based on organizational needs and view of what a superpower must have	Based on forces needed to deal with threats to important U.S. interests

1. Aspin, "Four Illustrative Options," Briefing Chart I.
2. Representative Aspin and his staff were all well aware that the Base Force was largely Powell's product. Whenever possible, they identified the base force with Secretary of Defense Cheney since he was a more suitable political target. To assail the position of the most popular military leader in years was deemed too risky politically. Interview with former Aspin congressional staff member.

forestalling more radical plans that might hurt the Democratic image during the presidential election.[21] The force options were a reasonable provision against charges of Democratic softness on defense while nonetheless providing an alternative to the current administration's defense policy and achieving additional budget savings. More specifically, the budget and aggregate personnel numbers of force option C became the Clinton campaign position and later the foundation for the Clinton administration's Bottom Up Review.[22]

Within the Pentagon, military leaders were well aware of Aspin's work. As the campaign progressed, the Joint Staff and the military services had the opportunity to study the plan in detail and develop counter arguments for those elements with which they disagreed. Some of this thinking was incorporated into the Base Force II plans that were being drafted concurrently.[23]

After President Clinton's inauguration, Secretary of Defense Aspin began the review he had advocated. The methodology used for the review started with an assessment of the post–Cold War era. Next, defense strategy was devised to protect and advance U.S. interests for the new era. Force building blocks were then constructed to support the strategy. Combinations of the building blocks were analyzed to determine overall force structure. At that point, decisions were made about modernization programs to support the force, defense foundations to sustain the force, and policy initiatives to support the program. The last step in the process was to convert the decisions ostensibly driven by defense needs into "a multi year plan . . . detailing the forces, program, and defense budgets the United States needs to protect and advance its interests in the post–Cold War era."[24]

One major difference between the Base Force and the Bottom Up Review was the number of participants. Unlike the Base Force, the Bottom Up Review had a large group of active participants. There were several subcommittees and working groups comprised of members of the military services, the Joint Staff and various civilian agencies within the office of the secretary of defense. As the report acknowledges,

Task forces were established—including representatives from the office of the Secretary of Defense (OSD), the Joint Staff, the unified and specified commands, each of the armed services and, where appropriate, other defense agencies—to review the major issues entailed in planning defense strategy, force, modernization programs, and other defense foundations.[25]

Furthermore, due to health problems, Secretary Aspin himself had to limit his participation. In the end, Undersecretary for Acquisition John Deutch chaired most of the substantive decision-making sessions.[26] With Deutch in charge of the review process, much of the supervisory effort focused on procurement and modernization issues.[27]

The first major piece of the review completed was the strategy section. The main responsibility for drafting the strategy belonged to Assistant Secretary of Defense for Policy Dr. Edward Warner. Coming from RAND, Warner had not been directly involved in Aspin's force option development in Congress. Warner took Secretary Aspin's guidance and crafted the two-major regional contingency (MRC) framework that defined the main threats around which U.S. military forces would be sized. The two threats closely identified with these contingencies were Iraq and North Korea.[28]

An alternative approach to force reconfiguration included suggestions from those who emphasized the enhanced role of air power in the post-Soviet era. Some suggestions for an avowedly "air dominant" approach to modernization and force structure were considered as part of the review.[29] However, in the staffing stages of the Bottom Up Review, unbalanced force reductions that would have altered the proportion of budget share for the four services were strongly opposed by the military services and ultimately were abandoned.[30]

A political difficulty in proposing unbalanced force changes in favor of the air force was the understanding that the air force would assume the 'hold' mission while ground, marine, and naval forces were assembled for the major combat phase to reverse any aggression. Particularly with respect to the second contingency, the air force was to provide the holding force while other forces, engaged in the first contingency, completed the main combat tasks in that theater before shifting to the second theater. The ground forces for the second contingency could come from shifting forces from the first theater to the second or through the mobilization of reserves. Either way, the reliance on active ground forces was clearly diminished in such an approach. Politically, several opponents of the plan did much to ensure that the 'hold' strategy for the second contingency became identified with a negative result—either as tantamount to losing or as a means of consigning the second ally to be out on a limb while the main body of U.S. forces were engaged elsewhere.[31] Furthermore, for deterrent reasons, many in Congress and the public thought that an explicit admission that the United States could really handle only one contingency at a time would be an invitation to potential adversaries to take advantage of the United States as soon as it was engaged elsewhere.

The intent was for the threats to drive the remainder of the process to determine the proper mix of forces and capabilities to address them. However, the appropriate forces selected would have to be within the guidelines of the president's campaign promises.

With respect to modernization, the focus of the review was on

[m]ajor programs that involve the potential for significant investment. These programs include: Theater air forces; Attack and reconnaissance helicopters; Ballistic missile defense; Aircraft carriers; Attack submarines; Space launch; Military satellite communications and V-22 Osprey tilt-rotor aircraft.[32]

For each of these programs, working groups developed and brought out a set of options for general consideration by Undersecretary Deutch. The main options considered and the decisions made are included in the BUR report.[33]

Other working groups of the review related to force structure and doctrine considerations included groups that looked at service roles and missions.[34] For service roles and missions, the work of the Bottom Up Review included efforts already initiated as a result of the Secretary Aspin's response and recommendations regarding the JCS chairman's *Report on Roles and Missions* submitted through Aspin to Congress in March 1993.[35] The BUR suggested further study of five areas raised by the chairman's report:

- Expeditionary ground-force roles and requirements
- Service air-power roles and force requirements
- Service contributions to meeting overseas presence needs
- Service responsibilities in new mission areas, such as peacekeeping
- Responsibilities assigned to the active and reserve components[36]

In short, the review accepted a broad agenda. However, the results were modest.

RESULT

As Secretary Aspin acknowledged in the report's introduction, there was still much work to be done, but he claimed that the Bottom Up Review process had taken a major step toward presenting a defense policy for the post–Cold War era.[37] However, the report's ultimate recommendations for force structure and doctrine offered little change. The process yielded incremental modifications from previous programs and not the comprehensive bottom-to-top review that Secretary Aspin had originally intended. As one participant noted, although the review was supposed to be a holistic approach to defense, "it boiled down to ... force shaping: how small can we make the force to come up with a strategy to meet these two threats that we see east and west—major regional contingencies."[38]

The operative word of the report was "maintain." In page after page of description and discussion about the decisions made, "maintain" or "retain" stands out as the dominant choice when confronted with options to modify or dramatically change existing programs and strategy. Particularly with respect to modernization (the largest portion of the report), the decisions made endorsed those made previously. In decisions regarding the modernization of theater air forces, attack and reconnaissance helicopters, aircraft carriers, attack submarines, space launch, and military satellite communications options for change that curtailed current programs while waiting for further development of innovative, so-called leap-ahead systems were routinely rejected.[39]

Similarly, with respect to service roles and missions and force structure, the BUR maintained the existing division of labor, the existing components of the force, and the traditional emphasis on war-fighting roles. For peace operations, the BUR acknowledged the new emphasis on such missions since the Cold War but maintained the idea that such missions would simply form a lesser-included task that the forces configured for war fighting would perform.

The mildly different outcome represented by the final report was a disappointment to many of the staffers and analysts who had constructed the Force Option report with Aspin while he was still chairman of the House Armed Services Committee.[40] Although the basic building blocks of using "Desert Storm equivalents" and returning to a threat-based approach were part of the BUR, the outcome itself represented few tradeoffs between services to respond to the challenges and opportunities of the new security environment.[41]

The specific changes to the force structure were determined by the military leadership. The Joint Staff and General Powell had already been working on the Base Force II plan during the latter stages of the Bush administration. As noted, the plan had not been publicly acknowledged during the election. The Joint Staff members aware of these plans did not discuss them during the Bottom Up Review and instead let the process take its course with the new team of civilian appointees. In the end, the services faced fewer cuts under the BUR than they would have if Powell and the Joint Staff version of the Base Force II had been implemented.[42]

In the course of the Bottom Up Review, it was clear that the Clinton administration wanted to use the two major regional contingencies as the primary sizing element for the armed forces while at the same time try to ensure that the new approach led to the savings necessary to meet the president's campaign promises. One way to accomplish this was to have a strategy that would address the two regional contingencies with some of the same forces being required for both contingencies. In other words, while the first contingency was still ongoing, forces not engaged there would become the hold force for the second contingency until some of the forces from the first could be freed up for redeployment. This "win-hold-win" trial balloon was floated publicly in the summer of 1993 but met strong negative reaction.[43] Aspin decided that the option presented must be one that explicitly supported the ability to win in two theaters at the same time.[44]

The way around the problem was an increase in sealift and the designation of fifteen enhanced readiness brigades in the National Guard to allow the U.S. the ability to conduct the two campaigns "nearly simultaneously."[45]

For the BUR, the needs of war fighting for the two major regional contingencies did not justify keeping twelve aircraft carriers. When Aspin challenged the level of twelve carriers, the navy worked hard to ensure that the rationale for rotational assignments was clearly understood by the new secretary. With help from congressional allies, particularly those interested in the maintenance of aircraft-carrier production lines, the navy was able to convince Aspin that presence should be a specific mission justifying the retention of one more aircraft carriers.[46] Similar pressure also operated for sustaining two shipyards capable of building submarines.[47]

One of the major contrasts between the Bottom Up Review and the Base Force was the difference between the capabilities versus threat-based rationale. The outcomes of the two reviews differed little in their size in and their emphasis on the two-war scenarios. However, whereas Powell had simply focused upon his considered military judgment that the United States armed forces need the redundancy of capabilities to deal with two unspecified regional conflicts, Aspin believed that it was important to tie the rationale for force structure to specific threats and a methodology for determining the appropriate force structure in light of those threats. Without delineating the specific threats, Aspin expressed the concern that there was no logical end to reducing the forces depending on the subjective assessments of appropriate capabilities from one analyst to the next. Aspin felt strongly that the more rigorous methodology based on historical parallels with representative scenarios of proven United States armed forces packages would provide a more solid justification for force structure and doctrine. Furthermore, such representative force packages tied to particular contingencies provided terms of debate for future assessments of appropriate force structure and doctrine.[48]

One of the prominent changes in the Bottom Up Review relative to the force options was the abandonment of peace enforcement or humanitarian assistance missions as the primary rationale for any of the building blocks of force structure. In the force options, Provide-Comfort-type operations had justified a portion of the force (as discussed earlier in this chapter).[49] In the Bottom Up Review, all forces were justified in terms of the two major regional contingencies. Peacekeeping, peace enforcement, and other intervention operations were acknowledged but were explicitly described as missions to which forces "maintained for other, larger military operations"[50] would be diverted if the need arose.

These capabilities [for a major intervention or peace enforcement operation] could be provided largely by the same collection of general purpose forces needed for MRCs, so long as the forces had the appropriate training needed for peacekeeping or peace enforcement.[51]

What remains in the Bottom Up Review is a description of the missions and the new demands that they create for the American military. Although it acknowledged options to size and shape forces specifically for such missions, the report backed down on implementing any change to the force structure to account for such missions and instead passed the buck for the time being.

Peacekeeping, peace enforcement, humanitarian assistance, and disaster relief operations place new demands on U.S. armed forces and require some redefinition of missions and functions, with an attendant impact on resource allocation. Of these potential missions, peacekeeping and peace enforcement operations will be the most demanding. Here again, the flexibility of complementary, multiservice capabilities is a tremendous asset....U.S. Atlantic Command [is] responsible for evaluating and refining joint and combined doctrine for peacekeeping and other peace support operations and for developing joint training programs and exercises.[52]

One other element that changed from the force options was the acceptance by Aspin of "Presence" as a separate mission for which to justify elements of force structure. Previously, Aspin had recognized presence as a lesser-included mission of forces that were otherwise justified for use in combat contingencies. In the course of the Bottom Up Review process, the navy was able to convince Aspin to accept presence as a separate mission that justified the retention of one additional aircraft carrier beyond those required for fighting wars.[53]

Sizing our naval forces for two nearly simultaneous MRCs provides a fairly large and robust force structure that can easily support other, smaller regional operations, However, our overseas presence needs can impose requirements for naval forces, especially aircraft carriers, that exceed those needed to win two MRCs ... for these reasons, our force of aircraft carriers ... is sized to reflect the exigencies of overseas presence, as well as the war-fighting requirements of MRCs.[54]

President Clinton approved the Bottom Up Review plan on 30 August 1993 with no modifications. Aspin's journal records the event and notes the dominant political concerns that framed the report at the level of the president's interest—jobs and budget savings.[55] To help achieve the 200,000 troop reduction, active army divisions were reduced by two (to ten), one of the twelve active aircraft carriers was moved from the active to the reserve rolls, and four Air Force Wings were deactivated. The Marine Corps was able to avoid any cuts and in fact won an increase of its end strength above what had been projected as part of the Base Force. Instead of the projected draw down to 159,000, the marines managed to get their end strength amended to put a floor of 174,900.[56]

As one former Aspin assistant described it, the Base Force represented a 25 percent reduction without restructuring, while the BUR represented an additional 7 percent reduction without restructuring.[57] The BUR's additional increment of reductions was simply added to those already underway for the Base Force. Programs to realize the recommended enhancements were added to the FY95 defense budget submission (submitted in February 1994).

Republican opponents of the plan focused on the military's readiness for the two-war requirement as their main criticism. Republicans used the readiness issue as an element of the "Contract With America" that they presented as part of their effort to regain control of Congress in the 1994 election. Under pressure from Republican criticism of military readiness, the Clinton administration returned much of the money to the defense budget that it removed as part of the BUR.[58] In December 1994, following the Republican victory in Congress, President Clinton proposed the addition of $25 billion for the defense budget. The following year, Congress added $7 billion dollars more for defense than the president's budget requested. In 1999, the president proposed the addition of another $100 billion for defense. The original $60 billion cuts have been returned, with interest.

SUMMARY AND ANALYSIS

The most important impetus for the review was the change of presidential administration due to the 1992 election. In the end, political concerns about presenting a positive front for civil-military relations within the administration gave the military a major advantage in the process. By most accounts, the force that resulted from the Bottom Up Review is just a smaller version of the Base Force that allowed President Clinton to meet his $60 billion defense funding cut and 200,000 troop reduction.[59] As minority party Representative Floyd Spence (R-SC)[60] assessed the outcome at the time,

Recent quotes by unnamed White House officials to the affect that the President's defense cuts were essentially set in stone regardless of what Secretary Aspin's Bottom Up Review concluded certainly lends weight to accusations that the administration has put the political and budgetary cart before the strategic review and global commitment horse.[61]

Similarly, JCS Chairman Powell noted the continuity with the Base Force and the campaign driven nature of the outcome:

Theoretically, BUR meant starting with a clean slate, as if the current armed forces did not exist and then building a new force to match current defense missions. This approach had a test-tube reasonableness, except that instead of starting from scratch, the new administration had inherited existing strategies, forces, treaty obligations, commitments, and crises all around the world, and instead of a clean slate, Clinton has already pledged during his campaign to cut forces by 200,000 troops and tens of billions of dollars below the Base Force level...It took us nine months to finish the BUR, and we ended up again with a defense based on the need to fight two regional wars, the Bush strategy, but with Clinton campaign cuts. The Base Force disappeared as a term, but, as Aspin acknowledged, it was the lineal ancestor of the BUR force.[62]

Clinton's choice of Les Aspin to be secretary of defense presumably allowed Aspin to implement the suggestion he had made to the previous administration to conduct a bottom-up review of defense policy. However, Aspin had little time to devote to the process. Most of the analysis was turned over to the Joint Staff and to many of the same military officers who had worked out the numbers for the Base Force. Detailed analysis by Aspin himself was difficult. As a former colleague of Aspin in both the House and the Department of Defense noted, one of the important differences between being the chairman of the House Armed Service Committee and being secretary of defense were the time demands of the job. In Congress, there are opportunities in the course of a year to conduct a thorough exploration of issues when there are lulls in legislative activity. As secretary of defense, unfortunately, there is so much to be done that the secretary has little time for the sort of "classic policy analysis" that used to take place in informal congressional session. Instead, the pressure in the Pentagon is to get things done.[63] For Aspin, the demands of the job, such as the gays in the military issue and the inherited mission in Somalia, took most of his time and left little time for contemplation of the details of the Bottom Up Review. Based on the evidence in his personal papers and the assessment of close aides, Aspin's active role in the process was greatest towards the end when it came to determining how to package the report for Congress and other agencies. It was with regard to these issues that Aspin's political instincts and techniques are more prominent than they were with respect to any of the substantive issues addressed by the BUR.[64] Furthermore, the management of the process by the incoming Democratic civilian appointees was adversely affected by Aspin's health problems.

Another important aspect of the Bottom Up Review was the fact that there was so much turn over and turmoil in the civilian side of the Pentagon. Whereas much of the military leadership and staff in the Pentagon carried over their experience from the Base Force process and the Bush administration, the civilian leaders showed the inexperience of twelve years outside the executive branch.[65] Furthermore, during the BUR, there were problems in the confirmation of key civilian appointees, such as Morton Halperin and Graham Allison.[66] These appointees, among others, were not confirmed quickly and therefore had difficulty influencing the process. Conversely, the advance knowledge the Joint Staff and military services had from Aspin's work of the previous year helps account for the fact that the military was well prepared for the review and was able to participate actively in every aspect of it.

General Powell (CJCS) and several other important leaders provided continuity from the previous administration. These military leaders were also well versed in the justifications and support for the Base Force plan. Furthermore, unlike the Base Force development process, during the Bottom Up Review all the military services and many of the civilian agencies in the office of the secretary of defense (OSD) had the opportunity to participate in the process. This more complex bureaucratic process made agreement among participants more difficult.

As a prelude to the BUR, the experience of the gays in the military issue made it difficult for Clinton to oppose military preferences. According to Secretary of Defense Aspin, this had much to do with generating one of the most important measures of success for the review—that General Powell be 'shoulder to shoulder' with the secretary and the president when the BUR was unveiled.[67] This political requirement to have the military firmly on board did much to water down the degree of change the review could engender. Furthermore, with the popularity of Colin Powell, there were additional concerns that he leave the administration on a positive note as he finished his fourth and final year as Chairman of the Joint Chiefs of Staff. As Aspin noted,

It seems to me that Colin Powell is a very key figure in terms of Bill Clinton's future political success. I'm a little worried that if Colin Powell joins the Republican Administration in 1996 he could take the black votes with him or a good chunk of them and tilt the balance. I think we want to be sure that Colin Powell does not have a falling out with the [Clinton] Administration.[68]

Ultimately, the administration's definition of political success in the BUR was meeting President Clinton's campaign target of a reduced defense budget.

Another interesting point about the Bottom Up Review is that it was presented to the public before the Clinton administration had even officially promulgated a national security strategy. The first National Security Strategy of the administration was published in May 1994—over seven months after the BUR was announced.

The Bottom Up Review's two-regional wars scenario solidified the defining element of defense strategy first introduced during the Base Force development. There appeared to be general consensus in governing circles that the goal of being able to handle two major regional contingencies simultaneously was the right one; although there was less agreement as to whether the armed forces themselves where properly sized and resourced to effectively support the strategy.

Another element that affected the outcome of the review was the fact that the review took place toward the end of Powell's tenure as Chairman of the Joint Chiefs of Staff. At that time, Powell was secure in his position with tremendous expertise and familiarity with the Pentagon and with an exceptionally high public standing. On the other hand, Les Aspin, although active on these issues well before becoming secretary of defense, had difficulty engaging on these issues as secretary of defense because of the greater scope of responsibilities he had as secretary and due to his health problems.

In the end,

Essentially, the BUR maintains the U.S. planning perspective that existed during the Cold War: It focuses on the near-term future, and on the most *familiar* threats, as opposed to the *greatest* or *most likely* threats to the national security, which will probably appear in the next decade, at the earliest.[69]

Concerning the restructuring of service roles and missions, the report of the Bottom Up Review analyzed some areas for reform, such as potential redundancies in expeditionary ground forces, air power roles; new mission areas, such as peacekeeping; and division of labor between active and reserve forces. No major changes were suggested by the BUR, rather, "The Bottom Up Review determined that it is necessary to maintain multiservice capabilities in all the areas listed above."[70] The report also acknowledged that continued review of service roles and missions was warranted.[71] The lack of significant changes in roles and missions contained in the BUR, coupled with the failure of the Chairman of the Joint Chiefs of Staff to make any major changes in his earlier roles and missions report[72] reinforced the modest nature of the changes made to force structure and doctrine in the first year of the Clinton administration. In

Congress, Senate Armed Service Committee Chairman Nunn and House Armed Services Committee Chairman Dellums were disappointed with the modest degree of change. These two leaders were instrumental in instigating the next major opportunity for defense policy reformulation through legislation creating an independent commission to review the roles and missions of the armed forces.

NOTES

1. Les Aspin (Secretary of Defense), *Report on the Bottom Up Review,* October 1993, 1. (Hereafter referred to as BUR.)

2. Message posted on the wall of Clinton campaign headquarters in Little Rock, Arkansas during the 1992 election campaign. James Q. Wilson and John J. DiIulio Jr. *American Government,* 6th Edition (Lexington, MA: D.C. Heath and Company, 1995), 217.

3. For Democrats, one tactic was to refer to the Base Force as the 'Bush-Cheney Base Force' to avoid the appearance of attacking General Powell.

4. Interviews with former Aspin staff members from the Armed Services Committee.

5. General John M. Shalikashvili (Chairman of the Joint Chiefs of Staff), "A Word From the Chairman," *Joint Forces Quarterly* (Summer 1996).

6. Details of Clinton's defense positions are contained in answers he and his campaign staff provided to questions from *Defense Week* editors. "Clinton Shines New Light on Defense Views As Nomination Nears," *Defense Week,* July 13, 1992, 13–15.

7. Bill Clinton (Arkansas governor and democratic presidential nominee), "Speech on Foreign Policy Before the Los Angeles World Affairs Council." 13 August 1992.

8. In particular, evidence that Clinton had deliberately tried to avoid military service during the Vietnam War made defense topics an undesirable focal point for him as a candidate.

9. Interview with former Aspin congressional staff member.

10. Les Aspin papers, Personal Journal, January to July 1993. Les Aspin papers, Mudd Manuscript Library, Princeton University. (Hereafter referred to as Aspin Papers or Aspin Journal.)

11. Pew Center for the people and the press, tracking polls of public attentiveness to various issues.

12. Gallup poll, 1991. Available from http://www.gallup.com/poll/releases/pr970815.asp; Internet; 11 April 99.

13. As one of the congressional Democratic stalwarts on defense, Nunn had been somewhat hobbled at this point because of his vote against giving President Bush support to begin offensive military operations against Iraq in the Gulf War. Aspin voted to support President Bush and offensive military operations against Iraq.

14. Interview with congressional professional committee staff member and interviews with former Aspin staff members from the House Armed Services Committee.

15. For a detailed presentation of the force options, see Les Aspin, (Chairman House Armed Services Committee). "An Approach to Sizing American Conventional Forces for the Post-Soviet Era: Four Illustrative Options," 25 February 1992. Aspin.

16. Also see Aspin papers, notes from files when he served as chairman of the House Armed Services Committee.

17. Aspin, "Four Illustrative Options," 2.

18. Aspin, "Four Illustrative Options," Briefing Chart II.

19. Provide Comfort was the operation to provide safe havens and humanitarian support in northern Iraq for the Kurds.

20. Aspin, "Four Illustrative Options," Briefing Chart II.

21. For example, Representative Ron Dellums led a group of Democrats that advocated defense spending cuts to achieve $400 billion in savings in five years—over five times the savings advocated by the Clinton campaign—to provide more funds for domestic priorities. Most savings would be achieved by cutting active forces substantially and transferring a greater role for defense to reserve and National Guard forces.

22. "Clinton Shines Light on Defense Views as Nomination Nears," *Defense Week*, July 13, 1992. 13–15.

23. Interview with senior military officer who worked on Base Force II plans.

24. BUR, 4.

25. BUR, 22–23.

26. Aspin journal and interviews with former Aspin staff members. Aspin had a heart problem that led to surgery in February 1993. Aspin's energy and ability to perform his duties was affected for several weeks before and after the operation.

27. This may also account for why the presentation of modernization analysis and decisions is the final report's largest single segment (38 pages out of 109), BUR, 33–70.

28. BUR, 14.

29. Within the Aspin Defense Department, key leaders of OSD strategy and plans brought a different perspective to the ideas of changing defense. In particular, Warner and one of his key assistants on strategy, David Ochmanek, brought with them experience as part of RAND's Project Air Force where they had explored the possibly greater role of air power in the post–Cold War security environment. An important example of this is the RAND study completed shortly before the 1992 election, Christopher Bowie, Fred Frostic, Kevin Lewis, John Lund, David Ochmanek, and Philip Propper, *The New Calculus: Analyzing Airpower's Changing Role in Joint Theater Campaigns*, (Santa Monica, CA: RAND, 1993).

30. Interview with senior civilian DoD leader.

31. Interviews with senior civilian DoD officials. Also, see Aspin Journal.

32. BUR, 34.

33. BUR, 33–70.

34. BUR, 85–96.

35. BUR, 85.

36. BUR, 86.

37. BUR, iv.

38. LTG (ret) Stroup, (Former U.S. Army, Deputy Chief of Staff for Personnel), interview by Dr. Richard Hunt, 13 April 1994, 5. Transcript on file at the Center for Military History.

39. BUR, 33–70.

40. One important reason for this dissatisfaction appears to be the result of the very different team that took up the issues of the Bottom Up Review within the Department of Defense versus those who had been the drafters and caretakers of the original force options in Congress. In particular, the BUR effort in DoD was spearheaded by John Deutch. Another major change is the inclusion of the Joint Staff and the military services in the review process.

41. For example, the force structure of Force Option C (which is generally regarded as the option from the plan Aspin formed in Congress that formed the foundation for the BUR) proposed only ten carriers versus the twelve endorsed in the BUR and a greater shift in force structure to the National Guard and reserves.

42. Interviews with a senior military officer, senior DoD civilian official, and a former Aspin staff member from the House Armed Services committee who participated in the Bottom Up Review process.

43. Representative Dave McCurdy was one of the most adamant in criticizing the win-hold-win approach and in counseling Aspin to find a way to create a win-win option. Interviews with a senior DoD civilian official.

44. Aspin Papers, journal entry, Saturday, 26 June 1993.

45. BUR, iii. Defined as the ability of the military to deploy an effective force for the second major contingency within forty-five days of the start of the first major regional conflict, interviews with a former Aspin Congressional staff member and a senior DoD civilian official.

46. Interview with a senior DoD civilian leader.

47. Production target for the Seawolf submarine was raised to three until the new attack submarine is ready for production (the next generation following Seawolf). John Pike, "Cancel New Attack Submarine," Federation of American Scientists, Military Spending Working Group, available at http://www.fas.org/pub/gen/mswg/msbb98/dd10subs.htm (updated May 1, 1998); Internet; accessed 16 January 1999.

48. Aspin Papers.

49. Aspin, "Four Illustrative Options," Briefing Chart II.

50. BUR, 9.

51. BUR, 23.

52. BUR, 89.

53. Aspin's unwillingness to accept presence as a separate mission while he was chairman of the House Armed Services Committee noted in interviews with former Aspin staff members from the House Armed Services Committee.

54. BUR, 24.

55. Aspin Papers, journal entry, Monday, 30 August 1993. Aspin lists as present, "all the Joint Chiefs there, Colin and me, Al Gore, Tony Lake, George Stepanopolous, Dave Gergen, Leon Panetta, Leon Feurth."

56. BUR, 28.

57. Interview with a former Aspin staff member.

58. From 1995 to 1999, the Clinton administration generally accommodated Republican concerns by increasing spending on readiness—particularly personnel.

59. The projected savings created by the BUR was $91 billion, BUR, 108.

60. Representative Spence became chairman of the House Armed Services Committee when the Republican party won control of Congress in the 1994 elections. He renamed the House Armed Services Committee the House National Security Committee.

61. Representative Floyd Spence, *Congressional Record*, "National Defense Authorization Act for Fiscal Year 1994" House of Representatives, August 4, 1993, H6058.

62. Colin Powell with Joseph E. Persico, *My American Journey* (New York: Random House, 1995), 579.

63. Interview with a senior Aspin staff member in the House of Representatives who came with Aspin to DoD. The point about the pace at which decisions and actions are executed at the Pentagon was reinforced in an interview with another former Aspin staff member from the House of Representatives who also worked with Aspin in the Pentagon. This person noted the difficulty for civilian appointees and workers to keep up with the pace of the military. "It's up to civilian leaders to step in and take control of the process, otherwise the military will do what it feels needs to be done."

64. Aspin Journal, several entries from July on (after the main part of review complete) focus on the plans for the public unveiling of the plan.

65. Christopher Gibson and Don Snider, "Civil-Military Relations and the Potential to Influence: A Look at the National Security Decision-Making Process." *Armed Forces & Society* 25, no. 2 (Winter 1999): 193–218.

66. Ultimately, Alison was confirmed to his post in the fall of 1993 by which time his office had been excluded from the process. Mort Halperin, who was to have had the lead on issues of democratization and peacekeeping, was never confirmed and eventually withdrew from consideration as an assistant secretary of defense.

67. Aspin papers, Personal Journal. Corroborated in interviews with senior DoD civilian officials.

68. Aspin Journal.

69. Andrew Krepinevich, *The Bottom-Up Review: An Assessment* (Washington, D.C.: The Defense Budget Project, February 1994), i. (Italics from original.)

70. BUR, 86.

71. BUR, 89.

72. General Colin Powell (Chairman of the Joint Chiefs of Staff), *Report on Roles, Missions and Functions of the Armed forces of the United States,* March 1993.

Chapter 6

The Commission on Roles and Missions
of the Armed Forces (1995)

We should not go into the future with just a smaller version of our
Cold War forces. We must prepare for a future with a fresh look at the roles
and missions that characterized the past forty years. We must reshape,
reconfigure, and modernize our overall forces—not just make them small.
—Senator Sam Nunn, 1992[1]

OVERVIEW

Another opportunity to address some of the fundamental force structure and
doctrinal issues of the post–Cold War era was the congressionally mandated
Commission on Roles and Missions (CORM). Chartered by a Democratic-
controlled Congress in 1993, the final report was submitted to a Republican-
controlled Congress in 1995. The requirement was established by members who
were disappointed with the roles and mission report submitted by JCS Chairman
Powell in March 1993 as well as by the lack of substantial change in DoD's
Bottom Up Review issued in October 1993. Critics of these efforts hoped that an
independent commission could more effectively review defense capabilities.

In June 1992, Senator Sam Nunn noted the major changes in the international environment and the substantially different challenges confronting the
United States. As in similar circumstances in U.S. history, Nunn suggested that
it was time to revisit the issue of military roles and missions for the various
military services to determine whether they were sized and shaped properly for
the likely future scenarios that would demand their use. "We must find the best
way to provide a fighting force in the future that is not bound by the constraints of the roles and missions outlined in 1948."[2]

The response was the formation of an eleven-person Commission on
Roles and Missions (CORM) under the leadership of John P. White.[3] Although
billed as a group of independent private citizens, five of the members were
retired senior military officers (a former general or admiral from each active
service and one from the National Guard). In its final report, the commission

acknowledges Senator Nunn's charter and goes on to explain why there is no need, in the commissioners' opinions, to revisit this fundamental issue. Instead, they focus on how to achieve operational improvements in the performance of joint military commands. In essence, the CORM sidestepped the issue of change in basic service roles and missions.[4]

In the final analysis, the CORM's report had minimal impact on force structure and doctrine. It was regarded by many of its initial proponents as another missed opportunity to adjust the United States armed forces for the post–Cold War era.[5] The CORM did, however, recognize the need for continued reassessment of military capabilities and recommended that the secretary of defense conduct a review of defense policy quadrennially, in the year following a presidential election.[6] This recommendation was accepted by Congress and incorporated in the 1996 Defense Authorization bill as the requirement for the 1997 Quadrennial Defense Review (QDR).[7]

HISTORICAL CONTEXT

International Environment

A month after the presentation of the Bottom Up Review, eighteen American soldiers were killed in Somalia.[8] The fallout from the mission brought into question the policies of the administration and, ultimately, cost Secretary of Defense Aspin his job. His deputy, William J. Perry, replaced him. By early 1994, the United States had pulled all of its troops out of Somalia. Around the same time, the Clinton administration also stepped up efforts to end the conflict in Bosnia. With the U.N. perceived as having been largely ineffective in ending the conflict, NATO assumed a greater role and included the use of U.S. air strikes to attack Serbian positions. The end to the fighting was marked by the Dayton accords.

In Rwanda, massacres of ethnic Tutsi occurred in spite of the presence of a small U.N. force. The failure of the U.N. to stop the massacre added to a list of difficulties, along with Bosnia, that signaled an end to widespread hope that greater U.N. involvement would be able to manage international security effectively.

In Haiti, the U.N.-endorsed, U.S.-led effort persuaded the military dictators—with invasion imminent—to abandon control of the country and return it to civilian rule under the democratically elected president.

This series of international crises seemed to refute any short-term expectations that the "end of history" might be reached. Optimism that a new era of peace and international cooperation were at hand substantially subsided.

Domestic Political Environment

The domestic political environment surrounding the Commission on Roles and Missions was similar to the one that President Clinton faced during the 1992 presidential election and the early part of his administration. Defense was not a major issue, but it was an issue area in which administration members felt they could generate substantial opposition if they were not careful. It was an issue area in which the main goal was not to make any major mistakes that could be used to partisan advantages by Republicans. It was not an issue area for which President Clinton had any important initiatives.

As the 1994 mid-term elections approached, the Republicans, the congressional minority, felt that defense was one area in which the Democrats were vulnerable. Republicans sought to make defense an election issue using the topic of military readiness. Republicans harped on what they perceived to be a disconnect between the strategy of the Bottom Up Review and the defense budget allocations to support the armed forces. One of the elements of the Republicans' "Contract With America" was the strengthening of American defense. The defense portion of the contract declared support for, "No U.S. troops under U.N. command and restoration of the essential parts of our national security funding to strengthen our national defense and maintain our credibility around the world."[9]

By 1994, general public interest in defense issues was low. Defense policy was generally an issue of only defense experts and those with personal stakes in defense, such as military communities and defense industry. As the 1994 Chicago Council on Foreign Relations poll noted, defense and foreign-policy issues had dropped considerably as public concerns.[10]

DEFENSE ISSUES AND ADVOCATES

The 1986 Defense Reorganization Act (Goldwater-Nichols) added a requirement for the Chairman of the Joint Chiefs of Staff to submit a report every three years assessing the roles and missions of the services. The requirement is as follows:

The Chairman shall submit ... a report containing such recommendations for changes in the assignment of functions (or roles and missions) to the armed forces as the Chairman considers necessary to achieve maximum effectiveness of the armed forces. In preparing each such report, the Chairman shall consider (among other matters) the following:

(A) Changes in the nature of the threats faced by the United States.

(B) Unnecessary duplication of effort among the armed forces.

(C) Changes in technology that can be applied effectively to warfare.[11]

In late 1989, General Powell submitted the first of these reports (drafted mostly by his predecessor, Admiral Crowe). This first roles and missions report was published during the Cold War. The Berlin Wall fell at about the same time the report was published. The first opportunity for the chairman to incorporate the implications of the end of the Cold War into the report was in the second report that General Powell submitted in March 1993.[12] Powell did not, however, make any recommendations for significant change to service roles and missions.[13] For many in Congress, this was disappointing. For Senator Nunn in particular, discussions with General Powell had led him to believe that this report would propose a major reorganization of the services.[14] Along with many others in Congress, Nunn had held back from pressuring for more change until Powell first had his chance to make recommendations.[15] Many critics of the report nonetheless reserved final judgment on the efforts to adjust roles and missions until the new administration had the opportunity to complete its overall defense review, the Bottom Up Review. When the Bottom Up Review was published, it acknowledged the possible need for greater change but endorsed Powell's report without any specific recommendations for change to fundamental service roles and missions. Instead, the BUR echoed the chairman's acceptance of "balanced forces"[16] among the services. Balanced forces means that the services would retain the same basic functions, the same proportional size, and same budget share each had throughout the Cold War. In other words, with respect to roles and missions, the BUR endorsed the status quo.

One of the early proponents of a fundamental review of service roles and missions had been Senate Armed Services Committee Chairman, Sam Nunn. In a speech to the Senate in 1992, Nunn outlined some general concerns that the military had too much redundancy in capabilities given the end of the Cold War. For example, he questioned whether it was necessary to have two land armies and four air forces.[17]

The model for review that Nunn had in mind was the early Cold War evaluation and establishment of service roles in the 1948 Key West agreement. The end of World War II and the onset of the Cold War had presented an entirely new security environment for the United States and the military organization was substantially overhauled to create the air force as a separate service and to create the Department of Defense to coordinate all defense efforts. (Previously there had been separate Departments of War (Army) and Navy with no over-arching agency to manage the two.)

House Armed Services Committee Chairman Ron Dellums (D-CA) was another prominent member of Congress who had been disappointed in the lack of significant change represented by both the chairman's report and the Bottom Up Review. He therefore proposed the creation of an independent commission to evaluate the roles and missions of the armed forces and recommend appropriate changes. With support from Senator Nunn, this proposal was added to the FY95 Defense Authorization bill.[18]

The Bottom Up Review acknowledged some of the challenges for future roles and missions but made no recommendations for change. In the section of the BUR that addressed service roles and missions, the report acknowledged the changing demands of the post–Cold War era and the potential relevance for expeditionary ground forces (army and marines), theater air operations (essentially a validation of the need for all the services' air components—the "four air forces"), overseas presence (predominantly navy), service roles in new mission areas (mainly peace operations), and responsibilities assigned to active and reserve components (a proportionally greater shift to reserves relative to active forces).[19] These were the issues that the commission's advocates hoped could be addressed effectively by an independent panel of experts.

PROCESS OF THE REVIEW

When Congressman Dellums first proposed the commission on roles and missions, his idea had been to establish a commission for a period of three years and for the commission to make initial recommendations and then follow up with assessments of implementation. In other words, rather than being a one-time effort to render a report, the commission would have multiple iterations, which would allow the commission to produce an initial report, receive a response from DoD, and then have the opportunity to make subsequent recommendations, as well as to analyze and comment on implementation.[20] Since the requirement for the CORM was initially contained only in the House version of the appropriations bill, negotiation on the nature of the CORM was part of the conference committee work. The main negotiations occurred between Senate and House Armed Services Committee staff members (in particular staff members Senator Nunn and Representative Dellums).[21] In the end, Nunn's preference for the more traditional, one-report approach prevailed. The legislation required the appointment of the commission and that it render a report within one year, at which time the commission's work would be complete.

The impetus behind the report was spelled out in the legislation:

Congress makes the following findings:

1. The current allocation of roles and missions among the Armed Force evolved from the practice during World War II to meet the Cold War threat and may no longer be appropriate for the post-Cold War era.

2. Many analysts believe that a realignment of those roles and missions is essential for the efficiency and effectiveness of the Armed Forces, particularly in light of lower budgetary resources that will be available to the Department of Defense in the future.

3. The existing process of a triennial review of roles and missions by the Chairman of the Joint Chiefs of Staff pursuant to provisions of law enacted by the Goldwater-Nichols Department of Defense Reorganization Act of 1986 has not produced the comprehensive review envisioned by Congress.

4. It is difficult for any organization, and may be particularly difficult for the Department of Defense, to reform itself without the benefit and authority provided by external perspectives and analysis.[22]

The intent was for the commission to be independent, but the appointment of the commissioners was a responsibility of the secretary of defense. Quickly, the independence of the commission was hobbled by the bureaucratic allocation of commission seats to recently retired representatives of each of the military services and the National Guard. The original plan was to have seven commissioners, but after pressure from the services to include retired military representatives from each service, the commission was expanded to eleven to ensure that it included more civilian than military members (five retired senior military officers, six civilians).[23] The commissioners were named in early 1994. John White was named the chairman of the commission. Following his resignation as secretary of defense, Les Aspin was also appointed to the commission.[24]

Within a few months, each of the services created its own team to cover the roles and missions commission work. The teams monitored the activities and debates of the commission and provided service perspectives. The service teams worked closely with commission staff members and sometimes the commissioners themselves to provide information concerning the various issues under consideration. As the staff director of the commission noted, in addition to the professional staff, "There are people ... in the [services] who are working on [their service's] point of view. If you start to roll in all of those efforts, you get a very large enterprise."[25] Service participants also provided information of the commission's work and debates to the leaders of their services so that they would know what the commission was trying to do.

The legislation establishing the committee was passed in early 1994. By April, the commission was in the process of hiring staff and deciding on its agenda. As the commissioners established their agenda, they decided to cast their net widely to include several issues. From a large menu of sixty to a hundred issues, the commissioners pared down the study to twenty-six.[26] Even so, the number and diversity of issues disappointed many observers, such as Secretary of Defense Perry and Deputy Secretary John Deutch, who felt that the commission's utility would be greatest if it were to focus on a few key issues rather than a broad array.[27]

After selection of the commissioners, thirteen staff coordination groups were formed to work on various issue areas. The staff groups reported their work back to the commissioners who then resolved disputes between the reports. With constraints on the number of staff members that could be hired for the commission,[28] the most heavily tapped source of expertise became borrowed civilian and military personnel from within the Department of Defense as well as many federally contracted consultants to which Congress granted the commission liberal access.[29] Along with the questionable independence of several commissioners from the process, in essence the commission was an internal effort of the DoD to reform itself with little actual distance or independence from the issues, processes and organizational structures that it ostensibly had been charged to review.

Each of the services initially approached the commission as a potential threat to the well-established roles and missions division of labor that had been in place for much of the Cold War and had been endorsed by the most recent roles and missions assessments (the chairman's 1993 report and the Bottom Up Review). The teams each service provided to work with the commission were designed to protect and promote service interests. Reinforcing this was the ability of commissioners to exercise a veto on topics with which they disagreed. By requiring consensus, commissioners representing service interests were able to block effectively any major changes that did not meet service approval.[30]

The one effort that seems to have violated the unwritten rule among military leaders not to disturb that balance between the services was the air force's attempt to suggest real tradeoffs in mission priorities and to list the savings that could be obtained from cuts to other services' programs. With the exception of the air force, the services appear to have had a general agreement about the nature of the debate and declared satisfaction with the existing division of labor.[31]

Throughout the commission's operation, the army and the marines had a close understanding about the role they played to complement each other. The army and marines cooperated to put down any arguments that sought to equate them and then reduce the structure to have only one or the other. The marines and the army made a point of stressing their "simultaneously complementary capabilities."[32]

RESULT

The services successfully resisted changes to their roles and missions. The commission produced no major recommendations for changes in the military services but did present a shotgun blast of minor recommendations to improve managerial efficiency and to focus DoD better on the supporting joint forces under the commanders in chief (CINCs) of the varied unified commands.[33] In this formulation, the services provide the capabilities to the CINCs for military operations (missions) in accordance with the CINCs requirements. This makes the services suppliers to the CINCs' demands. The report declares,

Our recommendations ... are designed to

- improve the ability of the Secretary of Defense to provide unified strategic and programmatic direction to DOD;
- expand the role of the Chairman and Vice Chairman of the Joint Chiefs of Staff and the CINCs in ensuring better joint doctrine, training, weapons planning, and support;
- focus the military departments on providing the right mix of capabilities for unified military operations;
- improve capabilities to deal with new challenges of the post–Cold War world; and
- reduce the cost of the support infrastructure through increased outsourcing and better management—while increasing responsiveness to the needs of the CINCs.[34]

Specific recommendations of the commission included emphasis on greater outsourcing of DoD commercial type functions to civilian contractors; streamlining service staffs to eliminate dual civilian and military staffs (for service secretary and military chief of staff); the creation of "a new, functional unified command responsible for joint training and integration of all forces based in the continental United States;"[35] and for the DoD to make a greater differentiation of peace operations as separate from other contingency missions.[36]

The impact of the final report was lessened by having been commissioned by a Democratic controlled Congress and in the end having been reported out after the Republicans had taken control of the Congress in the 1994 mid-term elections. Readiness of existing forces for fighting wars had been the main campaign issue concerning defense for Republicans. The Republicans accepted the strategy of the Bottom Up Review to fight and win two major wars but focused on what they thought to be the shortfall of the resources necessary to carry out the two-war strategy. Other than the emphasis on readiness and the push for greater resources to support missile defenses, the Republicans had no major defense initiatives. When the CORM itself was released, the interest of the new Republican leaders for reshaping the military was low. Secretary William Perry and others within DoD implemented many of the recommended efficiency changes. DoD did enhance the joint doctrine creation and staffing process within the Joint Staff. It did not, however, create the joint forces command to focus on joint training and evaluation. Congress did little with the report other than create the requirement for the recommended Quadrennial Defense Review.

The press coverage of the report was sparse and the effects largely unnoticed outside the Pentagon.[37] Within the Pentagon, Secretary Perry did not consider the report useful to him for major policy issues. He dismissed it as generally insignificant but did acknowledge its utility to help make bureaucratic improvements and adjustments to the DoD.[38] The report did provide the basis for some efficiency improvements within the Pentagon. Within the Pentagon, the report also had the virtue of being the work of the man soon to become deputy secretary of defense. As Deputy Secretary of Defense, John White took the lead in implementing many of the efficiency recommendations the commission made.

SUMMARY AND ANALYSIS

The commission was chartered to examine the fundamental roles and missions of the armed forces. The report recommended no changes to the roles and missions of the armed services. A requirement for consensus and the presence of representatives for each military service as well as the efforts of the service teams designed to support the commission blocked any significant recommendations for roles and missions change. The commission's recommendations did not challenge the status quo.

In the end, what was intended to be an independent evaluation of defense issues became an internal DoD reform effort. The commissioners had very little distance or independence from the issues, processes, and organizational structures that they had been asked to address. The commission rejected a fundamental reassessment of service roles, missions, or basic force structure and instead chose to address managerial efficiency issues similar to the Clinton administration's National Performance Review.

The final report received little high-level attention. The fact that the commission lowered its sights from fundamental exploration of roles and missions to a series of minor details on the margins of the defense-policy process accounted for this lack of high-level interest. Many of those inside and outside DoD who had hoped for a more substantial outcome attributed the diminished interest to the lack of focus on the part of the commission.[39]

After resigning as secretary of defense in December 1993, Les Aspin became a member of the commission. Given his previous enthusiasm and leadership in defense reform efforts, many thought the presence of Les Aspin would allow him to address some of the bolder changes that had not been included in the BUR. Although Aspin had ostensibly resigned from the administration, the fact was that he was pushed out following the debacle in Somalia. Aspin was generally dispirited by his removal from office and by all that he had given up to take the office in the first place.[40] In general, Aspin seems to have had little enthusiasm for the commission, did very little work with the commission and had very little impact on its report.[41] Additionally, Aspin's health was deteriorating as the commission worked on its report. Aspin died shortly before the final report was issued. The commission's report is dedicated to Aspin's memory.[42]

The Commission on Roles and Missions also implicitly recognized its inability to recommend major changes to overall defense policy and suggested the mechanism by which such changes might be better considered. The CORM included a recommendation for the routine review of defense issues at the beginning of each presidential term. The recommendation for a quadrennial review of defense policy was later adopted by Congress as the requirement for the 1997 Quadrennial Defense Review.

NOTES

1. Senator Sam Nunn speaking in 1992 as quoted in Commission on Roles and Missions of the Armed Forces. *Directions for Defense: Report of the Commission on Roles and Missions of the Armed Forces,* Washington, D.C.: Government Printing Office, May 1995. (Hereafter referred to as CORM), 1–3.

2. Nunn in CORM, 1–3. From March 11–14, 1948, the military service chiefs delineated respective service roles and missions during a meeting at Key West, Florida. Available from http://www.hq.nasa.gov/office/pao/History/Timeline/1945–49.html; Internet; accessed 12 April 1999.

3. In an interesting turn, John P. White was named deputy secretary of defense shortly after the report was completed. At the Pentagon, one of Deputy Secretary White's responsibilities was to respond to the report he had helped write.

4. CORM, ES-1 to ES-9. This assessment is also supported by Andrew Krepinevich, *Missed Opportunities: An Assessment of the Roles and Missions Commission Report* (Washington, D.C.: Defense Budget Project, August 1995).

5. Interviews with senior DoD civilian leaders and a professional congressional staff member.

6. CORM, 4–9.

7. U.S. Congress, "National Defense Authorization Act for Fiscal Year 1997," Title IX, Subtitle B—Force Structure Review, Sections 922–924.

8. Eighteen soldiers were killed during a raid aimed at Somali warlord Aideed 3–4 October 1993.

9. *Contract With America*, 1994, http://www.nationalcenter.inter.net/Contractwith America.html; Internet; accessed 22 February 1999.

10. John E. Rielly, "The Public Mood at Mid-Decade," *Foreign Policy* 98 (Spring 1995): 76–93.

11. The Goldwater-Nichols Act of 1986 created the requirement by amending the U.S. Code, Title 10. Subtitle A, Part I, Chapter 5, 153. Chairman Functions, located at http://www.dtic.mil/jcs/core/title_10.html; Internet; accessed 12 April 1999.

12. General Colin Powell, "Chairman of the Joint Chiefs of Staff's report to Congress on the Roles and Missions of the Armed Forces," March 1993.

13. Interview with a congressional professional staff member.

14. Ibid.

15. Powell officially submitted the chairman's report on roles and missions in November 1989; however, that report had been written primarily by Powell's predecessor, Admiral Crowe. Powell provided an endorsement and some points of disagreement with Crowe's work when he submitted the report one month after assuming the chairmanship. Interview with a professional congressional staff member.

16. Aspin, Les (Secretary of Defense). *Report on the Bottom Up Review,* October 1993, 31. (Hereafter referred to as BUR.)

17. One example of this is Senator Sam Nunn's 2 July 1992 speech in Congress, "The Defense Department Must Thoroughly Overhaul the Services' Roles and Missions."

18. Interview with a House of Representatives staff member.

19. BUR, 89.

20. Interview with congressional staff member who worked on CORM legislation.

21. Interviews with congressional staff members of the Senate and House Armed Services committees.

22. U.S. Congress, National Defense Authorization Act for Fiscal Year 1994, Subtitle E—Commission on Roles and Missions of the Armed Forces, Sec. 951, Findings. Available from http://thomas.loc.gov/cgi-bin/query/; Internet; accessed 3 June 1998.

23. Civilians means members of the commission whose professional backgrounds were primarily in civilian office as opposed to the five commissioners who were recently retired general officers.

24. The members of the commission were: John P. White (chairman of the commission and later Deputy Secretary of Defense), Antonia Chayes, Admiral Leon Edney (USN, ret.), Major General John Matthews (Army National Guard, ret.), Robert

Murray, Franklin Raines, General Robert RisCassi (USA, ret.), Jeffrey H. Smith, Lieutenant General Bernard E. Trainor (USMC, ret.), General Larry Welch (USAF, ret.), and Les Aspin (who was added to the commission after he resigned as secretary of defense in early 1994). CORM, title page.

25. Transcript of interview with Mike Leonard, commission staff director for the Commission on Roles and Missions. Interview by Dr. Edgar F. Raines, 9 May 95. Transcript at Center For Military History.

26. Ibid.

27. Interview with senior DoD civilian official.

28. The commission itself was limited to twenty full-time equivalent staff members. However, the commission was able to "borrow" manpower from the services at no cost. This led to the appointment of fourteen military officers to work on the staff of the commission. See CORM title page.

29. The commission was provided a budget of $20 million by Congress specifically for the hiring for FFRDC (federally funded research and development center). From Leonard interview. Also see bill S.2182, *National Defense Authorization Act for Fiscal Year 1995*, Section 923, (f).

30. Interview with a military member of the commission staff.

31. During a brief period early in the process, the air force offered to give the army the Close Air Support mission while requesting responsibility for all air defense assets—tactical through strategic. The army would have been the major loser in this particular set of tradeoffs and therefore fought hard to prevent the switch. With the replacement of General McPeak by General Fogelman as the air force chief of staff, the contentious issues about pursuing air-defense control appear to have been dropped by the air force.

32. Transcript of interview with Brigadier General John Costello, Director of Army CORM Team, by Dr. Ed F. Raines, 6 April 1995.

33. CORM, 1–9.

34. Ibid, ES-2 to ES-3.

35. Ibid, ES-3.

36. Ibid, ES-4.

37. Andrew Krepinevich, *Missed Opportunities: An Assessment of the Roles and Missions Commission Report* (Washington, D.C.: The Defense Budget Project, August 1995), 5.

38. Interview with senior DoD civilian official.

39. Interview with senior DoD civilian official.

40. Aspin Papers. In a handwritten note from the day prior to his resignation, he has a list of points to make during a meeting with the president that clearly represent the argument he would make to President Clinton to keep his job. Whether the points were actually addressed with Clinton is not clear from Aspin's papers.

41. This is evident both from interviews with commission participants and Aspin protégés as well as by the lack of documentation in the Aspin Papers about the commission. There are many other items in the Aspin Papers indicating his activities and efforts during the time following his resignation as secretary of defense and his death, but very little about the commission.

42. CORM, v.

Chapter 7

The 1997 Quadrennial Defense Review

> We cannot afford, either fiscally or strategically, to continue to tinker
> at the margins of our military forces or to procure Cold War systems
> we have previously bought but only in diminishing quantities and at
> ever-increasing prices. We need the Secretary of Defense and the chairman
> of the Joint Chiefs to put their best minds to work on these ideas and issues
> in a focused and comprehensive and independent way.
> —Senator Joseph Lieberman, 25 June 1996[1]

OVERVIEW

The Quadrennial Defense Review offered yet another opportunity to address
the capabilities of the U.S. armed forces in the post–Cold War era. The mandate
for the review came from Congress. The impetus was Congressional dissatisfaction with the pace of reform that resulted from previous efforts to reformulate defense policy. In particular, the Commission on Roles and Missions of the
Armed Forces had "largely validated the Pentagon's then current strategy,
forces, roles and missions, stationing and infrastructure."[2] Within the report
by the Commission on Roles and Missions was the recommendation for a process to conduct a "comprehensive examination of the defense strategy, force
structure, force modernization plans, infrastructure, budget plans and other
elements of the defense program and policies."[3]

Instigated by the CORM, the 1997 QDR was the first in this iterative review
process. The intent was for a similar review to take place every four years at the
start of a new presidential term. The first review began in the fall of 1996 with
the report due to Congress in May 1997.[4]

The final report proved to be yet another disappointment to those who continued to push the DoD for significant change. Like the Bottom Up Review and
the Commission on Roles and Missions, the Quadrennial Defense Review accepted the basic premises of the path established by the Base Force and offered
only small additional cuts in the military services with no major changes to
force structure of doctrine.

As with the previous reviews, military leaders and their staffs had significant roles in all deliberations related to the review and entered the process predisposed to defend their current plans and programs. Furthermore, although the military leaders were many of the same ones who worked on the previous defense reform efforts, the civilian leadership for this review was in the midst of transition. The review began before the 1996 presidential election and immediately after the election, Secretary of Defense Perry stepped down and was replaced by former Republican Senator William Cohen. Many participants felt that the time provided to complete the report was too short to conduct a thorough review. Therefore, the path the administration had already set with the Bottom Up Review was largely reaffirmed and extended.

HISTORICAL CONTEXT

International Environment

In the approach to the 1996 presidential election, the sense of optimism about world affairs and the ability of the U.N. to serve as an effective means for the management of international security had significantly declined. With U.N. failures in Somalia, Bosnia, and Rwanda came greater emphasis on the need for the United States or other powerful states to take the lead in "coalitions of the willing" to address international problems.

Prominent foreign policy issues for the United States included efforts to implement the Dayton peace accord in Bosnia, the effort to expand NATO and efforts to manage the global economy. U.S. military involvement in Bosnia was just beginning while tensions with Iraq were ongoing. U.N. forces had withdrawn almost completely from Somalia and the operation in Haiti was winding down. The security of the United States seemed in little direct jeopardy from any major state competitor. Remaining security concerns were primarily related to terrorism and the proliferation of weapons of mass destruction.

Domestic Political Environment

The legislation mandating the QDR was inspired by the CORM report and was passed before the 1996 presidential election. The preliminary work on the QDR by DoD began prior to the election, but proceeded tentatively until the new leadership of the department was in place. In particular, Secretary of Defense William Perry had already announced his retirement before the election. After the election, re-elected President Clinton appointed former Republican Senator from Maine, William Cohen to become secretary of defense.

The issue of defense had been a minor factor in the presidential election. Neither presidential candidate presented any significant proposals for defense.[5]

In essence, the Democrats campaigned using the BUR. For the Republicans, the main issue was the readiness of the armed forces.[6] Additionally, public opinion reflected little concern about defense and reinforced the lack of attention defense issues received in the election. As with 1992, the general analysis was that the election was driven by domestic economic issues.

One domestic political element related to the election that did affect defense was the base realignment and closing (BRAC) process. Following the 1995 round of BRAC recommendations, President Clinton interceded on behalf of installations in California and Texas to keep them operating in spite of BRAC recommendations. This overt politicization of the base-closing process was perceived by Republicans as a presidential election ploy to appease political constituents in two of the most important states for presidential electoral votes. This politicized what was supposed to be an apolitical process.[7]

DEFENSE ISSUES AND ADVOCATES

The arguments about the shape of the armed forces had changed little since the CORM. Within Congress, many still advocated more radical reductions in the overall forces as a means to free up more fiscal resources for domestic programs. Also some Republican defense supporters focused on increased funding for military readiness.[8] There were also many who continued to decry the lack of change within the military to embrace more fully the revolution in military affairs to adopt more radical force structure designs and weapon programs. The QDR debate was predominantly influenced by the conflict between two major groups—the debate between those focused on present readiness concerns and those concerned with future military capabilities.[9]

The QDR process established by legislation was a compromise product. In Congress, Senators Lieberman, Coats, McCain, and Robb wanted the creation of an independent panel (manifested later as the National Defense Panel) to conduct a review of defense policy.[10] The intent was to get together a group of defense 'wise men and women' to think about defense issues 'outside the box.' Their sense was that there had already been attempts by the Pentagon to reassess strategy and force posture for the future (the Base Force, BUR, and CORM) but that the reviews had led to little change and were unsatisfactory. The congressional sponsors wanted an assessment of the institutional mechanisms for change to address the demanding challenges of the future. The leadership in the Pentagon preferred that the assessment be done by the DoD and cited the recommendation of the CORM for a Quadrennial Strategy Review as support for this approach.[11] The compromise was the creation of the two-part process with the Quadrennial Defense Review done inside the Department of Defense and the independent National Defense Panel created to look in from the outside.[12]

The NDP concept did represent a substantially different approach than had been used in previous post–Cold War efforts. In the creation of the NDP, the intent was to have a group of

Wise men and women, recognized defense experts ... to review the work of the Pentagon ... and to offer comments and suggestions on how America can most effectively meet our defense needs in the next century. The real hope here is that this nine-person, nonpartisan commission ... would essentially go out of the box and ask the questions that either we have not thought of or we have decided are unthinkable or that we should not think about, to force us to face the tough questions about our security needs.[13]

The NDP was apprised of the work of the QDR as it progressed and provided its report in December 1997.

Within the Pentagon, the Deputy Secretary of Defense and former Chairman of the Commission on Roles and Missions of the Armed Forces, John White, was the civilian leader tasked with routine oversight of the process. This was particularly important given the transition occurring between secretaries of defense. White was well aware of the charter for change promoted by the review's supporters in Congress. As he noted in a public speech to the Defense Science Board,

We must take a fresh look at the full spectrum of plausible military operations and associated capabilities given posited world conditions. We need to include a wider set of potential scenarios. One of the criticisms of the Bottom Up Review was that it placed too much emphasis on maintaining the forces necessary to fight two major regional conflicts nearly simultaneously, and too little emphasis on the day-to-day demands of overseas presence and smaller-scale contingencies. I agree with that view.... So we are committed to evaluating and testing force structure alternatives against the full range of plausible contingencies.[14]

Continuing to lead opposition to higher defense spending, Congressman Ron Dellums sought to dramatically cut funding of the active military forces and place more emphasis on the reserves and traditional concepts of mobilization for future crises.[15] The dominant motives for such cuts were focused on the achievement of fiscal savings in defense as a means to free up greater resources for domestic programs. This alternative suggested few major modifications to existing forces other than their size.[16] In contrast, Republicans in control of Congress chose to emphasize readiness of the armed forces.[17] Democrats, such as Dellums and his supporters in the congressional minority, did not have much support for their preference to cut military funding and move more funds back to domestic programs.

Another argument for lower defense spending included calls for change to the basic two-war strategy. Proponents argued that active forces to handle one major regional contingency effectively were adequate when coupled with reliance on reserve forces to meet other challenges as they arose. Additionally, budget savings were also identified through the elimination or severely limited production of various weapons programs associated with apparently outdated

Cold War justifications.[18] As many analysts argued, even if the pursuit of research and development of such systems might be justified to anticipate future challenges, the procurement in quantity of such systems made little sense given the lack of clear competition available to existing generations of American weaponry.[19]

I believe strongly that we should avoid buying new systems that maintain the United States and the world on a treadmill of weapons development. Pressing ahead with such invites an arms race that we would be well advised to avoid.... In addition, we must avoid making purchases of systems that are excessive, redundant, and are designed to replace systems that currently work perfectly well because they are far superior to anything that they confront in a potential theater and will continue to do so into the mid-term future.[20]

PROCESS OF THE REVIEW

Senator Lieberman, in particular, was interested in creating a process that would raise the level of debate on defense issues related to future forces and the threats they might be called upon to address. Believing that Congress cannot and should not dictate the outcome (in terms of specific forces and organizations) Congress nonetheless could provide a useful oversight role in creating and monitoring the operation of processes to address such issues.[21]

To Lieberman the mission was for "the secretary of defense to conduct a thorough study of alternative force structures for our armed services."[22] This would include consideration of the RMA and the assessment of force structures to account for revolutionary transformations.

Yet the changes are so dramatic, the world so uncertain, our fundamental responsibility to provide for our national security so great, that what we who will put forth the amendment are asking is that we step back from the day-to-day, that we look out over the horizon ... look out as far as we can see to the future security threats we may face and how we can best meet them; to ask the bold questions, the questions that unsettle the status quo, that do not always, in the normal course of the process, get asked here.[23]

Within the Department of Defense, a large and diverse group of bureaucratic actors was designated to participate in the review. As Deputy Secretary of Defense White noted shortly after the requirement for the QDR was received,

The QDR will be a highly collaborative effort. It will involve all key elements of DOD—the offices of the Secretary of Defense and the Chairman of the Joint Chiefs of Staff as well as the CINCs and the military services. As a result, it will tap expertise and ideas throughout DOD.[24]

Consequently, it also created a complex bureaucratic mechanism to assess issues and reconcile differences.

Three tiers of work were established to address the legislated requirements. The first tier consisted of seven panels each tasked with responsibility for a different issue.[25] For the purposes of this study, the panels of greatest interest were those addressing strategy, force structure, and modernization. After the work of the seven panels was completed, the reports and recommendations were provided to the second tier, the integration group, which was charged with assembling the input and reconciling conflicts. The integration group then forwarded the report to the top tier senior steering group (consisting of the Deputy Secretary of Defense, the Undersecretaries of Defense, the Director of PA&E, the Vice Chairman of the Joint Chiefs of Staff, the Assistant Secretary of Defense for Strategy and Requirements, and the senior service representatives of the four services). The Secretary of Defense and the Chairman of the Joint Chiefs of Staff then review the report.[26] Each of the tiers consisted of members from each of the services, the Joint Staff, and DoD civilian leadership.[27]

The DoD was directed to deliver the final report to Congress in May 1997. The timing of the QDR created several challenges. Although the legislation mandating the report came out in the summer of 1996, the coming Presidential campaign was largely responsible for deferring significant work until the outcome of the election was known. Furthermore, the announced retirement of Secretary of Defense Perry, regardless of the outcome of the election, also created uncertainty about guidance for the process.

As soon as the legislation passed, each of the services created a team to manage their service's participation in the process. The QDR began in earnest following the election in November 1996. The seven panels for the review were created with each service providing a team to cover each panel.[28] The main participants in the QDR process were the military services and the civilians in the Department of Defense. Within the Office of the Secretary of Defense, many of the individuals who worked on the Bottom Up Review were still present and had developed a much greater understanding of defense issues and the responsibilities of their offices.

Going into the review, the army, navy, and marines staked out predominantly defensive positions to preserve force structure and end strength. Given the short period of time available until the final report was due, the main effort for the services was to avoid any major changes to existing plans.[29] The air force was the one service to step forward with an aggressive plan to press for greater emphasis on modernization for the future coupled with reductions related to current operations and personnel. Whereas the other services maintained the existing balance in emphasis between support for current operations and support for modernization, the air force was in favor of an increased effort to develop and exploit technological advancements associated with the RMA, even at the expense of current force structure and readiness.[30]

Air Force Chief of Staff Fogleman had hoped that the QDR would be an opportunity for major changes. He said, "I sincerely believed that the nation was at a unique crossroads, ... that we had an opportunity ... to restructure our military into a smaller, better-focused institution to respond to the kinds of challenges coming in the next ten to fifteen years. I was hopeful that the QDR would start us down that path."[31] In the early stages of the review process, however, Fogelman received guidance intended to minimize dissension among the services. According to Fogelman, in September 1996 a representative from the JCS Chairman, General Shalikashvili, visited to emphasize support for the status quo.

> An Army two-star from the JCS came by to see all the chiefs, and when he came to see me, he . . . said, "I have a message from the chairman, and the message is, that in the QDR we want to work hard to try and maintain as close to the status quo as we can." From that point on, I really did not have much hope for the QDR.[32]

For the force structure panel, one of the most important aspects was an assessment of the forces available and the likely risks in the performance of various missions based on different force structures. This included analysis of the forces required for the execution of major theater war (MTW), smaller-scale contingencies (SSC, such as peacekeeping and humanitarian assistance), and for conflict with a potential regional or global great power competitor. To assess the capacity of various forces to handle the contingencies, several simulations were run. For major theater war analyses, the simulations were run using force structures that were balanced to reflect the existing proportions of forces between the military services. Subsequent simulations applied incremental differences of "10-, 20-, and 30-percent proportional reductions to each service's combat capability."[33] No simulations or analyses were conducted using the premise of unbalanced force packages, that is, with force packages that reflected combinations differing significantly in the relative proportions of forces from the various services (such as an army-dominant or air force–dominant force package).[34]

For smaller-scale contingencies, each of the services, the Joint Staff, and the CINCs provided representatives to run a series of war-gaming exercises. These war games took the patterns of peace operation and other missions short of war that had occurred in the past several years and used them to project the frequency of such missions for the future.[35]

> DOD's war game series called Dynamic Commitment examined the force's suitability to carryout a wide range of notional smaller-scale contingency operations and major theater wars projected to occur between 1997 and 2005. The contingencies consisted of disaster relief, evacuation, humanitarian relief, and other operations based on the history of the number and types of such occurrences since 1991. Series participants allocated forces to the operations based on military judgment. The assessment confirmed that the projected force is sufficient in size to meet projected requirements and that some capabilities already known to be stressed will continue to be stressed in the future.

The General Accounting office was bluntly critical of the QDR's methodology;

> Although the series provided participants with some insight into the challenges of conducting multiple, overlapping operations, it did not identify what force would be best suited to meet these demands. Specifically, DOD did not use the series to identify

force structure alternatives that (1) might result in better balance between forces required for smaller-scale contingency operations and major-theater wars, or (2) eliminate excess capabilities. Moreover, the Joint Staff, which sponsored the effort, did not summarize the results of the analysis.[36]

On modernization, seventeen working groups were established to look at various systems. Among others, the working groups assessed defense of the United States, theater air and missile defense, tactical air, rotary aircraft, deep strike, ships, global-positioning system, ground forces, special-operations forces, and C4ISR (command, control, communications, and coordination, intelligence, surveillance, and reconnaissance).[37] Each working group functioned independently of other groups and reported to the modernization panel with little cross fertilization and cross consideration with other modernization programs. In other words, no tradeoffs were considered between the groups.[38] Furthermore, when the modernization panel forwarded the reports to the next level, there was no attempt to identify contradictions or potential tradeoffs among the various programs. In short, each modernization program was considered in isolation from potential tradeoffs or opportunity costs calculated in terms of other modernization programs.[39]

RESULT

The strategy of the QDR is captured by the three-word summary, "Shape-Respond-Prepare." As a clarification of U.S. strategy, the review was useful. In adopting this strategy, the report acknowledged that there were alternatives for more radical adaptation for the future and for greater concentration on present challenges (although both were somewhat oversimplified straw-man alternatives). The report instead selected a middle course that would balance the objectives of both short-term and long-term demands. It emphasizes the short-term need to meet the challenges of the current security environment and suggests useful application of U.S. forces to a spectrum of missions aside from war fighting that, nonetheless, serve the broader security interests of the state (for example peacekeeping, humanitarian operations, and military-to-military contacts). The report focuses on the short-to-medium term requirement to maintain combat forces capable of responding to major theater wars in two regions.[40] The two major theater war contingencies continued to provide the central sizing rationale for force structure. Lastly, the strategy emphasized the need to prepare for the future through foresight and innovation to address potential challenges and opportunities. The latter emphasis on preparing for the future is most tightly bound up with modernization of equipment. In practical terms, the emphasis on modernization is best understood as the recapitalization of the force through increased procurement funding to acquire the next generation of major weapon systems. The RMA figures prominently in language throughout the report. The RMA is presented as a key consideration for the military services as they prepare for the future, but, in practical terms, there are no major recommendations to change procurement or force structure due to any insights derived from the RMA.

The QDR contained an additional increment of personnel reductions to take place before 2010. Overall the QDR included the reduction of 60,000 active duty personnel (reduction of 4.2%), 55,000 reserves (reduction of 6.2%), and 80,000 civilians (reduction of 11.1%) for an overall reduction of 195,000 personnel (reduction of 6.4%). The breakdown of personnel changes that the QDR included for the services were reductions of 15,000 active duty and 45,000 reserve personnel for the army; 18,000 active and 4,100 reserves for the navy; 26,900 active duty and 700 reserves for the air force; and 1,800 active duty and 4,200 reserves for the marines.[41]

For modernization, no major weapon systems were added or canceled. Among the most hotly debated items during the QDR were the fates of three future aircraft purchases that many critics thought reflected unnecessary redundancy. Among the F-18 E/F, the F-22, and the experimental Joint Strike Fighter (JSF), role redundancy and cost constraints led many to expect at least one of the systems to be canceled.[42] In the end, Secretary Cohen decided to preserve all three systems, but at lower overall levels of production.[43]

Fiscally, the services each accepted minor force cuts and several important procurement plans were scaled back, such as the plans for purchases of new aircraft. However, no major procurement programs were eliminated and none of the services suffered disproportionate cuts relative to the others. To address the short fall between projected budgets and the requirements needed to sustain current capabilities while increasing funding for modernization, the report chose to emphasize the need for achieving greater cost efficiencies within the DoD (to achieve a revolution in business affairs) as well as to pursue additional rounds of base closings to reduce infrastructure costs—something Congress had already declared unlikely for the near future.

The modest personnel reductions and the changes to out-year procurement plans were implemented as part of subsequent budget proposals and congressional authorizations. One important element that was not implemented was the suggestion to conduct further rounds of base closings. Given President Clinton's overt, apparently partisan intervention in the 1995 BRAC round, congressional Republicans rejected the idea of further base closings as soon as the QDR report came out. The general consensus among Republican leaders was that they would be unwilling to conduct additional rounds with Clinton in office.[44]

The unique aspect of the QDR process relative to previous defense reformulation efforts was the work of the independent National Defense Panel (NDP).[45] In contrast to the QDR, the NDP *did* provide ideas for future defense policy that deviated radically from the status quo and suggested bolder ways in which DoD could exploit the current era of U.S. advantage to adapt forces and strategy for more demanding future scenarios. In particular, the NDP was forthright about its perceptions that a revolution in military affairs was underway and that the U.S. defense establishment must adopt a strategy to adjust to the revolution.[46] An important characteristic of the revolution concerns information technology and the challenge to adapt weapons and organizations to exploit these advanced capabilities. The report looks out ten to twenty years in the future to discern the demands likely to be placed on U.S. armed forces and foresees the need for substantially different capabilities than those that currently exist or that are envisioned for the near future. Some of the NDP's policy suggestions included greater emphasis on institutionalizing innovation, experimentation, and change (particularly as a joint endeavor of all the military services); review of alliance and alliance-like commitments and opportunities; increased emphasis on national intelligence collection and analysis efforts; improvement of the interagency process to include expansion of the National Security Council; modification of the Unified Command Plan (adding a new joint force command and adjusting others); changing the industrial base and acquisition process to increase off-the-shelf equipment acquisition, exploitation of dual-use technology; modify equipment modernization plans to emphasize greater experimentation and innovation and place less emphasis on large-scale production; and reform the defense infrastructure to reflect the reduced size of the armed forces since the end of the Cold War as well as to improve managerial efficiency and strategic resource management.[47]

The DoD and Congress moved to implement the modest changes in force structure the QDR recommended as part of the 1999 budget authorization and appropriation process. The NDP's more dramatic view of the future has been helpful in shaping efforts to think about the long-range possibilities for defense (twenty to thirty years out). Its recommendations for a transformation strategy, to include changes to current procurement and force structure, have not, however, been adopted.

SUMMARY AND ANALYSIS

As one analyst summed up,

The QDR uses Cold War units of account (divisions, carrier battle groups) to denominate military power; its scenarios, physically located in the Far East and Persian Gulf, dwell mentally in a Cold War world of precise calculations of forces required to defend [sic] an opponent attacking after just so many days of warning and with just so many forces.[48]

Echoing many other analysts and the National Defense Panel, the QDR was assessed as offering little new. As Congressman Dellums put it, the QDR "was yet another attempt to reshape the defense establishment after the Cold War, but it too fell short of the mark, although it was a cautious step away from the BUR."[49]

The QDR avoided major decisions to reshape the armed forces. The patterns of Cold War structure and doctrine were thereby preserved. As a GAO assessment of the QDR noted, "The QDR determined that the military force structure required to meet the strategy would be very similar to that determined by the Bottom Up Review."[50] Senator Lieberman (D-CT), who sponsored the original legislation mandating the report, said that the QDR was "... largely a status quo product ... [that] makes only minor changes to the current force."[51] The *Washington Post* captured the opinion of many noting:

In its latest review [QDR] of how to size and shape U.S. armed forces in the wake of the Soviet Union's collapse, the Pentagon has done some tinkering but left basically intact the military's budget, structure and battle doctrine.... The Pentagon's response to the critics is that evolutionary rather than revolutionary change must prevail.[52]

The strategy associated with the QDR is the clearest yet on the importance of the military's role in peace operations to shape the international environment to better support American interests and establish the conditions that might prevent the need for future intervention. Relative to the Base Force and the BUR, the QDR represents an even smaller incremental reduction in the size of the military with each service taking its fair shares of the cuts. The review noted three possible paths. The first focused on the near term with emphasis on readiness and current operations. The second focused on the long term with substantial cuts in the current force structure as a way to support a more vigorous modernization and experimentation effort for the creation of future forces. The third was a path that tried to accomplish both. Unsurprisingly, the attempt to do both was the path chosen.

As with the CORM, the QDR reflected extensive participation by all the major elements within the DoD. Each of the services, the Joint Staff, and the major civilian agencies had places at the table.[53] The QDR was a comprehensive internal DoD review of defense. The outcome of the review appears to be little different from what the DoD produced during the Bottom Up Review. The requirement to fight two major theater wars was a restatement of the two major regional contingency requirement from the Bottom Up Review. Furthermore, even thought the basic task remained the same, there was no attempt to see whether there were other ways the services could be organized to improve its success in fighting such conflicts. The focus was on the use of forces configured just as they had been since the Cold War.

DOD did not refine its assessment to determine whether fewer or targeted changes to the services' force structure could be viable force options. DOD officials said they did not perform such analyses because they would not have been able to obtain consensus on the force changes among the services within the time available to complete the QDR ... [54]

All the panels tasked to deal with portions of the review worked concurrently with little opportunity to coordinate amongst each other and consider the work of other panels prior to the submission of reports to the integration groups. For example,

The modernization and force-assessment panels conducted most of their work independently and concurrently, which hampered their ability to explore linkages and trade-offs between force structure and modernization alternatives.[55]

After all the panels provided their input, the integration group did very little integrating. For the most part, the integration group accepted the panel reports and then forwarded the collected reports to the Senior Steering group. The integration group did not try to make any tradeoffs between conflicting proposals.[56]

The president had very little participation in the review and the resulting report. The only area that attracted the president's attention after the review was complete and before the report was issued was the issue of base closings. Satisfied that the report created no significant political controversies the president made no substantive comments on the report.[57]

The strategy piece of the QDR reflected a strong degree of conceptual continuity with the strategy of the Bottom Up Review. Given that Assistant Secretary of Defense for Strategy and Requirements, Dr. Edward Warner, and members of his staff had also put together the strategy for the BUR, the similarities are unsurprising.[58]

To many, the final QDR report included a mismatch between strategy and resources. In particular, critics charged that the forces provided by the report would not be able to execute effectively the two major theater wars that are the foundation of the strategy. This is significant in that analyses conducted to determine the ability of the force to execute various missions, which took place in the early stages of the process, were conducted using procurement assumptions that changed later in the review.[59]

Given the president's politicization of the BRAC process during the 1995 election campaign, the ability to obtain the funds necessary to overcome the mismatch between strategy and resources was limited. The review placed emphasis on the need for two more BRAC rounds as an important means for obtaining the additional savings to free up funds to meet the other objectives in the report, such as spending for readiness and modernization.[60]

Another important element that influenced the outcome of the QDR was the relatively short amount of time allocated to complete the review.[61] The time for the review was further limited by the 1996 election in that any major decisions were deferred until after the election was decided and the new secretary of defense had been appointed. The lack of time for a comprehensive review appears to have hardened defensive positions among the military services with each simply acting to ensure that no major changes took place to undermine established positions.

As the sponsors of the original QDR anticipated, the result of the DoD's internal review was a predictable continuity with the past that reflected no major effort to think outside the box. In many ways, this was unsurprising. The key civilian leaders from the president down to DoD political appointees were, in large part, the same group that had helped put together the same administration's earlier Bottom Up Review. The notable exception to the continuity of the civilian appointees was the new Secretary of Defense, William Cohen.

One valuable service of the 1997 QDR is as the maiden effort in a routine series of reviews of defense policy that take place during each new presidential term. It was one of the CORM's recommendations that such reviews take place routinely.[62] Congress mandated the next review for 2001, during the first year of the new president's administration. The 2001 review legislation did not, however, include an independent panel, like the NDP, to supplement the internal DoD review.[63]

NOTES

1. "Statement on the Senate floor in support of his amendment to the Defense Authorization Bill [Amendment requiring Quadrennial Defense Review and National Defense Panel], June 25, 1996. Available from, http://www.senate.gov/member/ct/ lieberman/releases/f062696a.htm; Internet; accessed 4 February 1997.

2. Center for Defense Information, "The Quadrennial Defense Review: A Sense of Deja vu," http://www.cdi.org/issues/qdr/qdr.html, accessed 4 February 1997.

3. Commission on Roles and Missions of the Armed Forces. *Directions for Defense: Report of the Commission on Roles and Missions of the Armed Forces,* Washington, D.C.: Government Printing Office, May 1995, 4–9. (Hereafter referred to as CORM.)

4. The Lieberman amendment did not mandate any subsequent reviews in later presidential terms.

5. See "Democratic National Platform: Security Freedom and Peace," posted at *New York Times* Web site, available from http://www.nytimes.com/specials/issues/ihome/ where/pltform/dem/dem-plat4.html; Internet; accessed 3 October 1996, and "Republican Platform: Restoring American World Leadership," posted at *New York Times* Web site, Available from http://www.nytimes.com/specials/issues/ihome/where/pltform/ rep/plat8.html; Internet; accessed 3 October 1996.

6. Floyd D. Spence, (chairman House Committee on National Security). "Military Readiness 1997: Rhetoric and Reality," 9 April 1997.

7. Interview with a Senate civilian staff member. Sheila Foote, "House Panel Approves Restrictions on Depot Privatization," *Defense Daily,* 6 June 1997, 408.

8. Spence, *Military Readiness 1997.*

9. William S. Cohen, *Report of the Quadrennial Defense Review,* (Washington, D.C.: Department of Defense, May 1997), 7–9. (Hereafter referred to as 1997 QDR.)

10. Interview with Senate civilian staff member.

11. CORM, ES-8.

12. U.S. Congress, H.R. 3230, National Defense Authorization Act for Fiscal Year 1997, Title IX Subtitle B—Force Structure Review Sec. 923. Quadrennial Defense Review and Sec. 924. National Defense Panel. Available from http://www.cdi.org/ issues/qdr/qdrlegsl.htm; Internet; accessed 4 February 1997.

13. Lieberman statement, 25 June 1996.

14. "Deputy Secretary of Defense John White Outlines Quadrennial Defense Review Before Defense Science Board," Press Release, Reference Number: No. 594–96, 18 October 1996.

15. Dellums, "Envisioning a New National Security Strategy."

16. Interview with a House of Representatives staff member.

17. Spence, *Military Readiness 1997.*

18. For an example of such analysis, see Military Spending Working Group, "1998 Top Ten & Dirty Dozen," available from http://www.fas.org/pub/gen/mswg/msbb98/ index.html; Internet; accessed January 16, 1999. "Top Ten" refers to programs for continuation or augmentation. "Dirty Dozen" refers to programs for reductions or termination.

19. Military Spending Working Group, "Invest in 'Generation After Next' Research and Development," available from http://www.fas.org/pub/gen/mswg/msbb98/ tt10rd.html; Internet; accessed January 16, 1999. Also, Dellums "Envisioning a New National Security Strategy."

20. Dellums, "Envisioning a New National Security Strategy."

21. Interview with a Senate staff member.

22. Senator Joseph Lieberman, "Statement on the Senate floor in support of his amendment to the Defense Authorization Bill [Amendment requiring 1997 QDR and NDP], June 25, 1996, available from http://www.senate. gov/member/ct/lieberman/ releases/f062696a.htm; Internet; accessed 4 February 1997.

23. Ibid.

24. White, Press Release, Reference Number: No. 594–96, 18 October 1996.

25. The panel issues were intelligence, strategy, force structure, human resources, modernization, infrastructure and readiness.

26. Information on the structure of the process is combined from several sources. There is a brief description of the structure in the QDR report. Details on the service participation were provided by each of the services and corroborated with the GAO analysts tasked to assess the process. Also from interviews with a senior civilian analyst in the Government Accounting Office. Also from panel presentations and discussion, Panel discussion on the 1997 QDR, ISSS conference, Norfolk Virginia, 25 October 1997. Panel members at the ISSS conference consisted of presenters from each of the four services. The military officers on the panel were all members of their respective service "QDR cells." [COL B.J. Thornburg USA, COL Greg Parlier USA, CAPT Paul Ryan USN, LTC Stephen McNamara USAF, COL Robert Work USMC.] (Hereafter, ISSS QDR Panel, 25 October 1997.)

27. The level of attention was very high in each of the services. For example, for each of the seven panels and the integration group, the army assigned a general officer or, in one case, a high-ranking civilian, to represent its interests. From army briefing slides on the QDR, provided by COL Thornburg, ISSS QDR Panel, 25 October 1997.

28. Teams varied in size based on the issue areas. Service teams were generally led by a general officer. For example, the navy team included fourteen individuals but could draw on a vast array of Navy Department staff personnel in the Pentagon. From ISSS QDR panel, 25 October 1997.

29. ISSS QDR Panel, 25 October 1997. Also see, John Robinson, "Navy Won't Reinvent Itself for Strategy Review, CNO Says," *Defense Daily*, 19 November 1996, 280.

30. ISSS QDR Panel, 25 October 1997.

31. Richard H. Kohn, "The Early Retirement of General Ronal R. Fogleman, Chief of Staff, United States Air Force," *Aerospace Power Journal* XV, no. 1 (Spring 2001): 11–12.

32. Ibid, 12.

33. United States General Accounting Office (GAO), *Quadrennial Defense Review: Opportunities to Improve the Next Review (GAO/NSIAD-98–155)*, Washington, D.C.: Government Printing Office, June 1998, 6. (Hereafter GAO/NSIAD-98–155.)

34. Ibid.

35. Ibid, 7.

36. Ibid.

37. 1997 QDR, 44–48.

38. Interview with GAO official.

39. GAO/NSIAD-98–155, 8–9.

40. This is little different from the requirement to fight two near simultaneous regional contingencies—two MRCs—as presented in the BUR (which in turn had descended from the two-contingency capability of the Base Force).

41. Data from 1997 QDR, 29–31. Percentages from table "Slimming Down the Military," in Philip Shenon, "Pentagon Releases New Strategic Blueprint," *New York Times*, 20 May 1997, available from http://www.nytimes.com/yr/mo/day/news/washpol/pentagon-review.htm; Internet; accessed 20 May 1997.

42. For examples of this see Sheila Foote, "Weldon Says Changes Needed in DoD's Fighter Plan," *Defense Daily*, 10 January 1997, 45, and Jeffrey Record, "Three Planes, One Wallet," *Baltimore Sun*, 25 February 1997, 13.

43. 1997 QDR, 45–46.

44. Interview with Senate staff member.

45. National Defense Panel, *Transforming Defense: National Security in the 21st Century*, Washington, D.C.: Government Printing Office, December 1997. (Hereafter referred to as NDP.)

46. Ibid, i–vii.

47. Ibid, 57–86.

48. Eliot Cohen, "Calling Mr. X: The Pentagon's Brain-Dead Two War Strategy," *The New Republic* 218, No. 3 (19 January 1998): 17–19.

49. Dellums interview with Christopher Gibson, 12 June 1997.

50. GAO/NSIAD-98–155, 3.

51. Quoted in Philip Shenon, "Pentagon Releases New Strategic Blueprint," *New York Times*, May 20, 1997, accessed from Web site, May 1997 (http://www.nytimes.com/yr/mo/day/news/washpol/pentagon-review.htm).

52. Bradley Graham, "Pentagon's Plan for Future Draws Heavily from Cold War Past," *Washington Post*, May 11, 1997, A19.

53. This was particularly clear from the description of the QDR given by members of the ISSS QDR panel, 25 October 1997. The officers described the views of each of their services and how they would assess the nature of the outcome. They also discussed the

participation of the Joint Staff, OSD, and a variety of civilian contractors used for the process. Each officer had represented his service QDR team. Also corroborated during numerous interviews with other participants within the military and civilian leadership at DoD.

54. GAO/NSIAD-98–155, 6.

55. GAO/NSIAD-98–155, 5.

56. Interview with GAO official and GAO/NSIAD-98–155, 12.

57. Interview with a member of the NSC staff.

58. Noteworthy civilian leaders of the strategy review included Director of Strategy, Michele Flournoy and members of her office. From interviews with senior DoD civilian officials.

59. For one detailed analysis of the potential mismatch between strategy and defense budgets, see Michael O'Hanlon, *How to Be a Cheap Hawk: The 1999 and 2000 Defense Budgets* (Washington, D.C.: Brookings Institution Press, 1998), 4–20.

60. 1997 QDR, viii-ix.

61. The lack of time to conduct a thorough review to consider major changes was a comment from several participants to include the members of the QDR panel discussion at the ISSS QDR Panel discussion, October 1997 and interviews with senior DoD civilian officials.

62. The Commission on Roles and Missions recommended the creation of a process for a quadrennial strategy review at the beginning of each administration, but, only the 1997 requirement was required by the initial legislation (Lieberman Amendment).

63. William Matthews, "Worries Spur 4-Year Defense Plan Reviews," *Army Times,* 6 September 1999, 12.

Chapter 8

The 2001 Quadrennial Defense Review

As President, I will begin an immediate, comprehensive review of our military—the structure of its forces, the state of its strategy, the priorities of its procurement—conducted by a leadership team under the Secretary of Defense. I will give the Secretary a broad mandate—to challenge the status quo and envision a new architecture of American defense for decades to come.... The real goal is to move beyond marginal improvements.
—Governor George W. Bush, 23 September 1999[1]

OVERVIEW

The National Defense Authorization Act for Fiscal Year 2000 formally established the quadrennial defense review as a requirement in the first year of each presidential term.[2] In 2001, this review provided the first defense assessment of President George W. Bush's new administration. The report was due to Congress by 30 September 2001. In the months before September, there were many reports of major debates concerning force structure changes. There were also assertions by the new administration, particularly Defense Secretary Donald Rumsfeld, that the review would represent a major change in defense policy. As the deadline for the review approached, however, resistance to change, especially from military leaders, became the dominant theme. Secretary Rumsfeld's efforts to make major immediate changes to force structure and doctrine of the forces were frustrated.

The review was thrust to the background by the terrorist attacks on the World Trade Center and Pentagon on 11 September 2001. The report was nonetheless released as promised on 30 September 2001 with a strong emphasis on homeland defense. Furthermore, the war stance pushed remaining concerns about reductions and reshaping of existing military forces to the background. The focus became the execution of the war against global terrorism. Falling short of President Bush's expressed desires for major changes in military capabilities, the report suggested only marginal improvements. The report did, however, provide strong rhetoric for transformation and laid out a subsequent agenda and process to try to push for transformation. The rhetoric and commitment to transformation appeared strong and genuine even if immediate results were minimal.

HISTORICAL CONTEXT

International Environment

The 11 September 2001 attacks on the World Trade Center and the Pentagon represented a direct threat to the United States and its citizens at home. Aside from the direct destruction and death caused by the attacks, the attacks illustrated U.S. vulnerability to asymmetric threats in a profound way. In response, President Bush declared war against terrorism with a global reach.[3] A few weeks later, the United States launched its first combat operations as part of this war with military operations in Afghanistan. With strong international support, the United States worked closely with internal Afghan opposition forces to defeat Afghanistan's Taliban government and the terrorist network it harbored. Relying heavily on air power coupled with Afghan ground forces and U.S. special operations forces, the coalition toppled the Taliban government and paved the way for an international security force.

In follow-on operations for the war on global terrorism, the United States committed small numbers of forces to support military operations and training in the Philippines, Georgia, and Yemen. In South America, the United States provided strong support to the government of Colombia in its efforts to defeat rebels closely aligned with drug cartels. In the Middle East, tensions between Israelis and Palestinians included an escalating cycle of violence that seriously threatened efforts to create a stable and lasting peace.

In addition to emphasis on the war against global terrorism, President Bush used his January 2002 State of the Union address to highlight the threat of weapons of mass destruction. In particular, President Bush identified Iraq, Iran, and North Korea as members of an "...axis of evil, arming to threaten the peace of the world."[4] With respect to Iraq, the effort to unseat Saddam Hussein appeared to be a major goal of the Bush administration. Continued tensions on the Korean peninsula reinforced U.S. commitment to maintain a robust armed-forces presence in South Korea. The threat of weapons of mass destruction married to long-range ballistic missiles in all three states provided continued impetus to the administration's pursuit of ballistic-missile defense.

Between the 1997 QDR and 11 September 2001, the most significant U.S. military event had been Operation Allied Force, the air war launched against Serbia in 1999. The first war in NATO's fifty-year existence, Allied Force achieved Serbian withdrawal from Kosovo after a seventy–eight-day air campaign. Following the air war, U.S. and other international armed forces assumed responsibility for long-term security duties within Kosovo. Although the situation improved markedly with the departure of Yugoslav dictator Slobodan Milosevic, significant tensions remained within the former republics of Yugoslavia, particularly between Serbians and Muslims. A stable resolution to the tensions of the region does not seem likely to occur soon. Participation in peace operations in Bosnia, Kosovo, and Macedonian is an ongoing, open-ended commitment for American armed forces.

When the QDR report was presented at the end of September 2001, the international environment appeared much more threatening for the United States than at any other time since the end of the Cold War. There was no consensus about a name for this new era, but it seemed clear that the so-called post–Cold War era—one characterized primarily by peace—was over.

Domestic Political Environment

The most important element of the domestic political environment was the change in presidential administrations from Democrat Bill Clinton to Republican George W. Bush. Although the Republican party had been out of power in the executive branch for eight years, the new administration was able to place in office several prominent individuals from previous Republican administrations. With respect to defense policy, notable individuals included former Secretary of Defense Dick Cheney as the new Vice President, former Chairman of the Joint Chiefs of Staff Colin Powell as the new Secretary of State, and former Secretary of Defense in the Ford administration, Donald Rumsfeld, for a second tour as Secretary of Defense. Other prominent figures of previous Republican administrations that returned to important posts in the executive branch included Paul Wolfowitz as Deputy Secretary of Defense and Condoleezza Rice as National Security Advisor.

The first months of the Bush administration also included a brief period of unified control of both the executive and legislative branches of the government. In addition to the White House, the Republicans held a slim majority in both the House of Representatives and the Senate. In the House, Republicans had a slight majority. In the Senate, the split was exactly fifty-fifty with control in the hands of the Republicans by virtue of the vice president's tie-breaking role. In May 2001, Republicans lost control of the Senate when Senator James Jeffords of Vermont left the Republican party and became an independent.[5]

DEFENSE ISSUES AND ADVOCATES

During the presidential election, both the Democrats and the Republicans expressed strong support for defense and proposed legislative packages that would increase defense spending in the course of the next presidential term. During the campaign, Democratic candidate Al Gore proposed a much greater spending increase on defense than Republican candidate Bush.[6] Other areas about which the candidates differed significantly included Bush's emphasis on transformation to include skipping the next generation of weapons,[7] whereas Gore emphasized funding the next generation.[8] The Bush campaign also expressed a strong aversion to non-war-fighting missions and promised an immediate review of the U.S. overseas commitments, while the Gore campaign endorsed the Clinton administration's ongoing commitments.[9] Both expressed strong support for military personnel and were committed to improving their quality of life.[10]

The Republicans had consistently attacked the Clinton administration as not having done enough to ensure strong national defense. Although they did not argue against the two-war policy, the gist of their critique was that the Clinton administration had not provided adequate defense spending to meet realistically the demands of the strategy with the forces at hand. Republican Presidential candidate George Bush also proposed major changes to defense policy to incorporate the opportunities suggested by the revolution in military affairs. In the primary defense policy statement of his campaign, Governor Bush declared " ... I will begin creating the military of the next century."[11] Additionally, President Bush also pressed strongly for pursuit of a national missile-defense system. Within the Bush campaign and the Bush administration, the dominant theme became the effort to transform the U.S. armed services.

PROCESS OF THE REVIEW

As the previous chapter noted, many in Congress were disappointed in the modest changes induced by the 1997 QDR. This led to the establishment of the quadrennial defense review as a permanent requirement within the first year of each presidential term.[12] With the creation of the recurring requirement for the QDR in 2000, the agencies of the Department of Defense began to assemble the personnel and organizations to support the review. Well before the 2000 presidential election, each military service established an office to participate in the anticipated review.[13] A group at the RAND Corporation identified one of the key challenges the new Bush administration would face as it prepared to enter office in late 2000.

There is great momentum (some would say inertia) behind every major component of the defense program, and the Pentagon has been working for months on position papers, options, and analyses intended to present your new administration with available choices. Left on "autopilot," this process is quite capable of building a program and carrying it out without direction by you or your new defense team. But such a "business as usual" approach would be likely to avoid the tough questions, thus producing a total defense structure that is more costly than necessary.[14]

After the beginning of the new administration, Secretary of Defense Rumsfeld tried to reserve judgment for a few key issues to a small group of senior executives. This was a cause of some concern among many military leaders who perceived that they were being shut off from key decisions and that their services might therefore suffer.[15] Prior to the 11 September attacks, there were numerous reports in the press from unidentified military sources in the Pentagon who felt that Secretary Rumsfeld was not considering their views and would therefore make decisions these unnamed sources felt would be injurious to interests they represented.[16] This first stage of the review, called by some the "Rumsfeld Review," consisted of several panels that explored various issues related to the QDR.[17] Among them were panels dealing with strategy, conventional forces, personnel, and transformation.[18] The review panels helped Rumsfeld crystallize the key themes for the review. Significantly, the "Rumsfeld Review" bypassed the military QDR offices created by each service and the Joint Staff. In May and June, Secretary Rumsfeld also used meetings with senior civilian and military leaders to develop detailed guidance on strategy for the review. As Rumsfeld noted in testimony before congress in June 2001,

Over the past several weeks, the Chairman of the Joint Chiefs of Staff, the Vice Chairman, each of the Service Chiefs of Staff, on occasion the CINCs, and the few senior civilian officials in the Department who have been confirmed, held a series of meetings to discuss the U.S. defense strategy. We did not include staff, and met daily, two to three hours at a time, often on weekends—for a total of some 20–25 hours—to produce detailed strategy guidance for the execution of the congressionally-mandated Quadrennial Defense Review (QDR).[19]

The result was a twenty-two-page document of "Guidance and Terms of Reference" delineating overarching defense strategy themes and establishing the process for a detailed review of key subjects.[20]

The terms of reference clearly established transformation as the focus of the QDR effort.[21] The guidance Rumsfeld provided acknowledged that, "U.S. forces overall remain unrivalled, but are largely a downsized legacy of the Cold War investment and therefore may not be optimized for the future."[22] In order to secure a peaceful world, in cooperation with friend and allies, the members of the QDR effort were directed to, "focus on the task of transforming the U.S. defense posture to stay ahead of and hedge against the uncertain eventualities of the future while continuing to meet current U.S. security responsibilities. The current period of U.S. military preeminence is the best time to transform for the challenges of the future."[23]

The defense strategy guiding the review includes four goals:

- Assure allies and friends by demonstrating the U.S.'s steadiness of purpose, national resolve, and military capability to defend and advance common interests.
- Dissuade, to the extent possible, potential adversaries from developing threatening forces or ambitions.
- Deter threats and counter coercion against the U.S., its forces, friends and allies.
- Decisively defeat an adversary at the time, place, and manner of our choosing.[24]

The guidance emphasized giving greater priority to experimentation for new forces.[25] It also emphasized the need for capabilities to hedge against a wide range of possible contingencies.

U.S. forces must be sized and shaped to do the following concurrently:

- (U) DEFEND THE UNITED STATES: Provide strategic deterrence and missile defense; support U.S. civil authorities, as appropriate, in response to NBC [nuclear, biological, and chemical] events; assure U.S. access to and the ability to operate in, through and from space; assure the critical defense-related information infrastructure; and maintain the training, sustainment and power projection base.

- (U) DETER FORWARD: In critical areas of the world (i.e., Europe, Northeast Asia, East Asian littoral, and Middle East/Southwest Asia) advance security cooperation, counter coercion and deter aggression by maintaining regionally-tailored forward stationed and deployed forces that are capable of swiftly defeating an enemy's effort with minimum reinforcement.

- (U) WIN DECISIVELY: When directed by the President, decisively defeat an adversary in any one of these critical areas of the world, This capability must be designed not only against present threats, but should also be able to counter future capabilities focused on anti-access, NBC weapons, information operations, and other asymmetric means of threatening U.S. interests.

- (U) In addition, U.S. forces will be capable of conducting small-scale contingencies of limited duration in other areas of the world, preferably in concert with allies and friends.[26]

The organization for the review included three main tiers. At the highest level, the secretary of defense, deputy secretary of defense, under secretaries, Joint Chiefs of Staff, and service secretaries formed the Senior Level Review Group (SLRG). This group provided guidance, decisions, and taskings to support the review. Day-to-day work in managing the review was the responsibility of the deputy secretary of defense working with the Vice Chairman of the JCS.[27] To execute this day-to-day management, the deputy secretary had oversight of an Executive Working Group (EWG) responsible for monitoring, analyzing, and integrating the outputs of the eight integrated product teams The EWG was run by the special assistant to the secretary of defense supported by the undersecretary of defense policy (OUSD(P)), the director of program analysis and evaluation (DPA&E) and the Joint Staff directorate for Force Structure, Resources, and Assessment (J8). Senior members of other undersecretariats and the services also participated in the EWG.[28] The tier where the detailed analysis and proposals occurred was in the eight integrated product teams (IPTs). The teams created for the review were strategy and force planning, military organizations and arrangements, capabilities and systems, space information and intelligence, forces, personnel and readiness, and infrastructure and integration.[29]

Overall, the process reflected many of the improvements suggested by the GAO after the previous QDR. Initial guidance for the integrated product teams included a clear strategy for use of U.S. forces and the overall vision for defense transformation that the group efforts would support. Final briefings were also due to the senior level decision makers by mid-July 2001, therefore leaving plenty of time for reconciliation and integration into the final report due at the end of September.

When the terrorist attacks occurred on 11 September 2001, the QDR report was largely finished.[30] Changes to force structure that had been seriously considered in early stages of the review[31] had been stiffly and successfully opposed by military leaders. Although there was a slight chance that Secretary Rumsfeld might include force reductions in the final weeks before the report was due, this appeared highly unlikely even before September 11.

RESULT

The terrorist attack on the United States had some impact in shaping the final decisions on the report. Nonetheless, the majority of the study and preparation of the report took place prior to the 11 September attacks and remained largely intact in the final report. Understandably, the final report placed the issue of homeland security at the top of the priority list and sought to identify those areas in which immediate improvements in homeland defense could be realized. The report did not include any reductions or restructuring of U.S. armed forces.

The report emphasized the need for defense transformation and laid out the broad guidelines for the transformation effort. This was the most important element sustained from the president's September 1999 campaign speech concerning defense policy. Although rhetorically robust, the details of the transformation efforts were largely deferred. The creation of the Office of Force Transformation was an organizational effort to carry this emphasis forward after the report.[32]

To support the transformation effort, and to foster innovation and experimentation, the Department will establish a new office reporting directly to the Secretary and the Deputy Secretary of Defense. The Director, Force Transformation will evaluate the transformation efforts of the Military Departments and promote synergy by recommending steps to integrate ongoing transformation activities.[33]

The report embraces transformation and presses it as the central theme for the future of the armed services. The report establishes six operation goals to focus transformational efforts. The goals are:

- Protecting critical bases of operations (U.S. homeland, forces abroad, allies, and friends) and defeating CBRNE weapons and their means of delivery;
- Assuring information systems in the face of attack and conducting effective information operations;
- Projecting and sustaining U.S. forces in distant anti-access or area-denial environments and defeating anti-access and area-denial threats.

- Denying enemies sanctuary by providing persistent surveillance, tracking , and rapid engagement with high-volume precision strike, through a combination of complementary air and ground capabilities, against critical mobile and fixed targets at various ranges and in all weather and terrains;
- Enhancing the capability and survivability of space systems and supporting infrastructural; and
- Leveraging information technology and innovative concepts to develop an interoperable, joint C4ISR architecture and capability that includes a tailorable joint operational picture.[34]

Focusing on the adoption of a capabilities-based approach, Secretary Rumsfeld noted that this new approach, "entails adapting existing military capabilities to new circumstances, while experimenting with the development of new military capabilities."[35] To support this, the report increased the role of Joint Force Command (JFCOM) with added emphasis on its responsibility for experimentation. This was intended to support better exploitation of the revolution in military affairs and advancements in technology. This was the strongest step to date in operationalizing a process for military change.

Another development was a shift in the two major theater war strategy as the central component of the strategy. The report includes a strategic requirement for forces to be able to defeat one major adversary and to hold a second adversary at the same time. Following defeat of the first adversary, forces could be shifted to accomplish the decisive defeat of the second. In essence this represents the resurrection of the win-hold-win approach. In practical terms, this standard requires adequate air power to halt enemy forces in two major theaters and enough ground forces to conduct offensive operations in one theater to defeat and occupy and opponent's territory.

U.S. forces will remain capable of swiftly defeating attacks against U.S. allies and friends in any two theaters of operation in overlapping timeframes.... U.S. forces will be capable of decisively defeating an adversary in one of the two theaters in which U.S. forces are conducting major combat operations by imposing America's will and removing any future threat it could pose. This capability will include the ability to occupy territory or set the conditions for a regime change if so directed.[36]

This did not completely end the two-war standard; however, it did more realistically reflect the capabilities of the forces available. Additionally, rather than explicitly identify the strategy with specific threats of Iraq and North Korea, the 2001 QDR noted several critical regions that might require the use of U.S. armed forces as well as the need to execute concurrent small-scale contingencies. Among critical regions, Asia was singled out as a particularly important concern to a greater extent than in previous reviews. The capabilities to meet the full spectrum of national security demands will be the central force-sizing construct. Present identified threats are certainly still a concern; however, "A Capabilities-based model—one that focuses on how an adversary might fight rather than who the adversary might be and where a war might occur—broadens the strategic perspective."[37]

As with previous reviews, the 2001 QDR suggested efforts to improve the execution of joint operations. The 2001 QDR included the requirement to create better joint and combined command and control, creation of standing joint task force headquarters (details to be determined by subsequent efforts), examination of possible establishment of standing joint task forces, creation of a joint presence policy, and exploration of actions to sustain better joint logistics capabilities.[38]

SUMMARY AND ANALYSIS

The events of September 2001 overshadowed many of the contentious issues that had been at the core of the review. Force structure and program cuts that seem to have been seriously considered in the preliminary stages of the review were not part of the final report.[39] The report did not recommend any force-structure cuts and did not eliminate any major weapons programs.[40] This disappointed many in Congress and the defense-policy community who had hoped for immediate changes.

The lack of force structure or end strength changes puzzled Senate Armed Services Committee Chairman Carl Levin, who told Wolfowitz at [a] hearing that the QDR "seems to me full of decisions deferred." Paraphrasing Shelton's QDR assessment, he described it as more of a vision "than the comprehensive roadmap to the force of the future" that had been promised.[41]

Organizationally, the report did provide recommendations that hold the promise of improved mechanisms for facilitating military transformation. But, this exhortation for transformation and the creation of mechanisms, such as the Office of Force Transformation, are themselves a recognition of how far the armed forces need to go and, implicitly, an indication of the ineffectiveness of previous measures. One effect of this emphasis on transformation, from the president and the secretary of defense in particular, is that all the services have declared their loyal support for transformation. The military services have also made great efforts to demonstrate their commitment to transformation and to demonstrate that what they are doing contributes to transformation efforts. An unfortunate side effect is that just about everything is now somehow or the other related to transformation and the concept is in danger of becoming a meaningless buzzword.

The emphasis on a capabilities-based force structuring mechanism positively incorporates elements of General Powell's early capabilities-based justification of the Base Force and Representative Aspin's force-structure building blocks for specific types of operations.[42] This combination provides a concept for force-structure design and justification that better suits the full spectrum of military capabilities that military leaders have already identified. "The new construct for the first time takes into account the number and nature of the tasks actually assigned to the armed forces. Unlike previous force-sizing constructs, the new construct explicitly calls for the force to be sized for defending the homeland, forward deterrence, war-fighting missions, and the conduct of smaller-scale contingency operations."[43]

NOTES

1. George W. Bush (governor of Texas and presidential candidate), "A Period of Consequences." Speech given at The Citadel, South Carolina, 23 September 1999.

2. National Defense Authorization Act for Fiscal Year 2000, Public Law 106–65, 106th Congress, Sec 901. (Law amends Chapter 2 of Title 10, United States Code by adding Section 118 that requires "The Secretary of Defense shall every four years, during a year following a year evenly divisible by four, conduct a comprehensive examination (to be known as a 'quadrennial defense review') of the national defense strategy, force structure, force modernization plans, infrastructure, budget plan, and other elements of the defense program and policies of the United States with a view toward determining and expressing the defense strategy of the United States and establishing a defense program for the next 20 years."

3. George W. Bush, "Address to Joint Session of Congress and the American People," Text of presidential speech, Washington, D.C. 20 September 2001, available from http://www.whitehouse.gov/news/releases/2001/09/20010920–8.html; Internet; accessed 12 March 2002.

4. George W. Bush, "President Delivers State of the Union Address," Text of presidential statement, Washington, D.C. 29 January 2002, available from http://www.whitehouse.gov/news/releases/2002/01/print/20020129–11.html; Internet; accessed 15 February 2002.

5. James Jeffords, "Declaration of Independence," Statement, Burlington, VT, 24 May 2001, available from http://www.senate.gov/~jeffords/524statement.html; Internet; accessed 12 March 2002.

6. Gore proposed $100 billion in new spending compared to a proposed increase of $45 billion by Bush. Stuart A. Ibberson, "Candidates Offer Differing Views on Future of Military," *Journal of Aerospace and Defense Industry News*, 3 November 2000, available from http://www.aerotechnews.com/starc/2000/110300/Bush_Gore.html; Internet; accessed 13 March 2002.

7. Bush, "A Period of Consequences."

8. Association of the United States Army, "Gore, Bush Give Detailed Answers on Defense, National Security to 6 Leading Associations," 4 October 2000, available from http://www.ausa.org/; Internet; accessed 13 March 2002.

9. Ibberson, "Candidates Offer Differing Views on Future of Military."

10. Ibid.

11. Bush, "A Period of Consequences."

12. U.S. Congress, Public Law 106–65, *National Defense Authorization Act for Fiscal Year 2000*. 106th Cong., 2nd Sess., Title IX, Subtitle A, Section 901, Permanent requirement for quadrennial defense review.

13. Cindy Williams, "Strategic Defense Review in Context: Schedule of Pentagon Reviews and Budgets," *Foreign Policy in Focus,* May 2001, available from http://www.fpif.org/media/0105briefingbook/williams01.html; Internet; accessed 12 March 2002, and Gordon I. Peterson, "Sea Services Prepare for 2001 Defense Review," *Seapower,* September 2000, available from http://www.navyleague.org/seapower/sept00/washrep.htm; Internet; accessed 12 March 2002.

14. Frank Carlucci, Robert Hunter, Zalmay Khalilzad, *Taking Charge: A Bipartisan Report to the President Elect on Foreign Policy and National Security* (Washington, D.C.: RAND, 2000), 16.

15. Lisa Burgess, "Red Flags Flying On Rumsfeld Review," *European Stars and Stripes,* 22 May 2001, 2.

16. Thomas Ricks, "Post Interview with Defense Secretary Donald H. Rumsfeld," *Washington Post* 20 May 2001, available from http://www.washingtonpost.com/wp-srv/nation/transcripts/rumsfeldtext051701.html; Internet; accessed 12 March 2002 and Philip Gold, "Why the Pentagon Fears Rumsfeld's Review," *Seattle Times,* 13 June 2001, available from http://www.discovery.org/viewDB/index.php3?program = Defense&command = view&id = 652; Internet; accessed 12 March 2002.

17. John A. Tirpak, "QDR Goes to War," *Air Force Magazine* 84, no. 12 (December 2001), 29.

18. Panels identified included Defense Strategy (chaired by Andrew Marshall), Transformation (chaired by Gen (ret) James McCarthy), Conventional Forces (chaired by David Gompert), Nuclear Forces (chaired by Steven Maaranen), National Missile Defense (chaired by Steven Cambone), Intelligence/Space (chaired by Richard Haver), Crisis Management/Crisis Response (chaired by Adm. (ret) Joe Lopez), Acquisition Reform (chaired by Jack Welch), Financial Management (chaired by Stephen Friedman), and Morale (chaired by Adm. (ret) David Jeremiah). Other panels or studies included Electromagnetic Spectrum, Encroachment and Environmental Impact, Sustainment, Restructuring the Office of the Secretary of Defense, Allied Relations and Costs. Panels and studies identified by William M Arkin, "Rumsfeld Top-to-Bottom Review Evolves," *Defense Daily* 16 April 2001, 5. Also see Ricks, "Post Interview with Defense Secretary Donald H. Rumsfeld."

19. Donald H. Rumsfeld, "Prepared Testimony to the Senate Armed Services Committee," 21 June 2001, available from http://www.defenselink.mil/speeches/2001/s20010621-secdef.html; Internet; accessed 13 March 2002.

20. Donald H. Rumsfeld, (secretary of defense). "Guidance and Terms of Reference for the 2001 Quadrennial Defense Review," (Washington, D.C.: Department of Defense, 22 June 2001).

21. Ibid, 2.

22. Ibid.

23. Ibid.

24. Ibid, 6–7.

25. Ibid, 9.

26. Ibid, 9–10.

27. Ibid, 16.

28. Ibid, 16–17.

29. Ibid, 18–22.

30. Department of Defense, *Quadrennial Defense Review Report*, 30 September 2001 (hereafter referred to as 2001 QDR), v.

31. Tom Bowman, "Pentagon Faces Transformation," *Baltimore Sun* 13 March 2001, available from http://ebird.dtic.mil/Mar2001/e20010314faces.htm; Internet; accessed 14 March 2001.

32. 2001 QDR, 29.

33. Ibid, 29.

34. Ibid, 30.

35. Ibid, iv.

36. Ibid, 21.

37. Ibid, 14.

38. Ibid, 32–35.

39. Jonathan Weisman, "Cuts Get Cut From Pentagon Budget," *USA Today,* January 8, 2002, 4.

40. The report of the 2001 QDR did not include any specific weapon program cuts, but did highlight general themes concerning appropriate capabilities for the future armed forces. The report declared general principles to begin a process of transformation. 2001 QDR, vi.

41. Tirpak, "QDR Goes to War," 29.

42. Regarding the Base Force, see Lorna Jaffe, *The Development of the Base Force, 1989–1992.* (Washington, D.C.: Office of the Chairman of the Joint Chiefs of Staff, July 1993), 21–23. For the force building blocks concept see Les Aspin, *Report on the Bottom Up Review.* October 1993, 13.

43. 2001 QDR, 18.

Chapter 9

Explaining Decisions about Military Capabilities since the End of the Cold War

Policies once set in motion tend to go on and on, without much regard, at times, for changes in the circumstances that first occasioned them. In part this is related to the need for agreement; the best way to maintain a consensus is not to disturb it. It also reflects the fact that the time and energy of the policy elites are limited. Most policy problems are very difficult; so, too, is the process of reaching an agreement on what to do about them. The combination of the two difficulties can easily lead the policy elites, once they have thought and fought their way through to an operational consensus, to adopt an attitude of leaving well enough alone. And so they do, until some drastic change occurs in their environment which sharply and dramatically challenges the wisdom and feasibility of the previous course of action. The policy consequence is "outmoded policy."[1]
—Professor Warner Schilling, 1962

OVERVIEW

Although writing about the beginning of the Cold War, Warner Schilling captures the main theme of defense policy since the end of the Cold War. With agreement that the threats confronting the United States are less than they were during the Cold War, there has been consensus only for reduction of the armed forces. Policymakers have not challenged long-established agreements about force structure and doctrine.

Each of the five major reviews is a part of the process U.S. defense leaders have employed to help them organize the U.S. armed forces for current and future demands. This chapter summarizes the description and explanation of defense-policy formulation contained in previous chapters.

What emerged in previous chapters was a story of incremental adjustment to the end of the Cold War by the major figures engaged in formulating American defense policy. These adjustments in force structure and doctrine can be characterized as reduction without any significant restructuring.

The explanation for why this occurred the way it did is that within the policy making process, the military was able to control the outcome and achieve its preferences. Unsurprisingly, military leaders preferred a path of incremental change that was under their control. The efforts of General Powell in the closing stages of the Cold War—even before the collapse of the Soviet Union—defined the path that force structure and doctrine took from 1989 to 2001.

The major statement of this policy was the 1990 Base Force plan, for which Powell deserves the greatest share of the credit. After the change in presidential administrations in 1993, Powell was still Chairman of the Joint Chiefs of Staff. In that continuing capacity, he helped to ensure that the first major policy review of the new administration—the Bottom Up Review—took largely the same path as his Base Force. Like Powell, the military leaders embraced the approach that began under the Base Force and used its premises to govern their efforts within the policy process. General Powell encountered some resistance in getting the military leadership on board with the Base Force, but, once they agreed to the Base Force, they identified the path all four services were willing to follow. Since that time there has been little infighting among the services over the share of resources each receives as long as it has generally remained in line with the proportions at the time of the Base Force—which in turn represented substantial continuity with the Cold War era.

Close to the same time that military leaders agreed upon the Base Force as the plan they would pursue, the Gulf War occurred and helped to highlight the value of maintaining robust active duty war-fighting forces for immediate use. Combat success also reinforced the popularity of the military and individuals, such as General Powell in particular. This made it difficult for civilian leaders to openly oppose the military.

In 1992, military issues were not a major factor in the presidential elections. The focus was on economic issues and the recovery of the United States from a recent recession. When President Clinton was elected, he had a reputation on military issues that had been tarnished by evidence of youthful antimilitary actions during the Vietnam era. Immediately after the election, President Clinton induced a public disagreement with the military leadership, to include General Powell, and other defense supporters on the issue of gays in the military. In the end, President Clinton backed away from his plan to lift the ban against gays in the military, but the issue was a major distraction in the first six months of his administration.

President Clinton's Secretary of Defense, Les Aspin, argued strongly in favor of a major review, from the bottom up, of the entire U.S. defense posture in the wake of the Cold War. Political concerns about the public rift with the military, however, led civilian members of the administration to back away from any radical changes as part of the review. The result was an incrementally smaller force that did not substantially alter force structure or doctrine.

As the Cold War receded into the past and the armed forces remained essentially unchanged, some voices among the public and Congress expressed a need for greater change. In Congress, Senator Lieberman, Senator Nunn, and Representative Dellums led many who were dissatisfied with the changes that had occurred. As a result, Congress mandated the 1995 Commission of Roles and Missions of the Armed Forces and the subsequent 1997 Quadrennial Defense Review as attempts to induce greater change in the Department of Defense (DoD). In both efforts, the process included extensive participation of the military services and of individuals with a strong stake in the defense status quo. The reviews were both essentially conducted within the Department of Defense and ended up reiterating the established position of the Department of Defense—particularly the views of the military leaders. Furthermore, both the CORM and the 1997 QDR took place under the same administration that conducted the Bottom Up Review. With regard to these two reviews, President Clinton's stature on defense issues had not improved since the early days of the administration and he made no attempt to make defense a major issue. If anything, the president's ability to challenge the preferred positions of the military leadership was further inhibited by the Republican party's success in gaining control of the House of Representatives and the Senate in 1994. In one attempt to differentiate themselves from President Clinton and the Democrats, the Republicans took the position that the armed forces resulting from the Bottom Up Review were not sufficient to meet the two-war demands articulated by the President's own national security strategy. Republican congressional leaders argued that readiness was inadequate to meet national security needs both as a function of a mismatch in resources with stated policy and as a result of increasing operations tempo of American armed forces in support of peace operations. such as Somalia and Bosnia. To neutralize the issue, the president largely accepted the Republican critique and focused on the short- to near-term readiness of the force. President Clinton showed no interest in issues related to the long-term development of the armed forces.

In 2000, Congress created a permanent requirement for a quadrennial defense review with the next report due no later than 30 September 2001. Initially, the top-down efforts of Secretary Rumsfeld represented an end-run around the defense bureaucracy. In the latter stages of the process, however, the review took the bureaucratic trajectory of the BUR, CORM, and the preceding QDR, and was quickly smothered in a bureaucratic web of participants promulgating the same positions they had successfully defended in the previous reviews. Prior to September 2001, there were indications that President Bush and Secretary Rumsfeld were interested in significant changes that might represent major tradeoffs between the services and restructuring of basic service missions and functions. The attacks of 11 September intervened, however, before the 2001 QDR report was complete. The effects of the attacks on the 2001 QDR were an increased emphasis on homeland defense and at least a temporary end to attempts to further restructure or reduce military forces.

Presidents Bush (senior) and Clinton both voiced early calls for reassessment and restructuring of the U.S. armed forces. Both, however, showed little direct interest or concern with the details of force restructuring or strategic doctrine beyond endorsing the defense-policy reviews that took place during their administrations. As a candidate and then after assuming the presidency, George W. Bush expressed an interest in dramatic change of the armed forces. He did not, however, have an opportunity to demonstrate any substantive actions prior to the 11 September 2001 attacks.

As the 'superpower' of bureaucratic politics, the choice by the president not to get involved in long-range defense issues conceded the field to a wide group of subordinate actors. However, the participation of so many actors with no clear consensus on the nature of change simply helped perpetuate the existing agreements. The inertia of plans set in motion by the military leaders at the end of the first Bush administration persisted in the subsequent attempts to reformulate defense policy.

In short, the military leadership was able to set the trajectory for the force structure and doctrine of the armed forces at the end of the Cold War. The process has been characterized by lack of leadership by the president, general lack of interest by the public at large, and a general lack of interest by Congress. The result is that the policy set in motion by the Base Force has not been seriously challenged in the years since.

The remainder of this chapter details key characteristics of why there has been little change in the military, other than its size.

Strong Military Position: "No More Task Force Smiths"

Force structure and doctrine since the Cold War represent the preferences of military leaders. Military leaders entered this process with a firm conviction about what must *not* happen. That is, the military must not become a 'hollow force.' A hollow force is one where existing units are not provided with the resources—personnel and material—to prepare effectively for their stated missions.[2]

Military leaders insisted that the missions of the armed forces remain essentially unaltered and that the specific threats have changed mainly in degree rather than kind. Thus, to senior military leaders, the appropriate changes in defense policy following the collapse of the Soviet Union were the reduction in the overall size of the armed forces and the evolutionary adaptation of the forces to incorporate technological advances of existing systems. The emphasis was on enhancing the efficiency of the armed forces to execute the tasks that were well identified and understood during the Cold War.

The military leaders at the end of the Cold War were well aware of earlier problems the armed forces faced at the beginning of the Korean War. Between the end of World War II and the beginning of the Korean War, the active force was reduced dramatically. Additionally, since World War II, the main activity of this residual active force was the occupation of Germany and Japan. Training and readiness for war received little time and few resources. When North Korea invaded South Korea in June 1950, the United States resolved to defend South Korea. In the vanguard was an army task force hastily assembled and deployed from Japan. Named for its commander, Task Force Smith moved to Korea and raced forward to meet the attacking North Korean forces. In the ensuing battle, tenacious as their spirit was, Task Force Smith was overwhelmed and driven back by a better-trained and better-equipped enemy.[3] Although the American military recovered to perform well in the Korean war, the initial danger created by a military largely unprepared for its primary role provided a powerful lesson. The manner in which the military had been demobilized following World War II and the degree to which the active force was neglected received much of the blame.

A similar concern stemmed from the era immediately following the Vietnam War when the military was once again substantially reduced. Poor choices concerning the amount and pace of cuts threw the military into disarray. The resulting impact on force structure and budget left a military many deemed 'hollow' and unprepared for the demands of war.[4]

Military leaders attributed the problems in Korea and following the Vietnam War to poorly conceived peacetime policies that neglected the active forces and severely undermined the ability of the armed forces to perform their primary wartime mission. During the post–Cold War reductions, military leaders tried to ensure that the armed forces were not hollowed out in a time of low threat only to pay an enormous price in blood and effort during the next war.

The military's position was also a strong one because military leaders commanded a tremendous amount of political capital to support their efforts. This included tremendous popular support and prestige among the public at large[5] and strong support for their position among powerful defense constituents in the business world and among many communities near military installations.[6]

Facing the end of the Cold War and the pressures for a reduction in military capabilities, military leaders used the rallying cry of 'No more Task Force Smiths' to indicate their resolve to avoid the negative effects of cutting the military too far, too fast. This concern was echoed by civilian leaders, such as Secretary of Defense Cheney, who were concerned about 'breaking the force' by removing too much structure too quickly and not allowing the force time to adjust to new circumstances.[7]

The dominant plot line that emerges from the five major reviews is the successful control of the transformation of military capabilities by a core group of military leaders influenced by their negative experiences as junior military leaders. These leaders went through the very difficult and tumultuous period of the Vietnam War and the post–Vietnam War draw down and the resulting 'hollow' force structure of the 1970s. These leaders were also well-versed in the political process and, hence, much more capable of expressing and pressing their views within the policymaking process.[8] These leaders were largely responsible for the successful renovation of the U.S. armed forces from defeated and hollow forces of the Vietnam era to the formidable victors of Desert Storm. These leaders also presided over an institution that had risen from popular distrust and even contempt to the pinnacle of positive public regard.[9] The gains are impressive and laudable. The gains were hard won. Military leaders worked hard to successfully manage the draw down in the wake of the Cold War to avoid the precipitous demobilizations that followed most American wars.[10]

Politically, the military received strong support from members of Congress with a material interest in the existing defense establishment. Primarily this translated into support from districts with remaining military bases and major defense-industry contractors. Additionally, the Republican party, which dominated Congress from 1994 to 2001, saw as one of its distinguishing characteristics (in a partisan sense) a greater emphasis and support for defense. The primary manifestation was with regards to readiness and modernization.

There is also a disparity in many cases between the political and analytical skills of the various players with respect to defense issues—with the advantage of experience and education to the uniformed military leaders. This was particularly true in the early years of the Clinton administration when there were a limited number of civilian appointees with executive branch experience in defense matters. This was partly due to the twelve-year absence of the Democrats from the White House. Furthermore, they were dealing with a very strong group of military leaders who were well versed on the issues of defense reform. Such an advantage in political and analytical ability may help explain a dominance of military preferences over those of civilian leaders.[11]

Decrease in General Public Interest Concerning Defense

After the Cold War, defense declined as an issue of general public concern. Less public attention to defense issues also made such issues lower priority to public officials. The lack of general public attention also increased the influence of defense special interests.

For the three post–Cold War presidential elections (1992, 1996, and 2000), defense issues were low on electoral priorities as shown by opinion polls leading up to the elections. In 1998, one poll analyst noted that,

Worry about foreign policy, international relations or war is almost totally missing from the forefront of American concerns today. This stands in sharp contrast to many other periods since World War II when foreign-policy issues dominated the public's responses to [the Gallup Poll's] "most important problem" question. In the early 1950s, the Korean War was the nation's top problem. The threat of war, nuclear proliferation, and communism dominated in the mid-to-late 1950s, and into the 1960s. The Vietnam War moved to the forefront of the public's concerns in 1965 and remained a dominant problem well in to the early 1970s. War and peace issues also were highly likely to be top-of-mind through the mid-Reagan years of the 1980s, and again in 1990 and 1991 at the time of the Gulf War tensions.[12]

In the April 1998 poll of public perceptions of "the most important problem facing this country today," international issues/foreign affairs were cited by only 4 percent of the public and the military downsizing by only 1 percent. This was well below concerns about crime/violence (20%) ethics/moral/moral/family decline (16%), education (13%), drugs (12%) and poverty/homelessness (10%), welfare (8%), and Medicare/Social Security (8%).[13]

This lack of general public concern reinforced the lack of attention that such issues garnered from elected leaders. More difficult to discern is whether a lack of public interest drives lack of political interest or a lack of leadership by elected officials fails to put such issues in the fore of public debate. The truth is certainly a mixture of the two.

The more secure situation of the United States in the post–Cold War world drastically altered the context of the defense-policy process. The United States has always been able to distance itself from international relations to a greater extent than many other states. However, during the Cold War, the challenges of continuous competition with the Soviet Union and the threat the Soviet Union posed to the very existence of the United States worked to keep international affairs at the forefront of American politics. With the collapse of the Soviet Union, American politics once again put foreign policy on the back burner. Since the need for armed forces is most closely related to the perception of external threats, defense policy also moved to the political back burner. As the historic change represented by the collapse of the Soviet Union faded in the collective memory and no new clear threats emerged to provide a comparable challenge, the sense that what was done was adequate provided additional support for the defense-policy status quo. With increasing evidence that "it ain't broke," there was not much pressure for fixing it. This allowed leaders to devote greater time to other pressing issues and made it difficult for important leaders (especially the president, secretary of defense, and other senior civilian leaders) to focus on long-term issues that had little political currency in the short run.

Domestically, the shift of attention at the beginning of the 1990s from the drama of global competition with the Soviet Union to the challenges of domestic economic transformation helps account for the dramatically lower levels of attention defense issues garnered from elected civilian leaders, presidential and congressional. Furthermore, the generally healthy economic condition of the U.S. economy mitigated interest in the defense budget as a source for funds for other government programs (a concern after most previous major wars).

One effect of this lack of general public attention was the increased influence of defense special interests. With the end of the Cold War and the shift of defense issues to the background of American politics, there was less political capital to be gained from focus on defense issues—especially ones with long-range and uncertain implications. In 1998 Senator John McCain noted the difficulty in addressing defense issues,

I go on talk shows all the time . . . you start talking about national defense or foreign policy, the lines don't light up. Talk about Medicaid, Social Security, ITS, taxes—bang!—
they all want to be heard . . . I think we're stuck [regarding future national security] for
several reasons, and one of the major reasons is that most American don't care. The Cold
War is over. There's no perceived threat; the economy is good. Fewer and fewer Americans join the military. Politicians naturally gravitate to what interests their constituents.
Because people don't care, there's all sorts of political mischief being performed. And
we're not making the transition to the post–Cold War era.[14]

The effect of this general lack of interest was that the actors that remain most
active on defense are those with vested material interests in the status quo, such
as the defense industry. This substantial and diverse constituency of defense
industrial and military community beneficiaries reinforced the tendency of political leaders to focus on individuals or communities likely to bear the main
costs of change. For Congress, this material bias favored attention to the continued flow of resources to their districts. As during the opening stages of the
Cold War, a period subject to insightful treatment by Warner Schilling,[15] little
rational analysis was devoted to the manner in which the expenditure of resources addresses any particular strategic imperative. The concern, rather, was
upon the rational pursuit of maximizing dollar/resource delivery to districts.[16]

This general change in public interest to special interest can be characterized
as a shift of defense issues from the arena of majoritarian politics (where benefits and costs are widely distributed throughout society) to one of client politics (where the benefits are concentrated but the costs are widely distributed).[17]
Throughout the Cold War, as with wars in general, defense is more clearly understood as a benefit to society as a whole. In peacetime, the benefits of expenditure on defense are less clear for the public as a whole. Throughout American
history prior to World War II, this pattern was reflected in the rapid demobilization of armed forces, deep cuts in defense budgets and the general return of
resources and attention to peacetime applications in the immediate aftermath
of war.[18] Presidents Truman and Eisenhower were both concerned about the
level of defense spending as a drag on the economy in the years following
World War II. As the concern about unbalanced budgets subsided, and deficit
spending became routine, such concerns about the defense costs the economy
could sustain lessened considerably.

During the years since the end of the Cold War, few people appear to think of
the defense budget as a tradeoff to be measured against the general well being
of the economy. This may be a function of recent prosperity and, hence, there
has not been a need to examine government spending in detail. In the era of
budget surpluses, the importance of tradeoffs between budget categories was
less critical. The rising economic tide can float many boats. Therefore, logrolling
to share the gains seems to have precluded radical policy change. The competition for resources was not fierce because the resources were not scarce.

Inertia was reinforced by the relatively clear set of political losers that would
result from major changes in the military. Within the military, those well

versed in current methods of war might face difficulty having to learn new roles and responsibilities, or, worse yet, might be displaced all together. This was particularly true among senior military leaders who are also most likely to control decisions about changes. These changes apply to both the active and reserve military communities. Moreover, reserve communities, especially the National Guard, have tremendous influence on civilian political leaders. Within civilian communities, individuals potentially dispossessed by major change include those that produce goods and services for the armed forces (for example, defense industry, maintenance depots, base support activities, and so on). The material interests of these communities will likely translate into continued political pressure to retain the flow of national resources to existing beneficiaries. Examples of this at work include the decisions to keep open two submarine shipyards (in Connecticut and Virginia), President Clinton's intervention to save major depots in California and Texas during the 1995 round of base closings, and Congress' flat rejection of the 1997 Clinton/Cohen proposal for another BRAC round as part of the FY 1999 budget.[19] There was little political incentive for either the executive or the legislative civilian leaders to pursue major changes. There were great disincentives.

After September 2001, the public concern for national defense rose dramatically. The period of defense complacency appeared to be at an end. Although it remains to be seen what long-term effect the attacks will have, the initial public response about the importance of terrorism was greater than any other military action since the Vietnam War. In November 2001, a Gallup poll analysis noted that in the aftermath of the September 2001 attacks,

The importance of terrorism in the public's consciousness grew to parallel the importance given to the Korean War in 1951 and the Vietnam War in 1967. The economy—the top problem before September 11—significantly slipped into the background.[20]

This increased interest in national security and defense issues more generally is an important shift in the political landscape the effects of which remain to be seen.

Absence of Presidential Leadership

The first President Bush and President Clinton had little or no engagement on these issues. Other than monitoring by members of the National Security Council concerning hot-button political issues such as base closings, aggregate defense budget, both demonstrated little interest in the shape or specific capabilities of military forces. The second President Bush had little opportunity to demonstrate decisive engagement on these issues prior to September 2001. In general policy guidance, all three presidents advocated restructuring and reshaping of the military to meet the challenges of the post–Cold War era.[21] For the Base Force, President Bush was briefed on the details by Secretary of Defense Cheney and General Powell but did not request any major changes.[22] For Clinton, domestic political issues, such as health care and economic policy, were more important. The preliminary recommendations of the major reviews were briefed to him, but there is no evidence of any substantial engagement on his part leading to change in what was presented.[23] The second President Bush was waiting for the completion of the 2001 QDR before making any major defense policy decisions on these issues. However, the 11 September attacks intervened to set aside any major force structure decisions. Rhetorically, President Bush did remain strongly committed to defense transformation even as focus turned toward immediate efforts of the war on terrorism.

The lack of presidential leadership is important to the utility of a bureaucratic politics analysis. As a prominent critique of bureaucratic politics noted, "The bureaucratic paradigm will explain a great deal about foreign [and defense] policy formulation *if we assume that presidential preferences do not significantly constrain senior executive players in what they can do.*"[24] As the evidence in this study demonstrates, on major defense policy reviews concerning force structure and doctrine, the presidents, with a few narrow exceptions, have not shown much interest in the processes or the outcomes. As such, the political resultants of the bureaucracy do provide the dominant explanation for the policy outcomes. The dominant bureaucratic actor was the military. As the 'superpower' of bureaucratic actors, the president *does* have the ability to exercise tremendous influence on decision making.[25] The more salient point with respect to the president is whether he *chooses* to exercise that power with respect to a particular issue. Since the end of the Cold War, presidents have chosen not to intervene significantly on issues of force structure and doctrine.

As this study goes to publication, there are signs this may be changing. In mid-2002, Secretary Rumsfeld, with President Bush's support, signaled renewed effort to transform the armed forces—picking up to some degree where the administration left off just before the terrorist attacks of September 2001. Most dramatically, Secretary Rumsfeld terminated the Crusader howitzer system.[26] Many analysts had regarded Crusader as a legacy of Cold War thinking. The decision to cancel Crusader represented a significant step to operationalize efforts to move beyond Cold War-era systems and focus on next-generation, leap-ahead technology as the president had suggested. Similarly, the joint experimentation efforts of the Millennium Challenge 2002 exercise received a great deal of attention and support. Millennium Challenge was a key effort to move the president's military transformation interests from concept to reality.[27]

Diminishing Congressional Defense Interest and Expertise

The story that emerged from the various policy processes was one in which members of Congress, such as Senator Nunn and Representative Aspin, were prominent advocates for change and did much to institute the formal reviews of defense policy. As, the Cold War receded, however, the number of interested and knowledgeable members of Congress regarding defense issues dwindled.[28]

With the retirement of Senator Nunn, Senator Coats, and Representative Dellums, and the death of former House Armed Service Committee Chairman Aspin following his years as secretary of defense, the number of prominent members of Congress actively engaged on issues concerning military transformation diminished. In recent Congresses, members interested in the issues of future strategy and associated force structure were few. In the Senate, Joseph Lieberman (D-CT) and John McCain (R-AZ) were prominent advocates of continued emphasis on meeting the challenges of the future.

Among the remaining members of Congress, the dominant defense policy concerns were generally near-term and local issues that favor continuation on comfortable trajectories from the past. Support for industries producing the next in a series of weapons (submarines, fighters, destroyers, aircraft carriers, and so on) and for the bases serving the military were the main issues that engaged members of Congress. In other words, defense was of most concern to congressional efforts to direct dollars to members' districts. In many respects, this was unsurprising; as Barry Blechman noted, the incentives for parochial interests of congress members are strong.

The criteria applied in congressional decision-making are often inappropriate from a national perspective: the overriding criterion in congressional deliberations necessarily is to protect the interests of constituents. This often means that dollars allocated for defense are used inefficiently.[29]

Reinforcing the lack of attention from the public in general are the fewer personal ties to defense and the lower degree of personal experience with the national defense community among members of Congress. With fewer members who have served in uniform, there is less reliance of members of Congress upon their own judgment on such matters. Lower general public interest also reduced the incentives for political leaders to engage in political entrepreneurialism on defense issues as a means for improving electoral prospects. Similarly, there is decreasing interest in positions on defense related committees as the vehicles to advance the careers of ambitious elected officials. This leads fewer members to seek out positions on defense-related committees and subcommittees and to a greater tendency to move to other, more lucrative committee assignments. Hence, those members who do serve on committees dealing with defense issues are more likely to be junior members of Congress with less experience.

The events of September 2001 clearly elevated defense issues to an important concern for Congress as well as the American public. Whether this change is temporary or if it creates a sustained focus on long-term national-security issues remains to be seen.

Windows of Opportunity, Path Dependency, and Stagnation

John Kingdon noted it is often difficult to explain why a particular policy change takes place when it does. In attempting to explain how an agenda item becomes an agenda item, he notes that not only does there have to be a community and ideas associated with the policy but that the political stream of events must be favorable to action. The stream of political events creates windows of opportunity that policy entrepreneurs can use to institute plans and policies that significantly differ from the status quo.[30] Usually, such windows are caused by dramatic changes or catalytic events that suddenly thrust the topic to the top of the government agenda. It is often in the midst of transition or turmoil that the boldest options are available.

A window opens because of change in the political stream (e.g., a change of administration, a shift in the partisan or ideological distribution of seats in Congress, or a shift in national mood); or it opens because a new problem captures the attention of governmental officials and those close to them.[31]

Entrepreneurialism has its best hope in these periods of uncertainty when problems are thrust to the forefront of national attention. The end of the Cold War represented just such an opportunity. General Powell took advantage of the window of opportunity effectively and was also able to forestall, as he intended, potentially more radical plans. His plan emphasized the shift from global confrontation with the Soviet Union to the ability to undertake two major theater wars at the same time and the reduction of the armed forces without any substantial change to the basic force structure and doctrine. The initial window of opportunity for major change in defense policy, after the Cold War, appears to have closed at about the same time that the Base Force plan was adopted. Until September 2001, the absence of external shocks seemed to preclude any other windows of opportunity for major changes. Hence, subsequent attempts to review the general defense posture were limited by the course chosen by Powell for the Base Force.

With the collapse of the Soviet Union, the central justification for American armed forces was significantly altered. The new situation left the United States unchallenged by any major peer competitor and with none likely to arise anytime soon. The transition from the Cold War to the post–Cold War era was not, however, clear cut. As Saddam Hussein quickly demonstrated before the Soviet Union's dissolution, the absence of a global challenge did not mean that there were no dangers left to confront. As the world's sole superpower and with an array of global interests, the U.S. need for effective military capabilities remained. With a variety of potential challenges that might demand military force, it was difficult to identify any one clear path upon which to focus the development and training of military forces. However, there was a general consensus that the United States must be prepared to fight two major theater wars at the same time. The blurred ending of the Cold War, coupled with remaining evidence of other threats to important American interests, helps explain why the United States did not quickly demobilize after the Cold War, as it had often done after previous major wars.

There is little doubt that U.S.-Soviet relations had substantially thawed as Soviet President Gorbachev ended Soviet intervention in Afghanistan, unilaterally cut large portions of the Soviet conventional military, and abandoned the Brezhnev Doctrine that had justified Soviet intervention to preserve socialist governments. The end of the Brezhnev doctrine was most dramatically demonstrated by the opening of the Berlin Wall in November 1989. Nonetheless, the continued existence of the Soviet Union induced caution in many circles that the positive changes implemented by Gorbachev could be short-lived if reactionary elements could wrest control from him. Not until after the failure of the coup attempt of August 1991 were such concerns put to rest.

Before this final act of Soviet dissolution, the Persian Gulf War illustrated that the diminishing danger of the Cold War with the Soviet Union did not mean that the world was devoid of serious dangers to American security interests. This led to heightened emphasis on regional threats to U.S. interests. The combination of Soviet demise and Persian Gulf War led to a change of focus to regional or theater contingencies. The preparation for two major theater wars gained widespread acceptance in the policymaking community. The idea of the military being primarily sized to fight two major theater wars has been a constant in all five of the major reviews. Having used the two regional contingencies as an initial sizing tool in the Base Force process, it has become the accepted hook upon which each of the services can hang its arguments to continue to justify their relative portions of the defense budget and force structure. As the path chosen for military capabilities in the transition to the post–Cold War era, it has been a difficult path from which to depart.

For each review, the main participants were members of the Department of Defense itself. It is therefore unsurprising that the same group of participants, which included many of those who had been responsible for the creation of the Cold War force—especially in the military—would not be inclined to make dramatic alterations to a force in which they had vested interests. A common aspect of the process to review military capabilities is the fact that the main participants in each review were determined by the Department of Defense. Since the Base Force plan generated by the senior defense department leadership, each of the review processes included the participation of any military or civilian office that wished to be involved. Furthermore, the organizational structures of the defense-policy process are themselves largely a product of the Cold War.[32]

At the heart of this stagnation is the acceptance as almost canonical that the United States must be prepared to fight and win two nearly simultaneous major theater wars. With this premise at the center of all the reviews, service answers as to how to prepare properly for these contingencies has been similar.

In other words, the repetitive, almost routine nature of the process to weigh important defense issues is also limited by the continuing acceptance of the two-war premise as the central force-sizing tool. The shift in the 2001 QDR from two simultaneous theater wars to a more sequential win-hold-win standard provides a limited relaxation of the two-war force-sizing approach.

To summarize, there was a window of opportunity for defense change at the end of the Cold War. Defense leaders' choices during that opportunity, led by General Powell, established the policy path or trajectory for force structure and doctrine. This choice reflected a comfortable consensus among military leaders and is the path along which they continue to move.

The events of September 2001 represent a major national security shock and have undoubtedly opened a new window of opportunity concerning defense issues. The degree to which this window of opportunity can or will be used to address issues of long-term force structure and doctrinal change is as yet unclear. The outcomes of combat operations and the changing perceptions of national-security challenges will influence the manner in which the public and national leaders regard the imperatives for change or adaptation. As one commentator noted in late 2001,

During a 1999 visit to the Citadel, Bush delivered one of the defining promises of his presidential campaign: a pledge to radically transform the military into a leaner, more agile "Information Age" fighting force. But before the September 11 terrorist attacks, that effort had hit a wall, stalemated by opposition from the famed iron triangle of the Pentagon, the defense industry and Congress. Now, Bush and Defense Secretary Donald H. Rumsfeld are hoping the lightning progress in Afghanistan will help them shatter that resistance.... Bush argued that the success of new tactics and new weapons in the war against the Taliban should give the push for sweeping reform new momentum. But the military's very success in Afghanistan may allow traditionalists to argue that the massive change Bush seeks is not needed.[33]

Already, the policy agenda reflects the effects of homeland security. Although as yet undetermined, the force structure and doctrine of at least part of the U.S. armed forces will likely be forced to adapt to the new demands of the war on terrorism and national defense against terrorist attacks.

Number of Participants in the Policymaking Process

Another circumstance that helps explain the general outcome of the reviews is the number of principal actors involved in each effort. As many analysts have noted, the number of participants often effects the degree of change likely to result. The more participants there are, the less the process is likely to produce dramatic changes and the more likely such changes will reflect the lowest common denominator.[34]

The first major defense policy reformulation effort, the Base Force, was the work of a small group of decision makers that instituted the dramatic reduction of U.S. forces (25 percent). The Base Force plan was also explicit that reduction or draw down, not restructuring, was the primary objective. Most of the work on the Base Force took place only among the most senior military leaders (the Chairman of the Joint Chiefs of Staff and the chiefs of staff of the four services). Most deliberations and discussions took place in closed-door sessions among these senior leaders. Unlike the other four attempts to reformulate defense policy, the process was not publicized at all. The plan was unveiled to the public and Congress only after it was completed.

Conversely, the large number of actors and the diverse interests of the many groups that were involved in the last four policy reformulation efforts, unsurprisingly, yielded no more than incremental change.[35] In the other four policy reviews after the Base Force, the processes were widely known in advance and many individuals and agencies had the opportunity to participate in the decision-making process. The pulling and hauling of various powerful agencies in the course of many bureaucratic encounters helps explain the modest changes that emerged.

SUMMARY

At the center of this study was an attempt to describe and explain five important defense-policy efforts that sought to assess the challenges and opportunities of the U.S. armed forces in the post–Cold War era and suggest appropriate preparations for the future. The 1990 Base Force, the 1993 Bottom Up Review, the 1995 Commission on Roles and Missions, the 1997 Quadrennial Defense Review, and the 2001 Quadrennial Defense Review have been comprehensive efforts to address the manner in which U.S. military force should support U.S. national policy in the coming decades. They were comprehensive in the sense that each effort sought to assess the fundamental national security missions of the services, the appropriate mix of force structure and doctrine required by the military to fulfill these missions, and the appropriate levels of national resources required to support such forces. These five policy reviews form a coherent set of prescriptions that have occurred in rapid succession to one another, often involving the same prominent persons (albeit sometimes in different positions), with the same basic questions at the heart of consideration. In essence, each of the four main reviews sought to answer questions of how the United States armed forces should be organized and how they should prepare for the uncertain security environment of the post–Cold War era. Furthermore, military leaders have focused on the requirement to be able to fight two major theater wars near simultaneously as the element of the political guidance that provide the dominant characteristic for force sizing. Given the degree of effort and attention these reviews have engendered, it is remarkable that little aside from the size of the military has changed.

For all the sound and fury of the debate, the lack of change does, however, signify something. The debates concerning defense policy have sometimes proposed radical ways of changing the military for the future. The fact that little *has* changed does not reflect a lack of effort or lack of alternatives but rather the success of military leaders' strong defense against a series of diffuse and poorly coordinated efforts to change the armed forces. In the absence of strong effort to the contrary, particularly by the president, comfortable bureaucratic patterns of logrolling and inertia are likely to persist.

Among the main actors, clearly the most decisively engaged in the process have been military leaders. Given the implications for their organizational future, this is understandable and unsurprising. The U.S. Congress has been a source of pressure on the military to change. In each of the five reviews, key congressional leaders played a major role in prodding the Department of Defense to examine its policies. For all of the reviews other than the Base Force, Congress was the origin of the requirement.[36] On the substance of the issues, however, Congress developed no significant voting blocks around particular alternatives for change. In contrast, voting blocks have developed to support the status quo, such as the efforts of members of Congress to defend remaining defense depots from closure and loss of business.[37] In recent years, the strongest block on defense issues appears to have been congressional Republicans concerned about the readiness of the active force to perform current missions. The emphasis of this group is upon greater defense spending. In none of the reviews has the president himself been a major player.

The military has a strong justification for its current role. Among the services, there appears to be a general consensus about the present force structure and about the appropriate budget for each service. As the record shows, the American military leaders have been in charge of their organizational destiny and have generally controlled the outcomes of the policy reviews. The military services have been successful in holding the line against efforts to change the force structure and doctrine. These capabilities will therefore define what will be provided to decision makers when the armed forces are called upon to act.

While acknowledging the possibility of radically different futures, the military has so far pushed any major changes down the road to as yet unidentified future transitions while at the same time continuing to procure weapons, conduct training, and perpetuate doctrine that deviates little from patterns ingrained during the Cold War. The lack of interest in issues of force structure and doctrine was evident for the public, many members of Congress, and the president. Furthermore, deference to the judgment of military leaders representing an honored and popular institution is the dominant theme of those issues that have been considered by civilian leaders. A process for the analysis, selection, and, if necessary, innovation of capabilities crucial to the state as a whole should be a product of both civilian and military leaders. The record, however, presents a one-sided story of military leaders' success in securing their preferred force structure and doctrine.

NOTES

1. Warner Schilling, "The Politics of National Defense: Fiscal 1950." In *Strategy, Politics and Defense Budgets,* Warner R. Schilling, Paul Y. Hammond and Glenn H. Snyder, eds. (New York: Columbia University Press, 1962), 26.

2. The veneer of strength hiding the hollowness—lack of strength—for those units to perform their assigned missions effectively.

3. For an account of what happened to Task Force Smith, see Roy K. Flint, "Task Force Smith and the 24th Division: Delay and Withdrawal, 5–19 July 1950," in Charles E. Heller and William A Stofft, eds., *America's First Battles: 1776–1965* (Lawrence, KS: University of Kansas Press, 1986).

4. See David McCormick, *The Downsized Warrior: America's Army in Transition* (New York: New York University Press, 1998), 11–12.

5. See Gallup/CNN/USA Today Poll, "Confidence/Trust in Institutions," 25–27 June 1999. Available from http://www.pollingreport.com/institut.htm; Internet; accessed 24 January 2000. The military was listed as the most respected institution in an opinion poll.

6. William Grieder, *Fortress America: The American Military and the Consequences of Peace* (New York: PublicAffairs, 1998), vii–xix.

7. Interview with senior DoD civilian official.

8. Christopher Gibson and Don Snider, "Civil-Military Relations and the Ability to Influence: A Look at the National Security Decision Making Process" *Armed Forces and Society* 5, no. 2 (Winter 1999): 193–218.

9. The public has consistently rated the military as the government institution in which they have the most confidence. For evidence, see Frank Newport, "Small Business and Military Generate Most Confidence in Americans," Gallup Poll Releases, 15 August 1997, available from available from http://www.gallup.com/poll/ releases/pr970815.asp; Internet; accessed 11 April 99. See table, "Confidence in Institutions—Trend, 1973–1997."

10. McCormick, *The Downsized Warrior*, 111–112.

11. Gibson and Snider, 193–218.

12. Frank Newport, "No Single Problem Dominates Americans' Concerns Today," Gallup Poll, May 2, 1998, available from http://www.gallup.com/poll_archives/980502.htm; Internet; accessed 14 January 1999.

13. Gallup Poll, April 17–19, 1998, "What do you think is the most important problem facing this country today?," available from http://www.gallup.com/poll_archives/980502.htm; Internet; accessed 14 January 1999.

14. Senator John McCain, quoted in Greider, *Fortress America*, 139–140.

15. Schilling provides a brilliant analysis of seeming irrationality in policymaking with respect to the FY50 defense budget in "The Politics of National Defense: Fiscal 1950," 1–266.

16. Among many examples of this, see David Rogers, "Congress Approves Defense Bill Laden with Add-Ons for Firms in GOP States," *Wall Street Journal*, 26 September 1997, 1–2, and John Donnelly, "Top Contractors Won't Compete Against Depots," *Defense Week*, 29 September 1997, 1.

17. James Q. Wilson and John J. DiIulio Jr., *American Government*, 6th ed. (Lexington, MA: D.C. Heath and Company, 1995), 458–59.

18. Huntington, *The Soldier and the State: The Theory and Politics of Civil-Military Relations* (Cambridge: Harvard University Press, 1957), 156.

19. Rick Maze, "Congress Nixes Another Round of Base Closings." *Army Times*, 7 June 1999, 29.

20. Mark Gillespie, "Terrorism Reaches Status of Korean and Vietnam Wars as Most Important Problem, Economy Ranks a Distant Second," Gallup News Service, November 19, 2001, available from http://www.gallup.com/ poll/Releases/Pr011119.asp; Internet; accessed 5 January 2002.

21. George Bush, NSS 1991, 33 and Clinton speech before the Los Angeles World Affairs Council, 13 August 1992.

22. Interview with senior DoD civilian official.

23. Interview with NSC staff member.

24. Robert J. Art, "A Critique of Bureaucratic Politics," *Policy Sciences* 4 (December 1973): 467–90. [emphasis added]

25. Allison and Zelikow, *Essence of Decision*, 162. Allison's characterization of the president's special position is in his review of Richard Neustadt's work, *Presidential Power* (New York: Free Press, 1960).

26. Thom Shanker, "President Formally Seeks a Halt to Crusader Artillery System," *New York Times*, May 30, 2002.

27. Jim Garamone, "Rumsfeld Visits Millennium Challenge Experiment," American Forces Information Service, 29 July 2002, available from http://www.defenselink.mil/news/Jul2002/n07292002_200207295.html, Internet, accessed 14 August 2002.

28. William T. Bianco and Jamie Markham, "Vanishing Veterans: The Decline of Military Experience in the U.S. Congress, in *Soldiers and Civilians: The Civil-Military Gap and American National Security*, ed. Peter D. Feaver and Richard H. Kohn (Cambridge, MA: MIT Press, 2001), 275.

29. Barry Blechman, *The Politics of National Security: Congress and U.S. Defense Policy* (New York: Oxford University Press, 1990), 55.

30. See John W. Kingdon, "The Policy Window and Joining the Streams," chapter 8 in *Agendas, Alternatives, and Public Policies* (New York: HarperCollins College Publishers, 1995), 165–195.

31. Ibid, 168.

32. Donald M. Snow and Eugene Brown, *Puzzle Palaces and Foggy Bottom: U.S. Foreign and Defense Policy Making in the 1990s* (New York: St. Martin's Press, 1994), 2.

33. Ronald Brownstein, "Success in Afghanistan Clouds Military Transformation Plan," *Los Angeles Times*, 12 December 2001.

34. For a prominent example of these studies, see Mancur Olson, *Logic of Collective Action* (Cambridge, MA: Harvard University Press, 1971).

35. Kingdon, *Agendas, Alternatives, and Public Policies*, 79–83.

36. The origins of the Base Force were Powell's ideas about getting in front of political pressure for change in the waning days of the Cold War. I attribute the Bottom Up Review's origins to Les Aspin's efforts in the House Armed Services Committee, which

he imported with him to the Clinton Administration as secretary of defense. The Commission on Roles and Missions and the Quadrennial Defense Review were required by congressional legislation. With respect to the Base Force, the major congressional input came predominantly from the efforts of Senator Sam Nunn as he pressed the Department of Defense to respond to the decreased Soviet threat in 1990.

37. Sheila Foote, "House Panel Approves Restrictions on Depot Privatization," *Defense Daily*, 6 June 1997, 408, and "Authorization Remains Held Up in Conference by Dispute Over Depots," *Inside the Air Force*, 3 October 1997.

Chapter 10

Evaluation and Recommendations

> What transpires on prospective battlefields is influenced vitally years before in the councils of the staff and in the legislative halls of Congress. Time is the only thing that may be irrevocably lost, and it is the first thing lost sight of in the seductive false security of peaceful times.[1]
> —General Malin Craig, U.S. Army Chief of Staff, 1939

OVERVIEW

The preceding chapters have described a process characterized by inertia. With the military dominant in defining the nature of the changes in military capabilities since the end of the Cold War, this inertia may be unsurprising. Whether this is good or bad, however, is a matter of opinion. I argue that this inertia has two negative effects. First, it inhibits the military's efforts to prepare effectively for future war-fighting challenges associated with the revolution in military affairs. Second, it compromises the military's ability to execute efficiently the peace-operations missions that have been more prominent in the post–Cold War era. The continuity of Cold War patterns casts a lengthening shadow over the future and may have a negative effect on the United States' ability to pursue its goals and protect its interests. At a time when the United States is widely acknowledged to have a sizable advantage in military power over potential rivals and in a period of general uncertainty about long run threats, choosing continuity over innovation and restructuring is an inappropriate policy choice.

There are also some minor adjustments that need to take place to ensure appropriate measures for homeland defense. Homeland defense does not, however, require any significant restructuring of the U.S. armed forces. The National Guard, Coast Guard, and the civilian law enforcement agencies provide the foundations for an effective homeland defense with their current capabilities. Existing regular military forces provide valuable depth for homeland defense. Primary adjustments for homeland defense will be the identification of units to assist in crisis situations and the adjustment of mobilization and deployment plans to reflect the commitments of specific reserve or National Guard units to primary duties in support of homeland defense.

There is a general presumption in military affairs that stagnation or inertia is bad in that it allows opponents to counter strengths and identify asymmetric means to exploit weaknesses. The United States has attained an unmatched mastery of conventional war. This pushes potential challengers to asymmetric responses at both the high and low end of the conflict spectrum[2] and reduces the chance that the United States will become engaged in large-scale conventional war of the style demonstrated during the Persian Gulf War.[3] Much like a business competing in the market place, a military force's future success is not guaranteed by past successes. Successful military organizations, like successful companies, must constantly innovate and improve to remain successful. The terrorist attacks of 11 September 2001 and others that preceded it illustrate one example of an asymmetrical threat.

Additionally, it seems folly to hone military skills for war and wait for international circumstances to require the use of these war-fighting skills—a pound of cure—if an ounce of prevention provided by other uses of armed forces could forestall war. From this perspective, the training and employment of armed forces in peace operations is a valuable adjunct to preparing forces for war.

Preparing for the Next War: Anticipating the Revolution in Military Affairs (RMA)

Only one thing is certain: the greatest danger lies in unwillingness or an inability to change our security posture in time to meet the challenges of the next century. The United States needs to launch a transformation strategy now that will enable it to meet a range of security challenges in 2010–2020.[4]

—National Defense Panel, 1997

The United States must have forces well suited for fighting wars. It is naive and reckless to assume that peace operations will be sufficient to prevent future wars. However, current war-fighting capabilities make American armed forces well suited for the last war, but not necessarily the next. The revolution in military affairs generated by advances in computer technology requires fundamental rethinking of the military capabilities for future warfare. So far, there has been much talk about the revolution in military affairs and a general acknowledgement of its wide-ranging impact. Intellectually, the groundwork for reorienting and reshaping the armed forces to adjust is extensive. In application, however, there have been few changes to force structure and doctrine.

In the aftermath of the Cold War, the nature of the threats to U.S. interests has changed. There is no one, peer, state competitor against which armed forces can be optimized. There are several potential adversaries with a menu of options from which to choose. This requires that the United States vigorously pursue research and intelligence to discern the range of possible threats and to identify the array of capabilities required to counter them.

The nature of modern military capabilities and the time involved in their development makes it risky to wait until threats are clearly identified before creating the forces to address them. Hence, national leaders must decide well in advance what forces are needed to meet national objectives. In the absence of a central threat upon which to focus, such war-fighting capabilities must address a range of alternative threats and hedge against them.

States have paid a high price for failure to prepare properly in peace for the threats they will likely encounter in war. France in 1940 is a prominent case where the failure to integrate military doctrine with policy priorities contributed to catastrophic defeat. According to Barry Posen, an element of Germany's success and of Great Britain's ability to avoid France's fate was the successful integration of civilian policy and military capabilities.[5] Posen's explanation is that civilian leaders are more likely to consider the broader national goals for which military capabilities are but one instrument. As such, it is important for civilian leaders to remain aware and engaged concerning the identification of appropriate tasks for the military and the creation of the capabilities to accomplish these tasks.

Preventing the Next War: Supporting Effective Peace Operations

U.S. defense strategy seeks to defend freedom for the United States and its allies and friends, and it helps to secure an international environment of peace that makes other goals possible.[6]

—2001 QDR

Peace operations support key national security objectives and highlight the need for a reexamination of appropriate force structure and doctrine. Since the end of the Cold War, peace operations have dominated the activities of the U.S. military and reinforce the need to look beyond the patterns of the Cold War era military capabilities. Ongoing operations in Kosovo and Bosnia make it clear that peace operations will remain important military operations for the foreseeable future. The nascent peace operations taking shape on behalf of the long-term stability of Afghanistan following combat operations against the Taliban and Al Qaeda further demonstrate the importance of such missions. Speculations about a new war with Iraq deliberately seeking regime change imply a substantial commitment of armed forces to postconflict peace operations. These are missions that are not well suited to the normal routines and structure of a Cold War force designed to counter the Soviet Union.

American national-security strategy notes the importance of peace operations as a critical military contribution to shaping the international security environment to the long-term benefit of the United States.[7] The United State's willingness to participate in peace operations has been critical if not indispensable to several missions. Examples of this include the missions in Somalia, Haiti, Bosnia, and Kosovo. Although some policy analysts have argued that the

United States has a comparative advantage in war-fighting forces and that there are many allies and other countries that have forces already well suited to peace operations, the United States has a stated interest in supporting such missions and should be ready to set the example if not take the lead to provide armed forces to support effective peace operations.

Since the end of the Cold War, the preferred method for American participation in peace operations has been to deploy a segment of the armed forces that is therefore temporarily diverted from its established combat mission. American forces dispatched to such missions generally receive peace operations training before they deploy. Such training is regarded as a distraction from primary, war-fighting missions, and upon return from the mission, the forces involved need to be retrained for their war-fighting tasks.[8] Although the general performance of such forces has been good, the approach has been ad hoc and temporary. Additionally, because of the differing demands of peace operations, there is a premium on specific types of units and personnel (military police, construction engineers, military intelligence, electronic early warning units, civil affairs, and a variety of other service support specialties). Therefore, even though the operations to date have been executed successfully by the U.S. armed forces, the efficiency and effectiveness of such forces is problematic. It creates tremendous transaction costs in the shift from one type of mission to another.

Fighting the Current War: Homeland Defense and the Global War on Terrorism

The highest priority of the U.S. military is to defend the nation from all enemies. The United States will maintain sufficient military forces to protect the U.S. domestic population, its territory, and its critical defense-related infrastructure against attacks emanating from outside U.S. borders.... In addition, DoD components have the responsibility, as specified in U.S. law, to support U.S. civil authorities as directed in managing the consequences of natural and man-made disasters and CBRNE-related events on U.S. territory.[9]

—2001 QDR

A key theme of this study is the identification and preparation in peacetime to anticipate potential requirements for the future. Clearly, the events of 11 September 2001 and the subsequent war on global terrorism required response with the forces readily available. Adjustment of existing forces to meet identified needs defined the immediate response.

The United States has a robust domestic law-enforcement structure. It also has well-established mechanisms for augmenting domestic agencies with support from the military units in times of crisis or disaster. With regard to armed forces, the United States National Guard provides state governors an immediate resource to assist in critical homeland-defense tasks. As has been demonstrated numerous times, the active-duty armed forces also have been valuable as a source of manpower and logistics to meet overwhelming demands in times of disaster. The events of 11 September 2001 and the identified vulnerabilities of the United States to attack have commanded a sharp focus on defensive and preventive measure across the spectrum of governing institutions—from local to national level. All levels of society and government have had to assess security measures and consider adjustments. In general, the means to shore up homeland defense are present but are in need of better integration and organization. The Bush administration's effort to create the Department of Homeland Security is a promising attempt to achieve better integration.

The initial stages of the global war against terrorism included military operations in Afghanistan to defeat the Al Qaeda terrorist network and depose the Taliban government that supported Al Qaeda. As of publication, Afghanistan has been the only location of active combat involving U.S. armed forces. However, U.S. special forces were also dispatched to assist host governments with anti-terrorist actions in the Philippines, the former Soviet republic of Georgia and Yemen.

The military operations in Afghanistan illustrated fundamental strengths of the U.S. armed forces and are a substantial validation of the hope that the United States will successfully adapt and succeed in future armed conflicts. Special operation forces on the ground worked closely with local Afghan armed forces and American air power to achieve rapid success against Al Qaeda and Taliban forces. Special forces on horseback directed attacks from B-52 bombers, which are older than the horses and most of the riders, to devastating effect. Use of UAVs (unmanned aerial vehicles) and high-tech surveillance provided extensive battlefield awareness to support well-targeted attacks that limited collateral damage and danger to friendly forces. Moreover, these operations were undertaken with but a small fraction of American military and illustrated that existing military means are exceptionally capable. These operations also showed the tremendous intelligence, skill, and adaptability of military personnel.

Operations in Afghanistan also display a strong suit of U.S. military capabilities. U.S. forces are very good at conventional combat operations against identifiable concentrations of armed opposition (in this case, the Taliban and Al Qaeda military formations). To the degree that concentrations of armed opponents can be identified and attacked—whether associated with states (for example, Iraq) or harbored within states (for example, Al Qaeda in Afghanistan)—U.S. military capabilities are likely to enjoy continued success in the global war on terrorism. More problematic are the contributions that the armed forces can make to build and sustain long-term security in areas, such as Afghanistan, that suffer from years of societal deterioration and comprehensive failure of basic services mechanisms and governing institutions.

WHAT NEXT? POLICY RECOMMENDATIONS

The logic governing post–Cold War force structure is different from that which applied in the Cold War. . . . Paradox, asymmetry and uncertainty all argue for a flexible military force, not an optimized one. Utility with respect to the full spectrum of national security objectives should be the governing principle in determining the structure of U.S. armed forces.[10]

The governing logic of the Cold War defines the force structure and doctrine of U.S. armed forces. They are still useful and valuable for meeting familiar conventional military threats. With some significant inefficiencies and institutional resistance, the U.S. armed forces have also proven capable and generally successful in meeting the varied requirements for peace operations since the end of the Cold War. But the challenges of peace operations and the dangers of future warfare are increasingly diverging from existing American military capabilities.

This study presented historical evidence of how military and civilian leaders chose to reformulate American defense policy and how these efforts led to the current force structure and doctrine of American armed forces. Given the changes in the international environment and the identified policy objectives, understanding innovation in the past provides a useful way to evaluate the potential impact of peacetime decisions and their subsequent influence in times of crisis or war.

In Stephen Rosen's detailed study of military innovation in the past, *Winning the Next War,* he finds that although the impetus for military innovation is greatest in times of crisis or war, successful innovation is usually attained in peace, or at least started and well along before war breaks out. The main reason for this is that successfully implementing innovation in military organizations requires time—usually measured in years or decades. This time is needed to build promotion pathways for new personnel specialties and to build the organizational sub elements within the armed forces that can make innovations take hold.[11] Innovation is difficult to achieve without the combined efforts of military and civilian leaders to try to anticipate future demands. In times of crisis, existing military capabilities will define the options available to policymakers.

Williamson Murray and Allan Millett, in *Military Innovation in the Interwar Period,* draw on Rosen and extend the analysis of innovation to address the years between World Wars I and II to understand the nature of innovation in peacetime among the major belligerents of World War II.[12] The studies in their book draw out several points about the success or failure of national armed forces in World War II. Although the armed forces are the critical element in adopting new weapons, organizational structures, doctrine, and training, the importance of civilian leaders in establishing the strategic context for the military is crucial in focusing the national military forces on likely future adversaries, regions, and missions. In short, successful and unsuccessful innovations in the interwar period are a function of civilian and military leaders' actions or omissions.

With regard to traditional security threats, the present period does not have much in common with the Cold War period or the interwar period between World Wars I and II when the presence of antagonistic great powers provided ample incentive for innovation in military affairs. Today there are still threats to American interests, but none, thankfully, similar to the contentious great power competition of the interwar period. This situation will continue to frame the challenge of instituting fundamental change in the war-fighting capabilities of the military and, hence, the realization of the revolution in military affairs.

Ultimately, as a global power whose long-term well-being is closely bound with the international community, the United States needs to prepare effectively for both sets of demands. Although some evidence suggests that innovation for the future is a concern for both military and civilian defense-policy leaders, little has been done to transform Cold War military forces to meet future requirements.

Given the dominance of the military leadership in shaping the forces and doctrine of the future, generational change in military leaders and their supporting organizations are a potential source of innovation. In a peacetime environment where defense issues are of low salience to elected leaders, it is this source that is more likely to institute substantial change. The Goldwater-Nichols Act of 1986 altered the military organizational structure so that now there is the possibility that the JCS Chairman and his staff could be the catalyst for major change within the service cultures and inculcate the values of innovation and strategic thinking. In the past, advocacy and support by senior military leaders has been a successful path for innovation within military services.

The other potential source for major changes in military force structure and doctrine is strong civilian leadership. Most importantly from the president directly. Civilian leaders interested in transforming military capabilities must be willing to overcome the comfortable routines and alliances of several bureaucratic actors. Leaders also need the political support to withstand certain opposition from a well-entrenched and politically savvy bureaucracy. The greatest difficulty will be the unity of congressional and executive leaders to override opposition to more radical changes than have currently been undertaken. The war against global terrorism increases the likelihood that such defense issues will be a matter of concern to the broader public. This can strengthen the position of reformers who seek to challenge vested defense interests.

The actions and preferences of the military in pursuing established methods of operation display considerable logic, which is strongly supported by the logic of bureaucratic and organizational politics. In past military disasters, one of the most damning failures was the unwillingness, failure, or general lack of attention civilian leaders have exhibited to make sure that military leaders and the organizations they direct adopted the appropriate means to implement established national strategy.

Beyond selecting senior commanders ... the civilian heads of a military establishment must query their generals and not merely on broad problems of strategy but about the operational plans and concepts used to meet those problems and the fitness of the organizations at their disposal to implement those plans and concepts ... In peacetime, this cross-examination may take a different form, and concern, in particular the nature of the command systems—including the promotion and educational systems, as well as the shape of the organization charts—which govern the armed forces. The task is a delicate one, for ill-informed civilian intervention can do enormous damage, and efforts to dictate will backfire or be subverted by a recalcitrant bureaucracy. The great statesmen who have been most successful in reforming military organizations ... worked with senior officers to overhaul command systems shown to be unsuited for the tasks before them.[13]

The current era of uncertainty demands the attention of civilian leaders to the military capabilities that will condition the ability of the U.S. government to influence world affairs. Given the differing challenges of the present international environment and the uncertain challenges of the future, stagnation of military capabilities must be a broad political concern. The global war against terrorism further underscores the value of such attention.

The difficulties to be overcome are substantial. Continuing on, the present course is reinforced by high transaction costs in training, budget, and personnel dislocations inherent in any major change. The changes in force structure and doctrine required to fully respond to the implications of the revolution in military affairs and the differing demands of peace operations are potentially extensive. Such changes would require new specialties for personnel and significantly different organizational structures. These will be difficult changes to institute among leaders and followers who are well-versed in and comfortable with current systems. The stakes involved are critical to the long-range interests of the United States and therefore warrant the high costs likely to be involved. Fortunately, the consensus for increased defense spending prompted by the war against terrorism have temporarily reduced the need for immediate funding trade offs between this differing demands. In the short term, it should be possible to fund existing programs as well as to fund new programs. Eventually, however, resource competition will require choices among competing alternatives.

In addition to the broad principles suggested above, the following six recommendations would help better align American military capabilities with the challenges and opportunities of the post–Cold War era. The recommended changes include matters of substantive force restructuring and training, the defense policymaking process, and overall defense-policy leadership:

1. Restructure forces for RMA experimentation and adaptation

2. Restructure forces for peace operations

3. Adjust forces for homeland defense

4. Improve training and education of future military leaders

5. Reform the defense-review process

6. Increase civilian leadership

Restructure Forces for RMA Experimentation and Adaptation

As Secretary of Defense Rumsfeld pointed out,

Preparing for the 21st century will not require immediately transforming the entire U.S. military—just a portion. The Blitzkrieg was an enormous success, but it was accomplished by only a 13% transformed German army. And in some instances, transformation may not require new capabilities at all, but rather new ways of arranging, connecting, and using existing capabilities.[14]

This is a reasonable and workable objective that does not require a complete overhaul of existing forces. Transformation is possible while sustaining capabilities necessary to meet immediate or short-term security demands. Even using the existing forces structure, a modest portion devoted to experimentation and change imposes only modest risk on the remaining force that must handle immediate challenges.

To better prepare for the future, I propose the creation of a joint force that is shielded from short-term readiness requirements. This transformation force and its commander would focus on the challenges of the future with minimal concern for the immediate and short-term requirements that drive the operations of the present day CINCs. This is similar to the 1997 NDP's suggestion for a Joint Forces Command to take responsibility for the experimentation and training of forces that can work to understand the challenges of joint operations in light of the rapid advancements of technology and the changing emphasis of national security policy.[15] The intent would be to provide a commander with the forces and resources to train, experiment, and exercise new concepts and technologies. The command could draw on prototyping and innovative exercises to test operational concepts before large-scale production or wholesale force reorganization that could "leap into the future."

The Department of Defense is thus at a crossroads. On the one hand, it can incorporate the information revolution into its existing structures and doctrine, replicating present platforms in ever more sophisticated forms and creating a force designed to master today's challenges, notably the deterrence and suppression of major regional conflicts. On the other hand, the Defense Department may recognize that opponents in the mid-1990s pale in comparison with their potential successors and that some time beyond the next decade, more sophisticated competitors will present far greater challenges. A strategy to prepare for the latter eventuality would emphasize technology, education, and doctrine rather than replicating today's platforms, albeit in more capable versions.[16]

Joint experimentation is assigned to Joint Forces Command (JFCOM).[17] In October 2002, changes to the unified command plan for the combatant commands removed Joint Forces Command's regional responsibilities (which were assigned to Northern Command) and made it a functional command with responsibility for joint experimentation and for providing forces to other combatant commanders.[18] This is a major improvement, which gives the joint forces command the ability to focus on experimentation in support of transformation efforts. The command also has a mandate to use service forces to assist with joint experimentation efforts. The individual services retain the primary responsibility to train and equip their forces. This is a very positive development that substantially improves upon the previous arrangement, where JFCOM had a regional defense responsibility as well as the charter to lead joint experimentation and transformation. Nevertheless, as a major force provider to the regional combatant commanders, the JFCOM commander still must ensure that the forces in his command sustain considerable and important efforts to meet immediate or near-term military requirements. This detracts from the long-range focus on transformation.

The frame of reference of the current combatant commanders is on near-term readiness for specific tasks (geographic and functional). Joint forces command as reconfigured now has the lead role in the transformation effort. Nonetheless, JFCOM is still reliant on the services to provide the forces for experimentation and transformation efforts. Instead, I propose that a new combatant commander be separated completely from the near-term force provision requirements. Alternatively, this outcome could be achieved with a subunified command within JFCOM. This new unified command would be a separate, functional command focused on the future. It would be composed of assigned forces for experimentation from each service and the agencies focused on long-term transformation. It would not be responsible for providing and sustaining capabilities for other combatant commanders. This would more decisively divorce the command from short-term demands.

The mission of future preparations is big enough and valuable enough to warrant a separate combatant command. This force would focus on validating joint concepts through experimentation. The command would include apportioned forces from each of the services. The forces assigned to the command would not be readily available for operational deployments. The focus of the forces assigned to the command would be testing and evaluation of new equipment and concepts in regular war games and simulations. The command would be the natural test bed for prototype equipment before decisions on large-run production. The command should also include an opposing force of actual units and simulations designed to challenge experimentation exercises with anticipated as well as creative concepts of threats our forces might confront in the future.

To strengthen the command even further, it should be granted budget authority similar to SOCOM (meaning, a budget beyond the direct control of the military services). With this budget authority, the command would have greater latitude to reinforce promising developments to support transformation and experimentation.

Restructure Forces for Peace Operations

The United States can improve effectiveness in preventing war by creating forces better structured and trained for peace operations. Military forces have a demonstrably powerful role to play in helping to preserve a positive international environment. The United States has so far chosen to execute peace operations with capabilities designed for other roles. The United States should focus on peace operations as first-order missions and adopt new doctrine and force structure to more efficiently and effectively prepare for these missions.

Peace operations are important national security missions that require well prepared forces. Currently, American military leaders prefer to execute peace operations with units temporarily diverted from war-fighting preparation. Peace operations tasks are simply lesser-included missions of the armed forces in general. Regarding peace operations as lesser-included missions means that there are high transaction costs to prepare for such missions. Forces designed more closely to meet the demands of peace operations would help to alleviate the pressure on currently overused parts of the force. The result would be an increase in effectiveness of the forces conducting peace operations as well as maintaining a more reasonable war-fighting training pace for other forces. As one of the panel members of the NDP noted,

DOD needs to resolve the competition between MRC and peace operation requirement. As seen by the recent events in places like Somalia and Bosnia, so-called peace operation require significantly different kinds of strategy, doctrine, force structure, equipment, and training than do the major regional contingencies.[19]

These are missions that support critical global objectives. To meet the demands of these operations, the military should designate forces to prepare specifically for peace operations as their primary mission. These forces should be trained separately from conventional war-fighting units, thus ending discussions over diversion of traditional forces from war-fighting readiness. This does not rule out the possibility that these forces might be used in traditional war-fighting situations. These forces should also be trained in basic war-fighting tasks—but as a lesser-included mission. The benefits of this force include the elimination of significant training diversions for the forces that remain oriented to traditional war-fighting missions. Currently, the armed forces spend considerable time, money, and effort training forces for peace operations only to have to re-train the same forces for war-fighting roles after their commitment to peace operations is complete.[20] Being able to draw on forces specifically trained for peace operations would have the benefit of ending the current 'three-for-one' effect where for each unit engaged in a peace operation deployment, there is an additional unit training for the mission and another unit that is training to reestablish its proficiency in combat skills after the deployment.[21]

The fundamental differences between peace operations and war are substantial.

[Peace operations] are as different from "real" war as are special operations, for which the United States retains dedicated forces under a separate command. . . . The starting point of rules of engagement for such operations is the imperative of utmost restraint and discrimination in applying force. Firepower is an instrument of last rather than first resort. There is no big enemy to close with and destroy, but rather the presence of threatened civilian populations that must be protected in a way that minimizes collateral damage. Conventional ground-force preparation for peace operations accordingly requires major doctrinal and training deprogramming of conventional military habits and reprogramming with the alien tactics, doctrines, and heavy political oversight of peace operations.[22]

A letter from a lieutenant assigned to the NATO force in Kosovo further illustrates this point.

Right now [March 2000] you have KFOR enforcing the peace. This means you have soldiers—who are trained to aggressively seek the initiative in high-intensity conflict—negotiating, compromising, and providing humanitarian relief; all of which require a different type of patience and perspective than we have worked so hard to develop up to now. None of this means we can't do the job, it just means we are doing a job for which we aren't trained.[23]

Forces better structured and trained for peace operations can avoid the heavy transaction costs of training and retraining the same force to perform conflicting roles.

One way to do this would be to create or reorient five brigades to emphasize preparation for peace operations. One brigade could be assigned or apportioned to each of the major regional combatant commands.[24] These brigades would be heavy on military police, civil affairs, and other specialties that are in high demand for peace operations. Training for the force should include emphasis on cultural sensitivity and understanding of the region to which they're assigned.

To reinforce the separation from the primary war-fighting forces, for oversight and training these peace operation brigades should be assigned to Special Operations Command. Special Operations Command already includes civil affairs and psychological operations units that are often employed in peace operations. Furthermore, alignment with Special Operations Command would allow for better integration of personnel with regional and cultural expertise. These forces would specialize in peace operations and would be well-suited to serve American interests to provide basic security and assist in the arduous tasks of stabilizing areas of conflict. Within particular missions, such forces are the logical follow on to combat forces that have successfully fought and created the conditions for peace. Examples of situations for which the force would be appropriate include long-term peace and stability missions in Bosnia, Haiti, and Kosovo. In Bosnia, Haiti, and Kosovo, dedicated peace operations forces would have been deployed after the initial entrance of combat forces to end or deter conflict. Using Bosnia as an example, peace-operations forces would have been the U.S. component of the follow-on stabilization force (SFOR) that replaced the initial implementation force (IFOR).[25] In the global war against terrorism, such a force would be a logical and useful follow on to support peace operations in Afghanistan. One of these brigades, in conjunction with armed forces of allies and with other instruments of national power, would be a superb asset in creating the long-term conditions for peace and stability. Such forces could also work side by side with traditional war-fighting forces in situations where the likelihood for combat is still strong. Combat units could provide the complementary quick reaction forces with the ability to provide escalation dominance if fighting flares up.

Portions of the National Guard should also be reoriented from traditional war-fighting missions to preparation for peace operations. Five maneuver brigades should be similarly reoriented towards peace operations and aligned with one of the counterpart brigades in the active force. This would provide valuable depth to the forces available to support peace operations. These National Guard brigades could also provide useful depth in support of homeland defense.

Adjust Forces for Homeland Defense

As noted early in this chapter, there is no need for substantially restructuring the armed forces for homeland defense. The units and capabilities to augment civil authorities in support of homeland defense are well established. Minor adjustments to existing mechanisms will be adequate to strengthen American capacity to respond to threats from within the United States. The National Guard represents the armed forces' most important contribution to increase the depth of American domestic defenses. The active military forces can provide further depth in times of exceptional crisis or disaster. The focus of the armed forces should appropriately remain on the defense of the country from external attacks. The armed forces greatest contribution to defense of the homeland is the security provided by addressing the sources of external threats to U.S. security.

Organizationally, the establishment of the Department of Homeland Security is an appropriate mechanism to orchestrate broader readjustment. Similarly, the creation of the new Northern command (NORTHCOM) for homeland defense will better focus military efforts. This builds on previous organizational adjustments, such as the creation of Joint Task Force Civil Support, which was designed to assist lead domestic agencies in consequence management following the use of a weapon of mass destruction.[26]

Adjustments to the armed forces to support homeland defense should center on the National Guard. In particular, some National Guard units may be exclusively designated for homeland defense missions. The most important issue with regard to restructuring the armed forces is the degree to which units retained solely for use in homeland-security missions would effect mobilization and deployment plans for overseas contingencies. Additionally, National Guard units that retain global deployment missions may have secondary responsibilities to support homeland security as required by the national authorities. (That is, national authorities may need to activate National Guard units from one state to assist with homeland defense in other states.)[27] Forces that have been configured and trained for peace operations are also likely to be well suited to a variety of potential homeland-defense tasks.

Improve Training and Education of Future Military Leaders

Successful adaptation will require changes to the training and education of future military leaders in order for changes to take hold firmly within the military culture. This is a long-term process. Although civilian leaders play an important role in identifying the changes in the international environment and the manner in which these affect national priorities, for changes to take hold, they must be internalized and institutionalized by the armed forces themselves. This includes the acceptance of the new roles by military leaders, sponsorship of the promotion pathways for new personnel specialties, adaptation of organizational structures, and changes to the organizational culture to establish the innovations securely.

Samuel Huntington long ago noted the conservative nature of the military mind and the tendency towards worse-case scenarios, hedging, and inertia.[28] Given the nature of military leaders' responsibilities and the potentially catastrophic costs of failure—both personally and for their state—a predisposition for prudence and conservatism is logical and is a generally positive attribute.

As one recent study noted regarding successful military innovation between the World Wars, innovation can take place as an evolutionary process. In this light, the incremental changes that the military services have undertaken may contribute to the long-run transformation of U.S. armed forces into significantly different ones than fought the Cold War and the Gulf War. But it takes time and an effort to create the personnel systems that will value and encourage such innovation.

Evolutionary innovation depends on organizational focus over a sustained period of time rather than on one particular individual's capacity to guide the path of innovation for a short period of time. Military leadership has the most influence on innovation by long-term cultural changes rather than immediate short-term decisions.[29]

Some evidence of change exists in promotion systems of the armed services. The test will be whether leaders other than those in traditional war-fighting specialties can survive in the services to serve at the highest levels. New systems, such as the army's OPMS III,[30] hold some promise but are in the early stages of implementation. Successful promulgation and protection of new specialties will be difficult to assess for several years.

Additionally, the services should overhaul the officer professional military education system (PME) to better train officers for the uncertain demands of the future. "Every great period of strategic reform in the past ... has involved a radical change in America's military education system."[31] The lack of certainty about the future requires officers broadly educated and flexible enough to respond to differing crises as they arise. One way to do this might be to consolidate or standardize professional military education at the senior service level (Colonel/Captain level).[32] Rather than maintaining separate war colleges as the primary means of education for senior officers, officers selected for senior service education could receive the same joint education program that might then be followed by service-specific modules to deal with peculiarities related to the future assignments of officers within their services. This education should take place before any officer can be considered for promotion to flag rank (general and admiral). This education system could be built on the current structure using the existing National War College and the service-specific schools. For example, after attending the National War College[33] (joint PME), army officers would attend Army War College for education on ground warfare aspects, naval officers would attend the Naval War College to prepare for specifics related to naval operations, and so forth for the air force and marines. The professional education priority would be the joint school. Alternatively, greater focus on standardizing the joint curricula of the current schools could accomplish the same objective but without the need to move many officers to two locations to complete the program. With this alternative, a robust mix of students from all services would remain a key objective. Officers attending PME at a national or sister-service program would return to their service school for the service-specific portion of their education.

Reform the Defense-Review Process

Successfully adapting military capabilities to meet uncertain future needs requires an iterative policy process to review fundamental defense-policy issues. The process to review fundamental defense-policy issues should include the participation of the defense establishment as well as independent, outside, experts on defense. To accomplish this, lawmakers should institutionalize the national defense panel (NDP) and quadrennial defense review (QDR) model—with some important modifications—to reassess and reevaluate periodically the congruence of military capabilities with national goals.

1997 NDP member, Dr. Andrew Krepinevich, noted that with the changes in administration and some key players that have occurred over the past eight years and the notable similarity of the reviews that they have produced, the problem might be more with the process and less with the people involved.[34] The apparent trend of smaller but similar military forces that has been reinforced by each of the major reviews may reflect a need to adopt more innovative ways to structure the defense-review process to remove some of the parochial interests that currently seem to dominate future defense planning.

The role of the National Defense Panel was a valuable one that helped bring in views from outside the Department of Defense. As recommended by the Commission on Roles and Missions, Congress created a permanent mandate for the Department of Defense to conduct quadrennial reviews of defense in the first year following presidential elections.[35] However, Congress decided not to include the requirement for an outside independent panel, such as the NDP, to be part of the process.[36] An effort to institutionalize the national defense panel as part of the process was passed in the Senate but did not make the final authorization bill from the conference committee.[37] Conducting only the quadrennial defense review portion within the Department of Defense (without including the external work of an independent panel) seems unlikely to affect the key bureaucratic elements that have inhibited major change so far. Informally, Secretary of Defense Rumsfeld appears to have adopted a variant of the

NDP approach through the nineteen panels that he created and used to generate his guidance and terms of reference for the 2001 QDR. This was a useful mechanism to help focus the work of various issue teams around central themes.

The changes that have occurred in defense policy, albeit incremental, have been related to the major reviews. I recommend that Congress mandate a quadrennial requirement for an outside panel of experts to review the major themes of defense policy in the year immediately following a presidential election to be *followed* by a DoD internal review that includes a response to the panel's recommendations. This would reverse the order of the 1997 QDR and NDP process and place the DoD portion of the review in the second year of a new presidential administration. This would allow members of the defense-policy team to settle into their jobs before the review begins (to include getting through the confirmation process for political appointees). In August 2001, while working on the 2001 QDR, Secretary of Defense Rumsfeld noted that,

[The QDR is] a fascinating process. The congressmen mandated this be done every four years. Unfortunately it happens early in a new administration. And, as you may recall, we had practically no new people brought into the administration until, oh, just a month, a month-and-a-half ago [July 2001]. So ... it's been a very difficult thing to do although we're making good progress.[38]

Placing the DoD review after the NDP work would also allow the DoD staff to take advantage of the wisdom of the National Defense Panel to inform their review. One other useful technique would be to make appointment to the National Defense Panel a long-term commitment (for example twelve years) similar to the appointment of members to the Federal Reserve Board. With presidential appointment and congressional consent, this panel could provide a relatively unbiased assessment of the challenges and opportunities of defense. The focus of this review process should be on long-term defense needs as opposed to emphasis on the budget cycle a year or two out. In other words, thoughtful consideration of future defense demands should take priority over the only marginally malleable defense programs conditioned by short-term budget limitations.

Additionally, the DoD elements of the review should occur sequentially rather than concurrently. As noted in chapters 7, "1997 Quadrennial Defense Review," and 8, "2001 Quadrennial Defense Review," panels on strategy, force structure, and modernization worked concurrently and were unable to integrate fully the elements of other panels' final analyses into their own. Decisions on strategy should precede analysis and decisions concerning the appropriate strategic doctrine for the armed forces, with a greater emphasis on joint strategic doctrine as the guide to the subordinate military services. This should in turn precede consideration of overall force structure to support strategy and doctrine. Similarly, modernization decisions should be considered in light of the overall force-structure decisions. Within modernization, the consideration of complementary or redundant programs should be rationalized to better account for the capabilities that various programs provide and how they might influence tradeoffs with other programs.

Lastly, the president must play an important role in the process to ensure that it is more than just a restatement of organizational preferences. The executive branch portion of the internal review (QDR) should include the direct participation of the president at key points in the review.

Increase Civilian Leadership

Adapting military capabilities to the future requires strong civilian leadership, particularly from the president. Presidential initiative and leadership, directly or through well-supported civilian appointees—such as the Secretary of Defense—presents the most promising means to break out of the inertia-driven administrative patterns of the Cold War. One of the most powerful obstacles to change is the belief in almost immutable budget shares among the services. Whenever a new budget is proposed, one of the first things that each of the services does is to check and ensure that its budget share has not substantially changed relative to the other services.[39] The continued fair-share arrangements are bureaucratically driven and not strategically or capability driven. There are many ways to conceive of defense requirements that would shift the relative resource requirements among the services. For example,

- RMA related advances in precision strike and sensor-to-shooter improvements point to greater air force emphasis and to greater emphasis on artillery and other indirect fire systems in the army and marines.
- Information operations point towards greater emphasis on national intelligence capabilities and the collection assets of the services.
- Peace operations point to greater emphasis on special forces, light forces, military police, civil affairs, and combat service support units.

For such tradeoffs to occur, however, it will require intervention by the President or the Secretary of Defense. Their leadership is important to ensure that the development of national military capabilities are in consonance with national foreign and security policy—regardless of the disproportionate costs that might be born by various subordinate elements of the armed forces.

There is evidence that Secretary of Defense Rumsfeld tried to take such a role in the opening stages of the 2001 QDR. The fact that there were numerous leaks and complaints from disgruntled military leaders left outside of Rumsfeld's deliberation was one sign that he was making great efforts to avoid being smothered by the advice and restraints of the defense bureaucracy. Similar complaints from Capital Hill also indicate that Rumsfeld was threatening established interests. Although the events of 11 September intervened to overshadow contentious deliberations related to the final report, there were indications even before then that determined resistance among the military leaders had forestalled major changes. The truncated process also changed the role the president might have exercised over the final report.

Secretary Rumsfeld has devoted tremendous time and energy to the concept of transformation. In the February 2002 presentation of the administration's FY03 defense-budget proposal, Secretary of Defense Rumsfeld has re-emphasized the need for force transformation.[40] President Bush endorsed these efforts in a December 2001 speech at The Citadel[41] (a follow up to his foundational defense campaign speech of September 1999[42]) and in the 2002 State of the Union address.[43] Secretary Rumsfeld noted, "We have established a new Office of Force Transformation to help drive the transformation process, and have tasked each of the services to develop Service Transformation Roadmaps."[44] These are hopeful signs that the civilian leadership does place great emphasis on the need to better adapt U.S. military capabilities for the future. It remains to be seen whether civilian leaders can press the military leaders to help realize this ambitious agenda.

The new war has opened a window of opportunity concerning defense issues. The president should use this opportunity to take the lead in articulating the nature of the forces required to adapt to the demonstrated threats of global terrorism as well as to other emerging threats. President Bush's passionate support and leadership for national missile defense is an example of the type of support for military restructuring that is likely to overcome years of inertia. Although the terrorist attacks mitigated the impact of the 2001 QDR, the president can revisit the goals of the review in light of this new war and use it as the point of departure for articulating a clear vision of the military force structure and strategic doctrine that can best serve U.S. security interests in the long run. Taking the 2001 QDR as the starting point, the president should personally articulate the major programmatic objectives for transformation of the armed forces and their strategic doctrine.

More broadly, the events of 11 September 2001 have generated renewed attention in U.S. military capabilities by the public at large. The focus of such attention is on the near-term use of the armed forces to prosecute the global war against terrorism. This attention to the military and the challenges of the terrorist threats and other potential threats to U.S. interests provide a window of opportunity to implement significant changes to U.S. military capabilities. One way to take advantage of this window of opportunity might not even require head-on challenges to vested interests in the status quo. The consensus in favor of very large defense-budget increases on behalf of the global war on terrorism provides an opportunity to initiate transformational programs along side the established programs that have been so hard to modify. If or when the immediate security threats subside and opportunity costs among competing defense programs must be addressed, the wedge of transformational programs and organizations may have established durable constituencies to compete successfully against the current forces of inertia and status quo.

CONCLUSION

Since the end of the Cold War, there has been much activity on defense policy but little change—other than reduction—in American military capabilities. This lack of significant change limits the means by which the United States can achieve national objectives. Given national security interests to prepare effectively for the next war and to execute peace operations effectively to support a stable international environment, the changes to date are inadequate. There are many reasons to be concerned that policies reflecting substantial inertia regarding defense create significant risks or at least impose significant limits upon American ability to influence international relations.

The overwhelming emphasis within the armed forces on traditional warfighting missions seems to be partially decoupled from the strategic requirements outlined in the national security strategy. Radical, technology-driven innovations of the revolution in military affairs do not appear to have affected the structure and doctrine of the armed forces. Similarly, the changes in structure and doctrine required to adapt current forces to the different demands of peace operations have also not been evident. As the Cold War recedes, maintaining current trends seems less and less sustainable. The challenges of current operations in the uncertain international environment make it increasingly evident that the capabilities of the past are not necessarily the best for the future.

There is no one right way to organize and train the military for the future that will serve any potential contingency. The issue is not to get the answer exactly right but, more importantly, to ensure that it is not precisely wrong. I believe that this will require a hedge strategy that ensures that forces are available for a full range of contingencies from the low end to the high end of the conflict spectrum and includes the effective use of armed forces to support national objectives in both peace and war. Military capabilities constructed and trained for but a narrow band of the spectrum of possible missions serves national interests poorly. Civilian leaders are responsible for ensuring that comfortable but ill-suited preferences driven by bureaucratic inertia do not become binding constraints on the execution of policy.

Major changes to the military's current way of doing business require support from outside the military that is not yet in evidence. Nevertheless, we know that this is possible. This can happen just as the Goldwater-Nichols Act of 1986 greatly enhanced the power of the Chairman of the Joint Chiefs of Staff to lead rather than facilitate. Another example of this is the Nunn-Cohen Amendment of 1987 that helped protect special operations forces and create the political space away from the services to enhance their effectiveness. What is needed is civilian leadership with the foresight to look beyond the present annual budget battles and short-term procurement cycles to the long-term efforts required to adapt military capabilities to future challenges.

Prior to September 2001, these issues were not a matter of significant public debate or concern. The terrorist attacks of 11 September 2001 and the subsequent combat operation in the global war against terrorism have thrust defense issues back into prominence. A window of opportunity concerning defense issues has been created by the crisis. It remains to be seen how this crisis and the increased attention on national security will affect the efforts to shape American military capabilities for the future. The increased salience of national security issues should generate renewed public attention about the appropriate military capabilities for the future.

The stakes of the debate are important and multifaceted. These issues pertain to the manner in which the United States will prepare to defend itself and its interests for many years to come. Defense-policy decisions, whether the result of a new debate or the result of continued inertia by the present political status-quo alliance, affect the distribution of national resources for all programs. National leaders must place defense-policy decisions within the context of broader national debates concerning the appropriate priorities for national government and the allocation of resources under its control. The allocation of resources for defense represents an opportunity cost in terms of the contributions the same resources can make to other national objectives (such as domestic economic stimulus measures and education). The decisions concerning such opportunity costs are clearly the responsibilities of the country's civilian leaders.

What seems clear is that the security challenges are not what they were during the Cold War. Military and civilian leaders must do a better job of preparing the military capabilities for the future, not the past.

NOTES

1. General Craig, as quoted by Senator Dan Coats, "Joint Experimentation: Unlocking the Promise of the Future," *Joint Force Quarterly* No. 17 (Autumn Winter 1997–98): 19.

2. Asymmetric challenges at the high end could include weapons of mass destruction; whereas challenges at the low end are those related to low-intensity conflict, such as guerrilla warfare and terrorism.

3. Jeffrey Record, *The Creeping Irrelevance of U.S. Force Planning*, Carlisle, PA: Strategic Studies Institute, May 19, 1998, 4.

4. National Defense Panel, *Transforming Defense: National Security in the 21st Century*, Washington, D.C., Government Printing Office, December 1997. (Hereafter referred to as NDP), i.

5. Posen, *The Sources of Military Doctrine* (Ithaca: Cornell University Press, 1984), 233–236.

6. Department of Defense, *Quadrennial Defense Review Report*. 30 September 2001, 11. (Hereafter referred to as 2001 QDR.)

7. President Clinton, *A National Security Strategy For a Global Age*, (Washington, D.C.: The White House, December 2000), 1.

8. Mark S. Martins, *The "Small Change" of Soldiering? Peace Operations as Preparation for Future Wars*. Arlington, VA: Institute of Land Warfare, Association of the United States Army. Contemporary Professional Military Writing, No. 99–1 (May

1999). Martins provides evidence from surveys and interviews that many field commanders do hold this view.

9. Department of Defense, *Quadrennial Defense Review Report*, 30 September 2001. (Hereafter referred to as 2001 QDR), 18.

10. James Dubik, "Sacred Cows Make Good Shoes: Changing the Way We Think About Military Force Structure," Arlington, VA: Association of the United States Army Landpower Essay Series. 97–1, February 1997, 10.

11. Rosen, *Winning the Next War*, 251–253. Rosen focuses on organizational adaptation as the most important aspect of innovation. He notes that technology is indeterminate for innovation as is the role of national intelligence about specific enemy capabilities. Innovative ways of using new technology and the creation of new organizational approaches are required to exploit properly the capability provided by new technology. As Rosen notes with respect to the time between World Wars I and II, different actors had similar weapons, such as the tank and the aircraft carriers, which were used differently by various states based on their preferred doctrinal concepts. For example, the British saw the aircraft carrier as supporting battleships in the fleet-to-fleet battle rather than recognizing a more independent role of the carrier as an offensive weapon (as perceived by the United States and Japan).

12. Williamson Murray and Allan R. Millett, *Military Innovation in the Interwar Period* (Cambridge: Oxford University Press), 1996. The study was funded by the U.S. Office of the Secretary of Defense (OSD), Office of Net Assessment, under the direction of Dr. Andrew Marshall.

13. Eliot A. Cohen and John Gooch, *Military Misfortunes: The Anatomy of Failure in War* (New York: The Free Press, 1990), 245–246 and Posen, *The Sources of Military Doctrine*.

14. Donald H. Rumsfeld (Secretary of Defense), "Prepared testimony to the Senate Armed Services Committee," 21 June 2001, available from http://www.defenselink.mil/speeches/2001/s20010621-secdef.html; Internet; accessed 13 March 2002.

15. NDP, 71. This concept of joint experimentation was also advocated by Senator Dan Coats, "Joint Experimentation: Unlocking the Promise of the Future," *Joint Force Quarterly* No. 17 (Autumn Winter 1997–98): 13–19.

16. National Defense University, *Strategic Assessment 1996: Instruments of U.S. Power*, Hans A. Binnendijk, ed., Washington, D.C.: National Defense University, Institute for National Strategic Studies, 185.

17. "Cohen Charges Atlantic Command with Joint Experiments," *Defense Daily*, 22 May 1998, 4. Atlantic Command was renamed Joint Forces Command in 1999.

18. Department of Defense, "Special Briefing on the Unified Command Plan," 17 April 2002, available from http://www.defenselink.mil/news/Apr2002/t04172002_t0417sd.html, Internet, accessed 8 August 2002.

19. Andrew Krepinevich, *The Bottom Up Review: An Assessment*, Washington, D.C.: Defense Budget Project, February 1994, 62.

20. An excellent description of the training process to reorient and prepare a unit for peace operations is William Langewiesche, "Peace Is Hell," *Atlantic Monthly*, 288, no. 3 (October 2001): 51–80.

21. Don Snider, "Let the Debate Begin: The Case for a Constabulary Force," *Army* (June 1998): 14.

22. Record, *The Creeping Irrelevance of U.S. Force Planning,* 19.

23. 1LT Casey Randall, Battery Executive Officer, C Battery, 3rd Battalion, 320th Field Artillery, writing to family members in the United States for the unit newsletter. March 2000. His artillery unit was deployed for a six-month rotation to Kosovo as part of KFOR. The unit primarily conducted security patrols and provided protection for Serbians still in Kosovo. In other words, it did primarily nonartillery missions.

24. The five regional combatant commands are European Command (EUCOM), Central Command (CENTCOM), Pacific Command (PACOM), Southern Command (SOUTHCOM), and Joint Forces Command (JFCOM—which includes the continental United States).

25. Ideas for the appropriate use of such a force were suggested by Snider, "Let the Debate Begin: The Case for a Constabulary Force," *Army* (June 1998): 14–16. Snider notes that the lineage of this idea dates back to Morris Janowitz, *The Professional Soldier: A Social and Political Portrait,* (New York: The Free Press, 1960). Janowitz, however, suggested that all U.S. ground forces be adapted for constabulary missions where as Snider and I propose the dedication of only a portion of U.S. forces for such missions.

26. Joint Task Force Civil Support was set up under U.S. Joint Force Command in 1999 to provide support to civil authorities in the event of a nuclear or other weapon of mass destruction event. Details of the Joint Task Force's mission are available from http://www.jfcom.mil/About/com_jtfcs.htm; Internet; accessed 14 March 2002.

27. By definition, unless activated for federal service, National Guard units are under the control of their respective state governments. Governors and local authorities can designate the tasks and preparations needed to support local requirements.

28. Samuel P. Huntington, *The Soldier and the State: The Theory and Politics of Civil-Military Relations* (Cambridge: Harvard University Press), 1957.

29. Williamson Murray, "Innovation: Past and Present," chapter 8 in Williamson Murray and Allan R. Millett, eds. *Military Innovation in the Interwar Period* (Cambridge: Cambridge University Press, 1996), 308–309.

30. OPMS III is a meant to create greater opportunities for officers who are not in traditional, operations fields (warrior). The system created new specialties and changed the promotion system to place greater value on non-operational specialties in selection of officers for lieutenant colonel and colonel. It remains to be seen whether the system will balance the dominance of the traditional combat specialties (for example, infantry, armor, and artillery) with the retention and reward of officers in necessary specialties, such as foreign area officers, strategic plans and policy, acquisition, and so on.

31. Eliot Cohen, "Calling Mr. X: The Pentagon's Brain-Dead Two War Strategy," *The New Republic* 218, No. 3 (19 January 1998): 17–19.

32. Also see Cohen, Ibid., who suggests in a brief passage that educational reform "... might merge some of the war colleges and create new schools for teach joint operations are—the interweaving of ground, air, sea, and space forces that increasingly characterized modern warfare."

33. Currently the National War College is just one option among many for senior officers of the various services. Some officers of each service, as well as several civilians, attend the year-long course in Washington, DC. The school is not mandatory for all senior officers. My recommendation would be for all senior officers of all services to attend a national war college followed by a month or two of education at a service war college. Furthermore, the joint war college would focus on joint operations.

34. Andrew Krepinevich, colloquium with staff and faculty, USMA Department of Social Sciences, West Point, New York, 28 April 1998.

35. U.S. Congress, Public Law 106–65. *National Defense Authorization Act for Fiscal Year 2000,* 106th Cong., 2nd Sess., Title IX, Subtitle A, Section 901, Permanent requirement for Quadrennial Defense Review.

36. William Matthews, "Worries Spur 4-Year Defense Plan Reviews," *Army Times.* 6 September 1999. 12.

37. Proposal is posted at the Web site of the Center for Defense Initiatives. Senate Proposal to Re-Institute the National Defense Panel. Senate, July 14 2000, Congressional Record p. S6920. Displayed at http://www.cdi.org/issues/qdr/NDP.html, Internet, accessed 6 January 2002.

38. Donald H. Rumsfeld (Secretary of Defense), DoD news briefing, August 16, 2001, Interview with Ray Suarez, PBS Newshour, available from http://www.comw.org/qdr/fulltext/010816Rumsuarez.html; Internet; accessed 12 March 2002.

39. Colonel Thomas Davis, Army PA&E, Colloquium, Department of Social Sciences, U.S.M.A., 13 March 1997.

40. Secretary of Defense Donald H. Rumsfeld, "2003 Defense Budget Testimony," Remarks as prepared for delivery to the House and Senate Armed Services Committees, 5 & 6 February 2002.

41. George W. Bush (president of the United States). "President Speaks on War Effort to Citadel Cadets," Text of presidential statement. Charleston S.C., 11 December 2001. Available from http://www.whitehouse.gov/news/releases/2001/12/20011211–6.html; Internet; accessed 12 December 2001.

42. George W. Bush (governor of Texas and presidential candidate), "A Period of Consequences," Speech given at The Citadel, South Carolina, 23 September 1999.

43. George W. Bush (president of the United States), "President Delivers State of the Union Address." Text of presidential statement (Washington, D.C., 29 January 2002). Available from http://www.whitehouse.gov/news/releases/2002/01/print/20020129–11.html; Internet; accessed 15 February 2002.

44. Rumsfeld, "2003 Defense Budget Testimony."

Bibliography

GOVERNMENT PUBLICATIONS AND DOCUMENTS

Aspin, Les, "An Approach to Sizing American Conventional Forces For the Post-Soviet Era: Four Illustrative Options." 25 February 1992.

Aspin, Les, *Annual Report to the President and Congress*. Washington: U.S. Government Printing Office, January 1994.

Aspin, Les, *Report on the Bottom Up Review*. October 1993.

Boyd, Morris J., "Doctrine and Force XXI—Leading the Army into the 21st Century." Available from http://cslspdc/97refs/mildoc.htm; Internet; accessed 22 April 1998.

Bush, George H.W., *National Security Strategy of the United States*. Washington, D.C.: The White House, August 1991.

Bush, George W., "A Period of Consequences." Speech given at The Citadel, South Carolina, 23 September 1999.

Bush, George W., "Address to Joint Session of Congress and the American People." Text of presidential statement. Washington, D.C. 20 September 2001. Available from http://www.whitehouse.gov/news/releases/2001/09/20010920–8.html; Internet; accessed 12 March 2002.

Bush, George W., "President Delivers State of the Union Address." Text of presidential statement. Washington, D.C., 29 January 2002. Available from http://www.whitehouse.gov/news/releases/2002/01/print/20020129–11.html; Internet; accessed 15 February 2002.

Bush, George W., "President George W. Bush's Inaugural Address." 20 January 2001. Available from http://www.whitehouse.gov/news/inaugural-address.html; Internet; accessed 14 March 2002.

Bush, George W., "President Speaks on War Effort to Citadel Cadets." Text of presidential statement. Charleston S.C., 11 December 2001. Available from http://www.whitehouse.gov/news/releases/2001/12/20011211–6.html; Internet; accessed 12 Dec 2001.

Chairman of the Joint Chiefs of Staff, *National Military Strategy of the United States of America: Shape, Respond, Prepare Now: A Military Strategy for a New Era.* Washington, D.C.: Government Printing Office, September 1997.

Chairman of the Joint Chiefs of Staff, *Report on the Roles, Missions, and Functions of the Armed Forces of the United States.* Washington, D.C.: Government Printing Office, February 1993.

Cheney, Dick, *Defense Strategy for the 1990s: The Regional Defense Strategy,* January 1993.

Clinton William J., *A National Security Strategy of Engagement and Enlargement,* Washington, D.C.: The White House, February 1996.

Clinton William J., *A National Security Strategy For a New Century.* Washington, D.C.: The White House, May 1997.

Clinton William J., *A National Security Strategy For a New Century.* Washington, D.C.: The White House, October 1998.

Clinton William J., *A National Security Strategy For a Global Age.* Washington, D.C.: The White House, December 2000.

Clinton, Bill, "Speech on Foreign Policy Before the Los Angeles World Affairs Council," 13 August 1992.

Cohen, William S., *Annual Report to the President and the Congress.* Washington, D.C.: Government Printing Office, April 1997.

Cohen, William S., *Annual Report to the President and the Congress.* Washington, D.C.: U.S. Government Printing Office, 1998.

Cohen, William S., *Annual Report to the President and the Congress.* Washington, D.C.: Government Printing Office, 1999. Available from http://www.dtic.mil/execsec/adr1999; Internet; accessed 12 April 1999.

Cohen, William S., Remarks prepared for Delivery, Center of Strategic and International Studies, May 22, 1997. Department of Defense News Release, Reference number 258–97. Available from http://www.dtic.mil/defenselink/news/May97/b052297_bt258–97.html; Internet; Accessed 23 May 1997.

Cohen, William S., *Report of the Quadrennial Defense Review,* Washington, D.C.: Department of Defense, May 1997.

Commission on Roles and Missions of the Armed Forces. *Directions for Defense: Report of the Commission on Roles and Missions of the Armed Forces.* Washington, D.C.: Government Printing Office, May 1995.

Congressional Budget Office. *Options For Reconfiguring Service Roles and Missions.* Washington, D.C.: Congressional Budget Office, March 1994.

Dalton, John H., J.M. Boorda, and Carl E. Mundy Jr., *Forward...From the Sea,* Washington, D.C.: Navy News Service, 9 November 1994. Available from http://www.chinfo.navy.mil/navpalib/policy/fromsea/forward.txt; Internet; accessed 19 March 1997.

Dellums, Ronald V., *Envisioning a New National Security Strategy.* March 10, 1997. Committee Reproduction.

Department of Defense. "Department of Defense Budget for Fiscal Years 2000/2001, Program Acquisition Costs by Weapon System." Washington, D.C.: Government Printing Office, February 1999.

Department of Defense. *Quadrennial Defense Review Report.* 30 September 2001.

Executive Office of the President of the United States. *The Budget For Fiscal Year 1999, Historical Tables.* Washington, D.C.: Government Printing Office, 1998.

Executive Office of the President of the United States. *The Budget For Fiscal Year 2002, Historical Tables*. Washington, D.C.: Government Printing Office, 2001.

Executive Office of the President of the United States. *A Blueprint for New Beginnings: A Responsible Budget for America's Priorities*. Washington, D.C.: Government Printing Office, 2001.

Executive Office of the President of the United States. *The Budget For Fiscal Year 2000, Historical Tables*. Washington, D.C.: Government Printing Office, 1999.

Fogleman, Ronald R., "Statement to Congress on the Quadrennial Defense Review." Available from http://www.fas.org/man/congress/1997/h970522f.htm; Internet; accessed 23 May 1997.

Institute for National Strategic Studies. *Strategic Assessment 1995: U.S. Security Challenges in Transition*. Washington, D.C.: Government Printing Office, 1995.

Institute for National Strategic Studies. *Strategic Assessment 1996: Instruments of U.S. Power*. Washington, D.C.: Government Printing Office, 1996.

Jaffe, Lorna S. *The Development of the Base Force, 1989–1992*. Washington, D.C.: Office of the Chairman of the Joint Chiefs of Staff, July 1993.

Jeffords, James. "Declaration of Independence." Statement, Burlington, VT, 24 May 2001. Available from http://www.senate.gov/~jeffords/524statement.html; Internet; accessed 12 March 2002.

Johnson, Jay L. "Forward...From the Sea: The Navy Operational Concept." Available from http://www.chinfo.navy.mil/navpalib/policy/fromsea/ffseanoc.htm; Internet; accessed 4 May 1998.

Johnson, Jay L. "Statement to Congress on the Quadrennial Defense Review." Available from http://www.fas.org/man/congress/1997/h970522j.htm; Internet; accessed 23 May 1997.

Joint History Office, *The Chairmanship of the Joint Chiefs of Staff*, Washington, D.C.: Office of the Chairman of the Joint Chiefs of Staff, 1995.

Joint History Office, *The History of the Unified Command Plan 1946–1993*. Washington, D.C.: Office of the Chairman of the Joint Chiefs of Staff, 1995.

Krulak, Charles C. "Statement to Congress on the Quadrennial Defense Review." Available from http://www.fas.org/man/congress/1997/h970522k.htm; Internet; accessed 23 May 1997.

National Defense Panel. *Transforming Defense: National Security in the 21st Century*. Washington, D.C.: Government Printing Office, December 1997.

Nunn, Sam. "The Defense Department Must Thoroughly Overhaul the Services' Roles and Missions." *Vital Speeches* 20 (1 August 1992): 717–24.

O'Keefe, Sean, Frank B. Kelso II, and C.E. Mundy Jr.. . . *From the Sea: Preparing the Naval Service for the 21st Century*. Washington, D.C.: Navy News Service, 30 September 1992. Available from http://www.chinfo.navy.mil/navpalib/policy/fromsea/fromsea.txt; Internet; accessed 19 March 1997.

Office of Management and Budget, "National Defense and International Affairs," *Budget of the United States Government, Fiscal Year 1995*, Washington, D.C.: Government Printing Office, 1994, 213–32.

Office of Management and Budget, *Budget of the United States Government, Fiscal Year 1995: Analytical Perspectives*. Washington, D.C.: Government Printing Office, 1994.

Office of Management and Budget. *Historical Tables: Budget of the United Sates Government, Fiscal Year 1996,*. Washington, D.C.: Government Printing Office, 1995.

Office of the Under Secretary of Defense (Comptroller). *National Defense Budget Estimates for FY2000*. Washington, D.C.. March 1999.

Office of the Under Secretary of Defense (Comptroller). *National Defense Budget Estimates for FY200*. Washington, D.C.. August 2001.

Perry, William J. *Annual Report to the President and Congress*. Washington, D.C.: Government Printing Office, March 1996.

Perry, William J. *Annual Report to the President and Congress*. Washington, D.C.: Government Printing Office, February 1995.

Reagan, Ronald. *National Security Strategy of the United States*. Washington, D.C.: The White House, January 1988.

Reimer, Dennis J. "Statement to Congress on the Quadrennial Defense Review." Available from http://www.fas.org/man/congress/1997/h970522r.htm; Internet; accessed 23 May 1997.

Rumsfeld, Donald H. "2003 Defense Budget Testimony," Remarks as prepared for delivery to the House and Senate Armed Services Committees, 5 and 6 February 2002.

Rumsfeld, Donald H. "DoD News Briefing, August 16, 2001." Interview with Ray Suarez, PBS Newshour. Available from http://www.comw.org/qdr/fulltext/010816Rumsuarez.html; Internet; accessed 12 March 2002.

Rumsfeld, Donald H. "Guidance and Terms of Reference for the 2001 Quadrennial Defense Review," Washington, D.C.: Department of Defense, 22 June 2001.

Shinseki, Eric K., and Louis Caldera. "The Army Vision: Soldiers on Point for the Nation ...Persuasive in Peace, Invincible in War." October 1999. Available from http://www.army.mil/armyvision/vision.htm; Internet; accessed 9 January 2000.

Spence, Floyd D. "Military Readiness 1997: Rhetoric and Reality." 9 April 1997.

Spence, Floyd D. Statement at Fiscal Year 1998 SECDEF/CJCS Posture Hearing, Press Release, 12 February 1996.

Sullivan, Gordon R., and Togo D. West, Jr. *America's Army of the 21st Century: Force XXI*. Fort Monroe, VA: Office of the Chief of Staff, Army, Director, Louisiana Maneuvers, 15 January 1995.

U.S. Air Force, Air Force Manual 1–1, *Basic Aerospace Doctrine for the United States Air Force*. March 1992.

U.S. Congress. House. Committee on Appropriations. *Department of Defense Appropriations for 1992: Hearings before a Subcommittee of the Committee on Appropriations, Part 8, Base Force Concept*. 102nd Cong., 1st Sess., 21 September 1991.

U.S. Congress. House. Committee on Armed Services. *Building a Defense that Works for the Post-Cold War World: Hearings before the Defense Policy Panel of the Committee on Armed Services*. 101st Cong., 2nd Sess., 22, 28 February, 14, 21, 22, 27 March and 25 April 1990.

U.S. Congress. House. Committee on Armed Services. *The 600-Ship Navy and the Maritime Strategy: Hearings Before the Seapower and Strategic and Critical Materials Subcommittee*. 99th Cong., 1st Sess., 24 June, 5, 6, and 10 September 1985.

U.S. Congress. House. Committee on Armed Services. *U.S. Defense Budgets in a Changing Threat Environment: Hearings Before the Defense Policy Panel of the Committee on Armed Services,* 101st Cong., 1st Sess., 16 and 17 May 1989.

U.S. Congress. House. Committee on Armed Services. *What Have We Got for $1 Trillion? Report of the Staff to Accompany H.A.S.C. no. 99–66*. 99th Cong., 1st Sess., October 1985.

U.S. Congress. House. Committee on the Budget. *Defense and the Deficit: A Review of Defense Spending and Its Relationship to National Security: Hearings Before the Task Force on Defense and International Affairs.* 99th Cong., 1st Sess., 28 March 1985.

U.S. Congress. House. Committee on the Budget. *Defense Policy in the Post–Cold War Era: Hearing Before the Committee on the Budget.* 102d Cong., 1st Sess., 31 July 1991.

U.S. Congress. House. H.R. 2401, *National Defense Act for Fiscal Year 1994.* Subtitle E—Commission on Roles and Missions. (Sections 951–960)

U.S. Congress. Public Law 106–65. *National Defense Authorization Act for Fiscal Year 2000.* 106th Cong., 2nd Sess., Title IX, Subtitle A, Section 901. Permanent requirement for Quadrennial Defense Review.

U.S. Congress. Senate. Committee on Armed Services. *Assisting the Build-Down of the Former Soviet Military Establishment: Hearings Before the Committee on Armed Services.* 102nd Cong., 2nd Sess., 5 and 6 February 1992.

U.S. Congress. Senate. Committee on Armed Services. *National Security Strategy: Hearings before the Committee on Armed Services.* 100th Cong., 1st Sess., January 12, 13, 14, 20, 21, 27, 28; February 3, 23; March 25, 30; April 3, 1987.

U.S. Congress. Senate. Committee on Armed Services. *Threat Assessment, Military Strategy and Defense Planning: Hearings before the Committee on Armed Services.* 102nd Cong., 2nd Sess., January 22, 23; February 19; March 3, 20, 1992. Washington, D.C.: Government Printing Office. 1992.

U.S. Congress. Senate. Committee on the Budget. *After the Thaw: National Security Objectives in the Post–Cold War Era: Hearing before the Committee on the Budget.* 101st Cong., 1st Sess., 12 December 1989.

U.S. Congress. Senate. S.2182, *National Defense Act for Fiscal Year 1995,* Section 923, Amendment to National Defense Authorization Act of 1994, Commission on Roles and Missions.

U.S. Navy. *Naval Doctrine Publication (NDP) 1: Naval Warfare.* March 1994.

United States Army Command and General Staff College, *S551/4: Low Intensity Conflict.* Ft Leavenworth, 1993.

United States Army Command and General Staff College, *Student Text 20–5: The Strategic Environment.* Ft Leavenworth, 1993.

United States Department of the Air Force. *Global Engagement: A Vision for the 21st Century Air Force.* Washington, D.C.: 1997.

United States Department of the Army. *Field Manual 100–23: Peace Operations.* Washington, D.C.: Government Printing Office, 1994.

United States Department of the Army. *Field Manual 100–5: Operations.* Washington, D.C.: Government Printing Office, 1993.

United States Department of the Army. *Field Manual 3–0: Operations.* Washington, D.C.: Government Printing Office, June 2001.

United States Departments of the Army and the Air Force. *Field Manual 100–20: Military Operations in Low Intensity Conflict.* Washington, D.C.: Government Printing Office, 1990.

United States General Accounting Office (GAO). *Bottom Up Review: Analysis of DoD War Game to Test Key Assumptions (GAO/NSIAD-96–170).* Washington, D.C.: Government Printing Office, June 1996.

United States General Accounting Office (GAO). *Quadrennial Defense Review: Opportunities to Improve the Next Review (GAO/NSIAD-98–155).* Washington, D.C.: Government Printing Office, June 1998.

BOOKS

Allison, Graham and Philip Zelikow. *Essence of Decision: Explaining the Cuban Missile Crisis.* Second Edition. New York: Addison Wesley Longman, 1999.

Allison, Graham, and Gregory Treverton, eds. *Rethinking America's Security.* New York: W.W. Norton and Company, 1992.

Allison, Graham. *Essence of Decision: Explaining the Cuban Missile Crisis.* Boston: Little, Brown and Company, 1971.

Aspen Strategy Group Report. *The United States and the Use of Force in the Post–Cold War Era.* Queenstown: The Aspen Institute, 1995.

Avant, Deborah D. *Political Institutions and Military Change: Lessons from Peripheral Wars.* Ithaca: Cornell University Press. 1994.

Betts, Richard K. *Military Readiness.* Washington, D.C.: Brookings Institution, 1995.

Betts, Richard K. *Soldiers, Statesmen, and Cold War Crises.* New York: Columbia University Press, 1991 (1977).

Blechman, Barry M. *The Politics of National Security: Congress and U.S. Defense Policy.* New York: Oxford University Press, 1990.

Blechman, Barry, and Stephen S. Kaplan. *Force Without War: U.S. Armed Forces as a Political Instrument.* Washington, D.C.: Brookings Institution, 1978.

Bose, Meena. *Shaping and Signaling Presidential Policy: The National Security Decision-Making of Eisenhower and Kennedy.* College Station, TX: Texas A&M University Press, 1998.

Bowie, Christopher, Fred Frostic, Kevin Lewis, John Lund, David Ochmanek, and Philip Propper. *The New Calculus: Analyzing Airpower's Changing Role in Joint Theater Campaigns.* Santa Monica, CA: RAND, 1993.

Braestrup, Peter. *The Big Story: How the American Press and Television Reported and Interpreted the Crisis of Tet 1968 in Vietnam and Washington.* New York: Anchor Books, 1978.

Builder, Carl H. *The Masks of War: American Military Styles in Strategy and Analysis.* Baltimore: Johns Hopkins University Press, (A RAND Corporation Research Study): 1989.

Bush, George, and Brent Scowcroft. *A World Transformed.* New York: Alfred A Knopf, 1998.

Clark, Asa A. IV, Peter W. Chiarelli, Jeffrey S. McKitrick, and James W. Reed. *The Defense Reform Debate: Issues and Analysis.* Baltimore: Johns Hopkins University Press, 1984.

Clausewitz, Carl Von. *On War.* Princeton: Princeton University Press, 1976.

Cohen, Eliot A., and John Gooch. *Military Misfortunes: The Anatomy of Failure in War.* New York: The Free Press, 1990.

Crabb, Cecil V. Jr., and Pat M. Holt. *Invitation to Struggle: Congress, the President, and Foreign Policy.* Fourth Edition. Washington, D.C.: CQ Press, 1993.

Crowe, William J. *The Line of Fire: From Washington to the Gulf, the Politics and Battles of the New Military.* New York: Simon and Schuster, 1993.

Dawkins, Peter M., *The United States Army and the "Other" War in Vietnam: A Study of the Complexity of Implementing Organizational Change.* Ph.D. diss., Princeton University, 1979.

Delmas, Philippe. *The Rosy Future of War.* New York: The Free Press, 1995.

Demchak, Chris C., *Military Organizations, Complex Machines: Modernization in the U.S. Armed Services.* Ithaca: Cornell University Press, 1991.

Destler, I.M. *Presidents, Bureaucrats, and Foreign Policy: The Politics of Organizational Reform.* Princeton: Princeton University Press, 1972.

Ederington, Benjamin, and Michael J. Mazarr, eds. *Turning Point: The Gulf War and U.S. Military Strategy.* Boulder: Westview Press, 1994.

Endicott, John E., and Roy W. Stafford, Jr. eds. *American Defense Policy.* Fourth Edition. Baltimore: Johns Hopkins University Press, 1977.

Epstein, Joshua M. *The 1987 Defense Budget.* Washington, D.C.: The Brookings Institution, 1986.

Epstein, Joshua M. *The 1988 Defense Budget.* Washington, D.C.: The Brookings Institution, 1987.

Feaver, Peter D., and Richard H. Kohn, eds. *Soldiers and Civilians: The Civil-Military Gap and American National Security.* Cambridge, MA: MIT Press, 2001.

Flournoy, Michele A. ed. *QDR 2001: Strategy-Driven Choices for America's Security.* Washington, D.C.: National Defense University Press, 2001.

Foerster, Schuyler, and Edward N. Wright, eds. *American Defense Policy.* Sixth Edition. Baltimore: Johns Hopkins University Press, 1990.

Gaddis, John Lewis. *Strategies of Containment: A Critical Appraisal of Postwar American National Security Policy.* Oxford: Oxford University Press, 1982.

Gibson, Christopher P. "Countervailing Forces: Enhancing Civilian Control and National Security Through Madisonian Concepts." Ph.D. diss., Cornell University, January 1998.

Gingrich, Newt. *To Renew America.* New York: Harper Collins, 1995.

Goure, Daniel, and Jeffrey M. Ranney. *Averting the Defense Train Wreck in the New Millennium.* Washington, D.C.: The CSIS Press, 1999.

Greider, William. *Fortress America: The American Military and the Consequences of Peace.* New York: PublicAffairs, 1998.

Halperin, Morton H. And Arnold Kanter, eds. *Readings in American Foreign Policy: A Bureaucratic Perspective.* Boston: Little, Brown and Company, 1973.

Halperin, Morton H. *Bureaucratic Politics and Foreign Policy.* Washington, D.C.: The Brookings Institution, 1974.

Hamilton, Alexander, James Madison, and John Jay. *The Federalist Papers.* New York: New American Library, 1961.

Hays Peter L., Brenda J. Vallance, and Alan R. Van Tassel. eds. *American Defense Policy.* Seventh Edition. Baltimore: Johns Hopkins University Press, 1997.

Heller, Charles E., and William A. Stofft, eds. *America's First Battles: 1776–1965.* Lawrence, KS: University of Kansas Press, 1986.

Hillen, John, Project Director. *Future Visions for U.S. Defense Policy: Four Alternatives Presented as Presidential Speeches.* New York: Council on Foreign Relations, 1998.

Hilsman, Roger. *The Politics of Policy Making in Defense and Foreign Affairs: Conceptual Models and Bureaucratic Politics.* 3rd Edition. Englewood Cliffs, NJ: Prentice Hall, 1993.

Howard, Michael. *War and the Liberal Conscience.* New Brunswick: Rutgers University Press, 1978.

Huntington, Samuel P. *The Common Defense.* New York: Columbia University Press, 1961.

Huntington, Samuel P. *The Soldier and the State: The Theory and Politics of Civil-Military Relations*. Cambridge: Harvard University Press, 1957.

Huzar, Elias, *The Purse and the Sword: Control of the Army by Congress through Military Appropriations, 1933–1950*. Ithaca: Cornell University Press, 1950.

Ippolito, Dennis S. *Blunting the Sword: Budget Policy and the Future of Defense*. Washington, D.C.: National Defense University Press, 1994.

Jablonsky, David. *Time's Cycle and National Military Strategy: The Case for Continuity in a Time of Change*. Carlisle, PA: U.S. Army War College, June 1995.

Janowitz, Morris. *The Professional Soldier: A Social and Political Portrait*. New York: The Free Press, 1960.

Jordan, Amos A., and William J. Taylor Jr., *American National Security: Policy and Process*. Baltimore: Johns Hopkins University Press, 1981.

Kaufmann, William W. *A Reasonable Defense*. Washington, D.C.: The Brookings Institution, 1986.

Kaufmann, William W., and John D. Steinbruner. *Decisions for Defense: Prospects for a New Order*. Washington, D.C.: The Brookings Institution, 1991.

Kaufmann, William W., and Lawrence J. Korb. *The 1990 Defense Budget*. Washington, D.C.: The Brookings Institution, 1989.

Kaufmann, William W. *Assessing the Base Force: How Much Is Too Much?* Washington, D.C.: The Brookings Institution, 1992. (Brookings Institution Studies in Defense Policy)

Kaufmann, William W. *Glasnost, Perestroika, and U.S. Defense Spending*. Washington, D.C.: The Brookings Institution, 1990.

Kaufmann, William W. *The 1985 Defense Budget*. Washington, D.C.: The Brookings Institution, 1984.

Kaufmann, William W. *The 1986 Defense Budget*. Washington, D.C.: The Brookings Institution, 1985.

Khong, Yuen Foong. *Analogies at War: Korea, Munich, Dien Bien Phu, and the Vietnam Decisions of 1965*. Princeton: Princeton, 1992.

Knightley, Phillip. *The First Casualty*. New York: Harcourt Brace Jovanovich, 1975.

Krepinevich, Andrew F. Jr. *The Army and Vietnam*. Baltimore: The Johns Hopkins University Press, 1986.

Krepinevich, Andrew F. *Missed Opportunities: An Assessment of the Roles and Missions Commission Report*. Washington, D.C.: The Defense Budget Project, August 1995.

Krepinevich, Andrew F. *Restructuring for a New Era: Framing the Roles and Missions Debate*. Washington, D.C.: The Defense Budget Project, April 1995.

Krepinevich, Andrew F. *The Bottom-Up Review: An Assessment*. Washington, D.C.: The Defense Budget Project, February 1994.

Lambeth, Benjamin S. *The Transformation of American Air Power*. Ithaca: Cornell University Press, 2000.

Larson, Eric V. *Casualties and Consensus: The Historical Role of Casualties in Domestic Support for U.S. Military Operations*. Santa Monica, CA: RAND, 1996.

Larson, Eric V., David T. Orletsky, and Kristin Leuschner. *Defense Planning in a Decade of Change*. Santa Monica, CA: RAND, 2001.

Lynn-Jones, Sean M., and Steven E. Miller, eds., *America's Strategy in a Changing World*. Cambridge: MIT Press, 1993.

MacGregor, Douglas A. *Breaking the Phalanx: A New Design for Landpower in the 21st Century*. Westport, CT: Praeger, 1997.

March, James G., and Herbert A. Simon. *Organizations*. New York: John Wiley & Sons, 1958.

Marquis, Susan. *Unconventional Warfare: Rebuilding U.S. Special Operations Forces*. Washington, D.C. Brookings Institution Press, 1997.

Martins, Mark S. *The "Small Change" of Soldiering? Peace Operations as Preparation for Future Wars*. Arlington, VA: Institute of Land Warfare, Association of the United States Army. Contemporary Professional Military Writing, no. 99–1 (May 1999).

McCormick, David. *The Downsized Warrior: America's Army in Transition*. New York: New York University Press, 1998.

Meese, Michael J. *Defense Decision Making Under Budget Stringency: Explaining Downsizing in the United States Army*. Ph.D. diss., Princeton University, 2000.

Miller, Steven E., and Sean M. Lynn-Jones, eds. *Conventional Forces and American Defense Policy*. Cambridge: MIT Press, 1989.

Millett, Allan R., and Williamson Murray, eds. *Military Effectiveness* (3 Volumes: Volume I—The First World War; Volume II—The Interwar Period; Volume III—The Second World War). Boston: Allen & Unwin, 1988.

Millett, Allan R., and Peter Maslowski. *For the Common Defense: A Military History of the United States of America*. New York: The Free Press, 1994.

Millis, Walter with Harvey C. Mansfield and Harold Stein. *Arms and the State: Civil-Military Elements in National Policy*. New York: Twentieth Century Fund, 1958.

Murray, Williamson, and Allan R. Millett, eds. *Military Innovation in the Interwar Period*. Cambridge: Cambridge University Press, 1996.

Nagl, John. "Learning to Eat Soup with a Knife." Ph.D. diss., Oxford University, 1996.

Neustadt, Richard E. *Presidential Power and the Modern Presidents*. New York: The Free Press/Macmillan, 1990.

Nunn, Sam. *Nunn 1990: A New Military Strategy*. Washington, D.C.: Center for Strategic and International Study, 1990.

O'Hanlon, Michael. *Defense Planning for the Late 1990s: Beyond the Desert Storm Framework*. Washington, D.C.: The Brookings Institution, 1995.

O'Hanlon, Michael. *How to be a Cheap Hawk: The 1999 and 2000 Defense Budgets*. Washington, D.C.: Brookings Institution Press, 1998.

Oberdorfer, Don. *The Turn: From the Cold War to a New Era: The United States and the Soviet Union, 1983–1990*. New York: Poseidon Press, 1991.

Petraeus, David H. "The American Military and the Lessons of Vietnam: A Study of Military Influence and the Use of Force in the Post-Vietnam Era." Ph.D. diss., Princeton University, 1987.

Pfaltzgraff, Robert L. Jr., and Richard H. Shultz, Jr. eds. *War in the Information Age*. Washington, D.C.: Brassey's, 1997.

Porter, Bruce D. *War and the Rise of the State*. New York: Free Press, 1994.

Posen, Barry R. *The Sources of Military Doctrine: France, Britain, and Germany Between the World Wars*. Ithaca: Cornell University Press, 1984.

Powell, Colin with Joseph E. Persico. *My American Journey*. New York: Random House, 1995.

Reagan, Ronald, *An American Life*. New York: Pocket Books, 1990.

Record, Jeffrey. *The Creeping Irrelevance of U.S. Force Planning.* Carlisle, PA: Strategic Studies Institute, May 19, 1998. (Monograph of conference paper originally presented at the U.S. Army War College's Annual Strategy Conference held 31 March–2 April 1998.)

Rosen, Stephen P. *Winning the Next War: Innovation and the Modern Military.* Ithaca: Cornell University Press, 1991.

Rosencrance, Richard, and Arthur A. Stein, eds. *The Domestic Bases of Grand Strategy.* Ithaca: Cornell University Press, 1993.

Sarkesian, Sam C., and John Mead Flanagin, eds. *U.S. Domestic and National Security Agendas: Into the Twenty-First Century.* Westport: Greenwood Press, 1994.

Schick, Allen. *The Federal Budget: Politics, Policy, Process.* Washington, D.C.: Brookings Institution, 1995.

Schilling, Warner R. "The Politics of National Defense: Fiscal 1950." In *Strategy, Politics and Defense Budgets*, ed. Warner R. Schilling, Paul Y. Hammond, and Glenn H. Snyder, 1–266. New York: Columbia University Press, 1962.

Schraeder, Peter, ed. *Intervention into the 1990s.* Boulder: Lynne Rienner, 1992.

Shafritz, Jay M., and J. Steven Ott, editors, *Classics of Organizational Theory.* 4th edition. Belmont: Wadsworth Publishing Company, 1996.

Smith, Daniel, Marcus Corbin, and Christopher Hellman. *Reforging the Sword: Forces for a 21st Century Security Strategy.* Washington, D.C.: Center for Defense Information, 2001. Available from http://www.cdi.org/mrp/reforging-full.pdf; Internet; accessed 9 March 2002.

Snider, Don M. "A Comparative Study of Executive National Security decision-making during periods of fundamental changes: The beginning and end of the Cold War." Ph.D. diss., University of Maryland, 1993.

Snider, Don M., and Miranda A. Carlton-Carew, eds. *U.S. Civil-Military Relations: In Crisis or Transition?* Washington, D.C.: The Center for Strategic and International Studies, 1995.

Snow, Donald M., and Eugene Brown. *Puzzle Palaces and Foggy Bottom: U.S. Foreign and Defense Policy Making in the 1990s.* New York: St. Martin's Press, 1994.

Snyder, Jack. *Myths of Empire: Domestic Politics and International Ambition.* Ithaca: Cornell University Press, 1991.

Sorley, Lewis. *Thunderbolt: General Creighton Abrams and the Army of His Times.* New York: Simon & Schuster, 1992.

Spiller, Roger J. "'Not War But Like War:' The American Intervention in Lebanon," *Leavenworth Papers*, Ft Leavenworth: Combat Studies Institute, January 1981.

Sullivan, Gordon R. *The Collected Works of the Thirty-Second Chief of Staff of the United States Army, 1991–1995.* Center of Military History (no other publication or copyright data noted).

Summers, Harry G. *On Strategy II: A Critical Analysis of the Gulf War.* New York: Dell, 1992.

Summers, Harry G. *On Strategy: A Critical Analysis of the Vietnam War.* New York: Dell, 1982.

Thompson, Fred, and L.R. Jones. *Reinventing the Pentagon: How the New Public Management Can Bring Institutional Renewal.* San Francisco: Jossey-Bass Publishers, 1994.

Toffler, Alvin and Heidi Toffler. *The Third Wave.* New York: Bantam, 1980.

Toffler, Alvin and Heidi Toffler. *War and Anti-War.* New York: Warner Books, 1993.

Waltz, Kenneth N. *Man the State and War.* New York: Columbia University Press, 1954.

Waltz, Kenneth N. *Theory of International Politics.* Reading: Addison-Wesley Publishing Company, 1979.

Weinberger, Caspar. *Fighting For Peace: Seven Critical Years in the Pentagon.* New York: Warner Books Inc., 1990.

Wildavsky, Aaron. *The New Politics of the Budgetary Process.* 2nd Edition. New York: Harper Collins, 1992.

Wilson, George C. *This War Really Matters.* Washington, D.C.: CQ Press, 2000.

Wilson, James Q., and John J. DiIulio Jr. *American Government.* 6th Edition. Lexington, MA: D.C. Heath and Company, 1995.

Woodward, Bob. *The Commanders.* New York: Simon and Schuster, 1991.

JOURNAL, INTERNET, AND NEWSPAPER ARTICLES

Abizaid, J.P., and J.R. Wood. "Preparing for Peacekeeping: Military Training and the Peacekeeping Environment." *Special Warfare Magazine* 7, no. 2 (April 1994): 14–20.

Arnold, S.L., and David T. Stahl. "A Power Projection Army in Operations Other than War." *Parameters* 23, no. 4 (Winter 1993–94): 4–26.

Art, Robert J. "A Defensible Defense: America's Strategy after the Cold War." *International Security* 15, no. 4 (Spring 1991).

Art, Robert J. "Bureaucratic Politics and American Foreign Policy: A Critique." Reprinted from *Policy Sciences* Vol. 4, no. 4 (1973) in *American Defense Policy,* 4th Edition, Baltimore: Johns Hopkins University Press, 1977, 240–525.

Aspin, Les. "The Defense Budget and Foreign Policy: The Role of Congress." Reprinted from *Daedalus,* Summer 1975 in *American Defense Policy,* 4th Edition, Baltimore: Johns Hopkins University Press, 1977, 321–334.

Association of the United States Army. "Gore, Bush Give Detailed Answers on Defense, National Security to 6 Leading Associations." 4 October 2000. Available from http://www.ausa.org/; Internet; accessed 13 March 2002.

"Authorization Remains Held Up in Conference by Dispute Over Depots." *Inside the Air Force,* 3 October 1997, 1.

Baldwin, David A. "Security Studies and the End of the Cold War." World Politics 48, no. 1 (October 1995): 117–141.

Becker, Elizabeth. "Air Force Jet in Fierce Fight, in Capital." New York Times. September 8, 1999. Available from http://www.nytimes.com/library/politics/090899lockheed-martin.html; Internet; accessed 8 September 1999.

Bender, Bryan. "Cohen to be Briefed on Plan to Kill Arsenal Ship." *Defense Daily,* 22 October 1997, 1.

Bender, Bryan. "National Guard Faces Drastic Overhaul." *Boston Globe,* November 20, 2001, 12.

Biddle, Stephen, Wade P. Hinkle, and Michael P. Fischerkeller. "Skill and Technology in Modern Warfare." *Joint Forces Quarterly* (Summer 1999): 18–27.

Binnendijk, Hans. "America's Military Priorities." *Strategic Forum.* no. 20 (February 1995).

Blaker, James R. "A Vanguard Force: Accelerating the American Revolution in Military Affairs." *Defense Working Group Policy Brief,* November 1997. Available from http://www.dlcppi.org/texts/foreign.vanguard.htm; Internet; accessed 14 January 2000.

Blaker, James R. "Understanding the Revolution in Military Affairs: A Guide to America's 21st Century Defense." Washington, D.C.: Progressive Policy Institute. January 1997. Available from http://www.dlcppi.org/texts/foreign/def3exe.htm; Internet; accessed 5 March 1997.

Blechman, Barry M. "The Congressional Role in U.S. Military Policy." *Political Science Quarterly* (Spring 1991): 17–32.

Brownstein, Ronald. "Success in Afghanistan Clouds Military Transformation Plan." *Los Angeles Times,* December 12, 2001.

Builder, Carl H. "Keeping the Strategic Flame." *Joint Forces Quarterly* no. 14 (Winter 96–97): 76–84.

Bullock, Gavin. "Military Doctrine and Counterinsurgency: A British Perspective." Available from http://cslspdc/97refs/doctrine.htm; Internet; accessed 22 April 1998.

Bumpers, Dale. "The Fighter Jet That Doesn't Need to be Resurrected." *New York Times,* 4 September 1999. Available from http://www.nytimes.com/yr/mo/day/oped/04bump.html; Internet; accessed 4 September 1999.

Cannon, Michael W. "The Development of the American Theory of Limited War 1945–63." *Armed Forces & Society* (Fall 1992): 71–104.

Capaccio, Tony. "Nine More B-2s Carry $20 Billion Price Tag." *Defense Week,* 16 June 1997, 1.

"Clinton Shines New Light on Defense Views As Nomination Nears," *Defense Week,* 13 July 1992, 13–15.

Coats, Dan (U.S. Senator). "Joint Experimentation: Unlocking the Promise of the Future." *Joint Force Quarterly* no. 17 (Autumn/Winter 1997–98): 13–19.

"Cohen Charges Atlantic Command With Joint Experiments." *Defense Daily,* 22 May 1998, 4.

Cohen, Eliot. "A Revolution in Warfare." *Foreign Affairs* 75, no. 2 (March/April 1996) 37–54.

Cohen, Eliot. "Calling Mr. X: The Pentagon's Brain-Dead Two War Strategy." *The New Republic* 218, no. 3 (19 January 1998): 17–19.

Cohen, William S. "Report of the Quadrennial Defense Review." *Joint Forces Quarterly* no. 16 (Summer 1997): 8–14.

Conetta, Carl, and Charles Knight. "Defense Sufficiency and Cooperation: A U.S. Military Posture for the post-Cold War Era." Project on Defense Alternatives, 12 March 1998. Available from http://www.comw.org/ pda/opdfin.html; Internet; accessed 19 March 2000.

Cottle, Michelle. "High on the Hog." *New York Times Magazine.* 22 November 1998, 58–59.

Courter, Jim, and Alvin H. Bernstein. "The QDR Process—An Alternative View." *Joint Forces Quarterly* no. 16 (Summer 1997): 20–26.

Cox, Matthew. "M1A2 Upgrades Mean More Lethal Tanks." *Army Times,* 20 September 1999, 8.

Deibel, Terry. "Strategies Before Containment: Patterns for the Future." *International Security* 16, no. 4, (Spring 1992): 79–108.

Donnelly, John. "Top Contractors Won't Compete Against Depots," *Defense Week,* 29 September 1997, 1.

Dubik, James M. "Sacred Cows Make Good Shoes: Changing the Way We Think About Military Force Structure." Arlington, VA: Association of the United States Army Landpower Essay Series. 97–1, February 1997.

Eland, Ivan, "Defense Reform is Dead," Cato Institute, Available from http://www.cato.org/dailys/08–29–01.html; Internet; accessed 5 January 2002.

Farrell, Theo. "Figuring Out Fighting Organizations: The New Organizational Analysis in Strategic Studies." *The Journal of Strategic Studies.* 19, no. 1 (March 1996) 122–135.

Fogleman, Ronald R.. "The Air Force and Joint Vision 2010." *Joint Forces Quarterly* no. 14 (Winter 96–97): 24–28.

Foote, Sheila. "House Panel Approves Restrictions on Depot Privatization." *Defense Daily,* 6 June 1997, 408.

Foote, Sheila. "Weldon Says Changes Needed in DoD's Fighter Plan." *Defense Daily,* 10 January 1997, 45.

Fram, Alan. "Congressional Leadership Wants Money for F-22." *Leaf-Chronicle,* 21 September 1999, B5.

Freedberg, Sydney J. "Navy Nervous About Rumsfeld Review." Govexec.com. 17 July 2001. Available from http://www.govexec.com/dailyfed/0701/071701nj.htm; Internet; accessed 7 January 2002.

Friedberg, Aaron L., "Is the United States Capable of Acting Strategically?" *The Washington Quarterly* 14, no. 1, (Winter 1991): 5–23.

Gallup Organization. Poll Topics and Trends, "Military and National Defense" December 2001. Available from http://www.gallup.com/poll/topics/military.asp; Internet; accessed 5 January 2002.

Gallup Poll, 17–19 April 1998, "What do you think is the most important problem facing this country today?" Available from http://www.gallup.com/poll_archives/980502.htm; Internet; accessed 14 January 1999.

George, Alexander, "Case Studies and Theory Development: The Method of Structured, Focus Comparison," in Paul Gorden Lauren, ed., *Diplomacy: New Approaches in History, Theory and Policy.* New York: The Free Press, 1979.

George, Alexander, "The 'Operational Code': A Neglected Approach to the Study of Political Leaders and Decision-Making," *International Studies Quarterly* 13, no. 2, (June 1969): 190–222.

Gerstenzang, James. "Bush Offers New Vision of Military." *Los Angeles Times,* December 12, 2001, p. 1.

Gibson, Christopher P., and Don M. Snider. "Civil-Military Relations and the Potential to Influence: A Look at the National Security Decision Making Process." *Armed Forces & Society* 25, no. 2 (Winter 1999): 193–218.

Gillespie, Mark. "Terrorism Reaches Status of Korean and Vietnam Wars as Most Important Problem: Economy ranks a distant second," Gallup News Service, November 19, 2001, Available from http://www.gallup.com/poll/Releases/Pr011119.asp; Internet; accessed 5 January 2002.

Gold, Philip. "Savaging Donald Rumsfeld." *Washington Times,* 28 August 2001. Available from http://www.discovery.org/viewDB/index.php3?program=Defense&command=view&id=1045; Internet; accessed 12 March 2002.

Gold, Philip. "Why the Pentagon Fears Rumsfeld's Review." Seattle Times, 13 June 2001. Available from http://www.discovery.org/viewDB/index.php3?program=Defense&command=view&id=652; Internet; accessed 12 March 2002.

Goodman, Melvin A. "Who Does the CIA Think It's Fooling?" *Washington Post National Weekly*, 3 January 2000, 22.

Graham, Bradley. "Army Plans Modest Makeover of Combat Divisions." *Washington Post*, 9 June 1998, A1, A8.

Graham, Bradley. "Military Favors A Homeland Command." *Washington Post*, November 21, 2001, p. 1.

Graham, Bradley. "The Pentagon's Budget Battle: Defense Spending is out of Step with Modern Threats, Critics say." *Washington Post National Weekly Edition*, 6 September 1999, 6–7.

Gray, Colin S. "The American Revolution in Military Affairs: An Interim Assessment." *The Occasional*. Number 28. Camberley, Great Britain: The Strategic and Combat Studies Institute, 1997.

Hahn, Walter. "In Search of an American 'Defense Insurance Policy.'" In *Paying the Premium: A Military Insurance Policy for Peace and Freedom*. ed. Walter Hahn and H. Joachim Maitre, 1–11. Westport: Greenwood Press, 1993.

Harris Poll, "Confidence/Trust in Institutions." 7–12 January 1999. Available from http://www.pollingreport.com/institut.htm; Internet; accessed 11 April 1999.

Hillen, John, Project Director. *Future Visions for U.S. Defense Policy: Four Alternatives Presented as Presidential Speeches*. New York: Council on Foreign Relations. 1998.

Holsti, Ole R. "A Widening Gap Between the U.S. Military and Civilian Society? Some Evidence 1976–96" *International Security* 23, no. 3 (Winter 1998–99) 5–42.

Ibberson, Stuart A. "Candidates Offer Differing Views on Future of Military." *Journal of Aerospace and Defense Industry News*, 3 November 2000. Available from http://www.aerotechnews.com/starc/2000/110300/Bush_Gore.html; Internet; accessed 13 March 2002.

Joffe, Josef. "'Bismarck' or 'Britain'? Toward an American Grand Strategy After Bipolarity." *International Security* 19, no. 4 (Spring 1995): 94–117.

Johnson, Douglas, and Steven Metz. "Civil-Military Relations in the United States: The State of the Debate." *The Washington Quarterly* 18, no. 1 (1994): 197–213.

Johnson, Jay L. (Chief of Naval Operations). "The Navy in 2010: A Joint Vision." *Joint Forces Quarterly* no. 14 (Winter 96–97): 17–19.

Johnston, Alastair Iain. "Thinking About Strategic Culture." *International Security* 19, no. 4 (Spring 1995): 32–64.

Joulwan, George A. "Doctrine for Combined Operations." *Joint Forces Quarterly* no. 14 (Winter 96–97): 46–49.

Kaplan, Robert D. "The Coming Anarchy," *Atlantic Monthly*, February 1994, 44–76.

Keir, Elizabeth. "Culture and Military Doctrine: France Between the Wars." *International Security* 19, no. 4 (Spring 1995): 65–93.

Keller, Bill. "The Fighting Next Time." *New York Times Magazine*, 10 March 2002. Available from http://www.nytimes.com/2002/03/10/magazine/10MILITARY.html; Internet; accessed 10 March 2002.

Kohn, Richard H. "Out of Control: The Crisis in Civil-Military Relations." *The National Interest* no. 35 (Spring 1994): 3–17.

Kohn, Richard H. "The Early Retirement of General Ronal R. Fogleman, Chief of Staff, United States Air Force." *Aerospace Power Journal* XV, no. 1 (Spring 2001): 6–23.

Krulak, Charles C. "Doctrine for Joint Force Integration." *Joint Forces Quarterly* no. 14 (Winter 96–97): 20–23.

Krulak, Charles C. "Operational Maneuver from the Sea." *Joint Forces Quarterly* no. 21 (Spring 99): 78–86.

Lacquement, Richard A., Jr. "Maintaining the Professional Core of the Army." *Army* 47, no. 1 (January 1997): 8–12.

Lacquement, Richard A., Jr. "The Casualties Myth and the Technology Trap." *Army* 47, no. 11 (November 1997): 12–14.

Landler, Mark. "Biden Wants U.S. Troops to Join Peace Force." *The New York Times,* January 13, 2002, 12.

Langewiesche, William. "Peace Is Hell." *Atlantic Monthly* 288, no. 3 (October 2001): 51–80.

Luck, Edward C. "Making Peace," *Foreign Policy* (Winter 1992–93): 137–155.

Luttwak, Edward N. "A Post-Heroic Military Policy." *Foreign Affairs* 75, no. 4 (July/ August 1996): 33–44.

Mack, Christopher C., and William M. Raymond Jr. "Strike Force Fires for the Future." *Field Artillery,* III, no. 6 (November-December 1998): 16–19.

Mahnken, Thomas G. "Transforming the U.S. Armed Forces: Rhetoric and Reality." *Naval War College Review* LIV, no. 3 (Summer 2001): 85–99.

Matthews, William. "Deployments Don't Degrade Troops' Peacekeeping [sic*] Skills: Many Bosnia Units Performed Better, GAO Says." *Army Times,* 27 September 1999, 23.

Matthews, William. "NATO Reveals New Kosovo Damage Estimates: Air Strikes Caused Less Destruction Than Reported." *Army Times,* 27 September 1999, 10.

Matthews, William. "Worries Spur 4-Year Defense Plan Reviews," *Army Times.* 6 September 1999. 12.

Maynes, Charles William. "A Workable Clinton Doctrine," *Foreign Policy.* (Winter 1993–94): 3–21.

Maze, Rick. "Congress Nixes Another Round of Base Closings." *Army Times,* 7 June 1999, 29.

Maze, Rick. "Defense Spending not High on Hill's List of Priorities." *Army Times,* 20 April 1998, 8.

Moore, David W. "Terrorism Most Important Problem, But Americans Remain Upbeat: Trust in government surges; congress approval at record high." Gallup News Service, October 18, 2001, Available from http://www.gallup.com/poll/ Releases/Pr011018.asp; Internet; accessed 5 January 2002.

Murray Williamson. "Preparing to Lose the Next War?" *Strategic Review* (Spring 1998). Available from https://ca.dtic.mil/cgi-bin/ebin; Internet; accessed 29 April 1998.

Murray, Williamson. "Thinking About Revolutions in Military Affairs." *Joint Forces Quarterly* no. 16 (Summer 1997): 69–76.

Myers, Steven Lee. "Administration to Propose Largest Increase in Military Spending Since the Mid-1980s." *New York Times,* 2 January 1999. Available from http://www.nytimes.com/yr/mo/day/news/washpol/military-budget.html; Internet; accessed 2 January 1999.

National Defense Panel. "National Security in the 21st Century: The Challenge of Transformation." *Joint Forces Quarterly* no. 16 (Summer 1997): 15–19.

Naylor, Sean D. "Cohen Delays QDR-Mandated cuts in Guard, Reserve." *Army Times* 3 January 2000, 8.

Naylor, Sean D. "Fast & Furious: Shinseki's Breakneck Battle Plan for All-Wheeled Brigades." *Army Times* 22 November 1999, 14–15.

Naylor, Sean D. "Radical Changes: Gen. Shinseki Unveils his 21st-Century Plans." *Army Times*, 25 October 1999, 8, 10.

Naylor, Sean D. "Shinseki Pressured to Support F-22: Army Chief of Staff Faced Firestorm for not Backing Beleaguered Fighter." *Army Times*, 20 September 1999, 8.

Naylor, Sean D. "Sidelined: How America Won a War Without the Army," *Army Times*, 16 August 1999, 18–21.

Naylor, Sean D. "Strike Force Struck Down … For Now." *Army Times*, 4 January 1999, 7.

Newport, Frank. "No Single Problem Dominates Americans' Concerns Today." Gallup Poll, May 2, 1998. Available from http://www.gallup.com/poll_archives/980502.htm; Internet; accessed 14 January 1999.

Newport, Frank. "Small Business and Military Generate Most Confidence in Americans," Gallup Poll, 15 August 1997. Available from http://www.gallup.com/poll/releases/pr970815.asp; Internet; accessed 11 April 1999.

Nye, Joseph S., and William A. Owens. "America's Information Edge." *Foreign Affairs* 75, no 2, (March/April 1996): 20–36.

O'Hanlon, Michael. "Can High Technology Bring U.S. Troops Home?" *Foreign Policy* no. 113 (Winter 1998–99): 72–86.

Pike, John. "Cancel New Attack Submarine." Federation of American Scientists, Military Spending Working Group. Available from http://www.fas.org/pub/gen/mswg/msbb98/dd10subs.htm (updated 1 May 1998); Internet; accessed 16 January 1999.

Posen, Barry R., and Andrew L. Ross, "Competing Visions for U.S. Grand Strategy." *International Security* 21, no. 3 (Winter 1996/97): 5–53.

Powell, Colin L. "U.S. Forces: Challenges Ahead." *Foreign Affairs*, (Winter 1992–93): 32–45.

Powell, Colin L. "National Security Challenges in the 1990s: The Future Just Ain't What It Used to be." *Army* 39, no. 7 (July 1989): 12–14.

Powell, Colin, et al. "An Exchange on Civil-Military Relations." *The National Interest* no. 36 (Summer 1994): 23–31.

Priest, Dana. "The Battle That Never Was: Did NATO's Threat to Send Ground Troops Bring Milosevic to the Table?" *Washington Post National Weekly Edition*, 27 September 1999, 6–7.

Ratnam, Gopal. "Chiefs Ask Clinton for Additional $112 Billion." *Army Times*, 21 December 1998, 16.

Record, Jeffrey. "Three Planes, One Wallet." *Baltimore Sun*, 25 February 1997, 13.

Reilly, John E. "The Public Mood at Mid-Decade." *Foreign Policy* no. 98 (Spring 1995): 76–93.

Reimer, Dennis J. "Dominant Maneuver and Precision Engagement." *Joint Forces Quarterly* no. 14 (Winter 96–97): 13–16.

Ricks, Thomas. "Post Interview with Defense Secretary Donald H. Rumsfeld." *Washington Post* 20 May 2001. Available from http://www.washingtonpost.com/wpsrv/nation/transcripts/rumsfeldtext051701.html; Internet; accessed 12 March 2002.

Ricks, Thomas. "The Great Society in Camouflage." *Atlantic Monthly* 278, no. 6 (December 1996): 24–38.

Roberts, Steven V. "Democrats Defy House Leaders; Price loses Post: Aspin, Pentagon Critic, to Head Arms Panel." *New York Times*, 5 January 1985, A1.

Robinson, John. "Navy Won't Reinvent Itself for Strategy Review, CNO Says." *Defense Daily*, 19 November 1996, 280.

Rogers, David. "Congress Approves Defense Bill Laden With Add-Ons for Firms in GOP States." *Wall Street Journal*, 26 September 1997, 1–2.

Rosen, Stephen Peter. "Military Effectiveness: Why Society Matters." *International Security* 19, no. 4 (Spring 1995): 5–31.

Schlesinger, James. "Quest for a Post–Cold War Foreign Policy," *Foreign Affairs*, Vol. 72, no. 1, 1993, 17–28.

Schneider, Greg. "Navy Scuttles Arsenal Ship." *Baltimore Sun*, 25 October 1997, 1, 14C.

Shalikashvili, John M. "A Word From the Chairman." *Joint Forces Quarterly* no. 16 (Summer 1997): 1–5.

Shalikashvili, John M. "A Word From the Chairman." *Joint Forces Quarterly* no. 14 (Winter 96–97): 1–6.

Shanahan, Jack. "The Best Investment the Pentagon Could Make." *New York Times*. September 17, 1999. Available from http://www.nytimes.com/yr/mo/day/oped/17shan.html; Internet; accessed 17 September 1999.

Shelton, Henry H. "Coming of Age: Theater Special Operations Commands." *Joint Forces Quarterly* no. 14 (Winter 96–97): 50–52.

Shenon, Philip. "Pentagon Releases New Strategic Blueprint." *New York Times*, May 20, 1997. Available from http://www.nytimes.com/yr/mo/day/news/washpol/pentagon-review.htm; Internet; accessed 20 May 1997.

Sherlock, Richard J. "New Realities, Old Pentagon Thinking." *Wall Street Journal*, 24 April 1997, 1, 18.

Snider, Don M. "Let the Debate Begin: The Case for a Constabulary Force." *Army* (June 1998): 14–16.

Snider, Don M. "The U.S. Military in Transition to Jointness: Surmounting Old Notions of Interservice Rivalry." *Airpower Journal* (Fall 1996): 16–27.

Tirpak, John A. "QDR Goes to War." *Air Force Magazine* 84, no. 12 (December 2001): 26–31.

U.S. Commission on National Security/21st Century. "New World Coming." Available from http://www.nssg.gov/reports/New_World_Coming/New_World1/new_world1.htm; Internet; accessed 14 January 2000.

Van Creveld, Martin. "Military Strategy for an Era of Transition." In *Turning Point: The Gulf War and U.S. Military Strategy*. ed. Benjamin Ederington and Michael J. Mazarr, 263–278. Boulder: Westview Press, 1994.

Weigley, Russell F. "The American Military and the Principle of Civilian Control from McClellan to Powell." *Journal of Military History* 57, no. 5 (October 1993).

Weiner, Tim. "Clinton as a Military Leader: Tough On-the Job Training." *New York Times*, 28 October, 1996, 1.

Weiner, Tim. "Two-War Strategy is Obsolete, Panel of Defense Experts Says." *New York Times*, 2 December 1997, 1.

Weisman, Jonathan. "Cuts Get Cut From Pentagon Budget," *USA Today*, January 8, 2002, 4.

Wilson, George C. "Inside Moves." *Army Times*, 27 September 1999, 18–20.

Wilson, George C. "Whole New Defense Debate." GovExec.com. 8 January 2002.

Wittkopf, Eugene R. "What Americans Really Think About Foreign Policy." *Washington Quarterly*, 19, no. 3 (Summer 1996): 91–106.

Zakheim, Dov S., and Jeffrey M Rainey. "Matching Defense Strategy to Resources: Challenges for the Clinton Administration." *International Security* (Summer 1993): 51–78.

INTERVIEWS AND UNPUBLISHED PRESENTATIONS

My thanks to the following individuals for the interviews or unpublished presentations they provided to me for use in this study (name, rank and relevant positions at time of interview/presentation are shown).

BAKER, JAMES (Former Secretary of State); BARBER, ARTHUR III (Captain, US Navy, member of J8 during Base Force consideration. Member of Navy team on QDR); BLAIR, DENNIS J. (Vice Admiral, US Navy, Director of the Joint Staff, Former member of J8, Assessments, during the Base Force and Bottom Up Review); BORSETH, ANN (Government Accounting Office); Cheney, Richard (Former Secretary of Defense); CHU, DAVID (Former Director, Office of the Secretary of Defense, Office of Program, Analysis and Evaluation); COLLEGE, CRAIG (Army Office of Program, Analysis and Evaluation); CONOVER, GREG (Lieutenant Colonel, Training and Doctrine Command Army After Next Project); DAVIS, THOMAS (Colonel, Army PA&E); DEBOBES, RICHARD (Senate Armed Services Committee Professional Staff); DELEON, RUDY (Undersecretary of Defense for Personnel and Readiness; Former Aspin Aide); DELLUMS, RON (D-CA, former Chairman of the House Armed Services Committee); DOWNEY, FRED (Legislative assistant to Senator Joseph Lieberman, D-CT); FINCH, LOUIS C. (Deputy Under Secretary of Defense for Readiness); FINELLI, FRANK (Office of Senator Dan Coats, R-IN; Former member of QDR analysis team); GARWIN, TOM (Former legislative assistant to Congressmen Les Aspin and Ron Dellums); HALTERMAN, LEE (legislative assistant to Representative Ron Dellums, D-CA); HOEHN, ANDREW (Office of the Secretary of Defense, Strategy and Requirements); JAFFE, LORNA (Joint History Office); KAUFMAN, DANIEL J (Colonel US Army, Department Head, Department of Social Sciences, USMA, Member of transition team for the Chief of Staff of the Army); KILLIBREW, ROBERT (Colonel, U.S. Army, Army After Next Project); KIMMITT, JAY (Professional Staff, Senate Appropriations Committee); KREPINEVICH, ANDREW (National Defense Panel member, Director of Center for Strategic and Budgetary Assessments); LEONARD, MICHAEL (Director of Commission on Roles and Missions); MARQUIS, SUSAN (Office of the Secretary of Defense, Office of Program, Analysis and Evaluation); MCCURDY, DAVID (Former Congressman, D-OK); MCNAMARA, STEPHEN J. (Lieutenant Colonel, U.S. Air Force, Air Force QDR Team); MIZUSAWA, BERT (Professional Staff, Senate Armed Service Committee); MURDOCK, CLARK (Deputy Special Assistant to the Air Force Chief of Staff for Long Range Planning; former professional committee staff member for Les Aspin in House of Representatives); OCHMANEK, DAVID (RAND, Former Deputy Assistant Secretary of Defense for Strategy); PARLIER, GREG (Colonel, U.S. Army, Army QDR Team); PERRY, WILLIAM J. (Former Secretary of Defense); PUNARO, ARNOLD (Brigadier General, U.S. Marine Corps Reserve; Former staffer for Senator Sam Nunn, D-GA); RAINES, EDWARD (Historian, Center for Military History—Historian for Commission on Roles and Missions project); RESNICK, JOEL (Former Aspin Staff member); RYAN, PAUL J. (Captain, U.S. Navy, Navy QDR Team); SCOWCROFT, BRENT

(Former National Security Adviser); SEATON, JAMES (National Security Council Staff member—Assistant to Robert Bell); SMITH, LARRY, (Former Aspin Staff member); STROUP, THEODORE (LTG (ret) U.S. Army, former Deputy Chief of Staff for Personnel); THORNBERG, B.J. (Colonel, U.S. Army, QDR Team); WARNER, EDWARD (Assistant Secretary of Defense for Strategy and Requirements); WINSOR, STEPHEN A. (Colonel, U.S. Army, Staff member, Commission on Roles and Missions of the Armed Forces); WORK, ROBERT (Colonel, U.S. Marines, QDR Team).

Index

About the Author

RICHARD A. LACQUEMENT JR. is a United States Army Field Artillery Officer with over 18 years of active duty service. He is a 1984 graduate of the United States Military Academy and a combat veteran of the Persian Gulf War. He is a member of the faculty of the U.S. Naval War College.